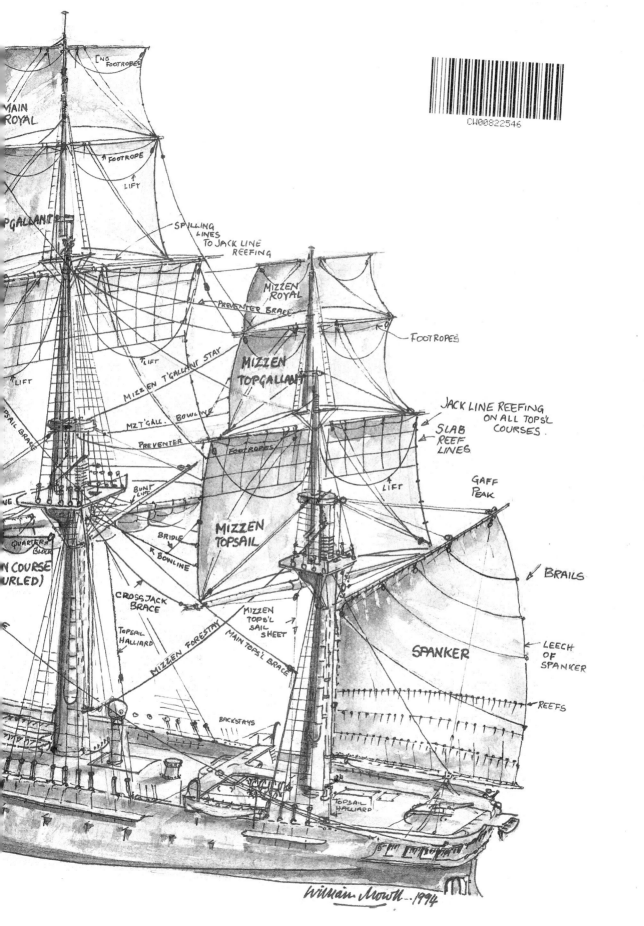

MAIN
ROYAL

[NO FOOTROPES]

FOOTROPE

LIFT

T'GALLANT

SPILLING
LINES
TO JACK LINE
REEFING

MIZZEN
ROYAL

PREVENTER BRACE

LIFT

MIZZEN
T'GALLANT STAY

MIZZEN
TOPGALLANT

FOOTROPES

MZT'GALL. BOWLINE

PREVENTER

LIFT

LIFT

BRACE

JACK LINE REEFING
ON ALL TOPS'L
COURSES.

SLAB
REEF
LINES

BUNT
LINE

FOOTROPES

MIZZEN
TOPSAIL

GAFF
PEAK

BRIDLE

QUARTER
BLOCK

BOWLINE

COURSE
URLED)

CROSSJACK
BRACE

MIZZEN
TOPS'L
SAIL SHEET

SPANKER

BRAILS

TOPSAIL
HALLIARD

MIZZEN FORESTAY

MAIN TOPS'L BRACE

LEECH
OF
SPANKER

BACKSTAYS

REEFS

TOPSAIL
HALLIARD

William Mowll - 1994

BUILDING A WORKING MODEL WARSHIP

BUILDING
A WORKING
MODEL
WARSHIP

HMS WARRIOR 1860

William Mowll

CHATHAM PUBLISHING

LONDON

For Susie,
the first and true love of my life.

The model of *Warrior* is now on permanent display at Portsmouth
in the *Warrior* visitors' centre.

Complete sets of plans of *Warrior* are available from:
The Plans Department, Nexus Special Interests,
Nexus House, Boundary Way,
Hemel Hempstead, Herts HP2 7ST

Frontispiece: HMS *Warrior* drawn by J E Wigston

Copyright © William Mowll 1997

First published in Great Britain in 1997 by
Chatham Publishing,
1 & 2 Faulkner's Alley,
Cowcross Street,
London EC1M 6DD

Chatham Publishing is an imprint of Gerald Duckworth & Co Ltd

British Library Cataloguing in Publication Data
A catalogue record for this book is available from the British Library

Hardback edition ISBN 0 86176 019 1
Paper cased edition ISBN 0 86176 041 8

Typeset and designed by Trevor Ridley ATD FRSA
Printed and bound in Great Britain by the Bath Press, Bath

CONTENTS

ACKNOWLEDGEMENTS

My grateful thanks are due to the following, without whom I would have been unable to bring such a major undertaking to completion.

Warrior: the model

Keith Lines, who laid up the GRP, and became such an ally in the early stages of the project. Geoff Sheppard, whose engi-neering skills in miniature are so carefully thought through: to him belongs the phrase 'Not only must it look right, but it has to work as well'. Dave Metcalf, for draughting the full set of scale plans for making the model (available from Nexus - see list of suppliers). Phyllis Checkley, my mother-in-law, whose exquisite needlework with the full wardrobe of miniature sails gives the authenticity required to what is perhaps the

Captain Henry Boys with his officers on the quarterdeck of *Warrior*, 1869. My great-grandfather sits cross-legged, fourth from the left.

most ethereal and difficult aspect of model shipwrighting.

Model shipwrighting

John Cundell, Editor of *Model Boats*, who for twenty years has risked covering the lengthy stages of bringing my three major models to completion, and given me endless gentle tips and advice on the way. He was the first person to explain to me that cameras had speed and aperture settings. Mike Taylor, Editor of the *Journal of the Scale Sailing Association*, for being the most adventurous and original working scale modelmaker I know. His attitude of 'Devil take the hindmost' was much in mind when I launched *Warrior* into the English Channel. He introduced me to metal casting in sand, and to many other techniques over the years. Tony Lench, who knows about miniature working sail, and is a near neighbour and mentor.

Research

Captain John Wells RN, without whose book, *The Immortal Warrior*, my work would have been much impoverished, if not impossible. Jean Bartram, PA to the Project Manager, Ray Hockey, at West Hartlepool; Walter Brownlee, who showed me over the ship in 1982; Keith Johnson, Bill Stevenson and Jim Wilson, all members of the original restoration team.

Portsmouth

Captain Colin Allen RN, who brought the ship home to Portsmouth under tow from restoration in West Hartlepool and was the first active Captain of the restored ship. Captain Fraser Morgan, for the kindnesses and attention received from him in the past five years.

Stanley Paine and Michael Leek, who supervised the illustration done by Stephen Ortega at Bournemouth and Poole College of Art and Design. John Longstaff, researcher. Len Paveley, who has come up with all sorts of interesting information from his extensive library. John Wigston, whose pen and ink sketches of *Warrior* have led to a prolonged friendship for the past fifteen years. John Smith, formerly MP for Westminster, who saved the ship for the nation, and has written several encouraging letters regarding the model.

Photography

Ray Brigden, Staff Photographer for the *Sunday Express* over many years, responsible for the official photographs taken of the model, and for the jacket of this book. Alison Fisher, who took the photographs of the sandcasting process, and to both Ben and Josh Mowll, who have on occasions had to answer a panic call to photograph some workshop procedure. Ian and Anne Andrews of Steam Powered Video, Dunkirk, for help and assistance.

Floating out trials

Richard, Hazel and James Linforth for the use of their pool.

Launch in the sea

Joe Brewer and Richard Judges for their strong backs and willing hands. Miss Alice Mannering, for her part in the official launch.

Script and editing

To Stephanie Rudgard-Redsell, who has made time to understand the technicalities of Victorian steam and sail, and made sense of my hastily written articles and notes. From an initial position of knowing nothing about this subject, she has not only grasped all the processes, but has also used her considerable skills with the English language to give the words of this book a correctness and a shiny polish that they never had before.

WILLIAM MOWLL
February 1997

THE FIRST AND LAST BATTLESHIP

HMS Warrior 1860: the Model for Nineteenth-Century Hybrid Model Ships

HMS *Warrior* was launched in 1860 at a critical moment in the history of ship development, when naval ships were no longer to be constructed from timber, but built from iron with armour plating, with rivets replacing nails and wrought iron bars used in place of wooden deck beams. Added to this was the issue of steam power, an invention which was progressively being adopted by both passenger ships and warships. Sail was still the major motive power, and had changed little in form or rig during the previous one hundred years, but made demands on the new technologies by requiring hoisting propellers and retractable funnels. The 1860s also saw enormous changes in armament, from smooth-bored 68pdr muzzle-loading guns, to breech-loading, shell-firing 110pdr Armstrong guns at the bow and stern of the ship, so that those ship-modellers who have a specialist interest in ordnance are also well served by the wealth of developments which were occurring in this mid-Victorian period. In *Warrior* we have the fleeting situation of the old and the new cheek by jowl, and anyone considering making a nineteenth-century model has this unique combination placed before them in the one famous prototype.

When compared with the pace of the enormous strides taken with the steam engines that powered the mills of industry

and pumped out the filthy waters of flooding mineshafts, the idea of raising steam inside the hull of a boat in order to propel a vessel mechanically through the water was relatively slow to catch on. This reluctance arose in part from the fact that the early engines took up the most desirable space in the vessel amidships. Steam power also made ships heavier, dirtier and more awkward to manoeuvre, besides which these auxiliary engines were nothing like as efficient as wind power. Added to these apparent disadvantages were the inherent risks associated with operating a steam engine aboard a vessel, whilst the difficulties of repairing and maintaining such an addition to the ship's equipment necessitated the employment of a special

John Fitch's first steam-boat on the Delaware River, USA 1785. 34ft long, with twelve vertical oars chain-driven via geared sprocket wheel. (Author)

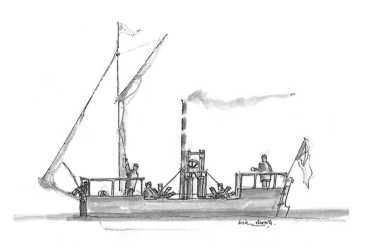

Miller and Symington's experimental steam-boat, Loch Dalswinton near Dumfries 1788. 'The first successful paddle steamer capable of doing service in the carriage of passengers or goods'.25ft long. (Author)

PT *Charlotte Dundas* 1801. The first stern-wheeler tug-boat, used on the Forth & Clyde canal. 56ft long. (Author)

the Delaware River, and Robert Fulton (1765-1815), are now both well-known and the importance of their innovative work recognised, but they suffered ridicule at the time. The unfortunate John Fitch was so depressed by the refusal of his contemporaries to see him as a serious inventor that eventually he committed suicide.[1]

On the other side of the pond in Scotland, Patrick Miller, an Edinburgh banker, and William Symington, a mining engineer, were experimenting in 1788 with the first successful paddle steamer on Loch Dalswinton. William Symington's engine was designed for powering carriages, but modified to fit into the hull of a boat. There appears not to have been a commercial outcome to this project, although Miller had poured his own money into the venture. Thirteen years later, in 1801, Symington's name reappears with his single-cylinder, double-acting engine, which became an established favourite for years to come, fitted to the mechanically very successful *Charlotte Dundas*, the first steam-powered tugboat. The prototype became the victim of critics who feared that the wash churned up by this stern-wheeler would destroy the canal banks, but this tugboat itself was seminal in every way.

workforce to stoke and trim the boiler and attend to the demands of the engine. The bunkering of coal also remained a weighty issue for shipping companies in more ways than one, particularly on long voyages, or on distant stations, whence the coal itself had to be ferried.

The earliest experiments were carried out on both sides of the Atlantic even before the turn of the nineteenth century, using inland waterways and lakes for these waterborne trials. The names of early American pioneers like John Fitch (1743-1798), with his three experimental craft on

Six years later in the USA, Robert Fulton's passenger ferry *Clermont*, unkindly referred to as 'Fulton's Folly', was the first steamer to prove that long-distance steam-powered ferrying was a practical possibility. On 21 August 1807 she made passage between New York and Albany, a distance of 150 miles, in 32 hours, averaging 5mph. Both Fitch and Fulton predicted the future of regular steam packet services, but sadly neither lived to see that day come to pass.

Five years on from the *Clermont*'s success, on the Clyde Henry Bell's *Comet* proved that it was possible to run a commercial paddle steamer in Europe, at a profit. His steamboat had the wonderful

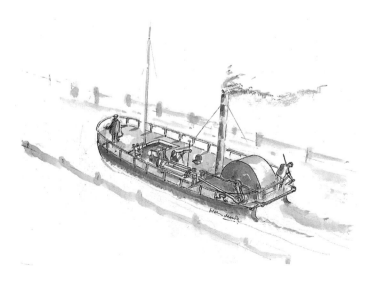

practical answer as to how one can mix sail and steam together by substituting a long, tall funnel in place of the mainmast. Why the sail did not catch fire is somewhat of a mystery.

The first brave attempt at taking a hybrid steam and sailing vessel across the Atlantic from west to east took place on 22 May 1819. The PS *Savannah* (1819) was no more than a converted windjammer, constructed in New Jersey and weighing in at 380 tons, with a single-cylinder engine and folding canvas paddlewheels. Although only fired up for eighty hours of steaming on a passage lasting twenty-nine days, she was the first engined sailing ship to cross from the New World to the Old, and the forerunner of all the powered ships built in the following fifty years, where steam and sail were employed as complementary motive forces.[2]

Eighteen years would pass before the epic voyage of the PS *Sirius,* the first ship to steam continuously on the North Atlantic passage from east to west. She snatched the crown from under the nose of Brunel's PS *Great Western,* which could rightly be claimed to have been built for this passage as the first *bona fide* packet ship, fulfilling the dreams of those early pioneers, Fitch and Fulton.

This slice of history includes some of the most famous ships ever built, including Brunel's three 'Greats': *Western*

(1838), *Britain* (1843), and *Eastern* (1859). In 1838, the same year as the PS *Sirius* and PS *Great Western* made their maiden voyages across the Atlantic, SS *Archimedes*, the first screw ship, was launched - a ship which so impressed Brunel that the moment he saw screw propulsion in action in October 1840, he stopped the engine building programme on the *Great Britain*, disposed of the paddle boxes, which were already attached to the hull, turned the engine through 90 degrees, and fitted her with a six-bladed propeller.

The list of hybrids continues on from the earlier part of the nineteenth century

Clermont 1807. Built by Charles Brown, Corlear's Hook, East River, New York to the order of Robert Fulton. Displacement 100 tons. 133ft long. (Author)

Bell's *Comet* on the Clyde 1812. The first steamer to run commercially in Europe. Displacement 28 tons. 51ft long, with two sets of radial paddles. (Author)

with lesser-known vessels such as the PS *William Fawcett* (1829), which picked up on the emergent contract mail service vital to the funding of this age of hybrid paddle ships, and the PS *Britannia* (1840) which, with her three sister ships *Acadia, Caledonia,* and *Columbia,* formed the Cunard Steamship Co. This established the first monthly transatlantic mail steamship service from Liverpool to Halifax and Boston. The last of the transatlantic paddlers, PS *Scotia* (1861), was the most beautifully-proportioned hybrid of them all with her rakish lines, and her lavishly gilded ribands and gal-

(Above)
PS *Sirius* 1837. The first ship to steam continuously across the Atlantic from the UK to America (1838). Displacement 703 tons. 208ft long. 9kts. (Author)

(Right)
SS *Archimedes* 1838. One of the earliest screw-driven steamships with a spiral propeller. Displacement 237 tons. 125ft long. 9kts. (Author)

PS *Scotia* 1861. The fastest passenger ship on the Atlantic run 1862-1867, with a time of 8 days 3 hours. Displacement 3871 tons. 379ft long. 14kts. Iron-built. (Author)

PS *Savannah* 1819. The first steam vessel to cross the Atlantic. Displacement 380 tons. 110ft long. (Author)

1. Armstrong, Richard, *Powered Ships: The Beginnings* (London: Benn, 1974), p29.

2. For those who would like to know where models of these early experimental steamers may be found, the American Museum in Bath (UK) has an excellent small model of *Clermont*. The United States National Museum Smithsonian Institution has the most accurate model of PS *Savannah* (USNM 319026), although the Science Museum in London also has a model of this vessel, beautifully represented, a gift of the Newcomen Society. The Science Museum also has models of some early experimental ships and boats which were concurrent with those of the American visionaries: the PT *Charlotte Dundas* 1801, a tugboat used on the Forth and Clyde canal, and Robert Fulton's First Steamboat (unnamed), which he launched on the Seine, as well as Henry Bell's PS *Comet* 1812, built for passenger service on the Clyde.

leries. At a perpendicular length of 400ft she was 20ft longer than *Warrior*, built from iron and launched in 1861, the same year as *Warrior*'s first commission. She paddled her way across the Atlantic in 8 days and 3 hours, and held the Blue Riband from 1862-1867.

From the 1840s to the 1860s was a time in history when hybrid ships in both the naval and merchant services were at their most graceful, possessing not only clipper bows, figureheads and acres of canvas, but also involving the challenge to engineering skills which accompanied the installation of steam power amidships, whether in the form of paddle or screw. In the restored form of *Warrior* we have living proof of the ultimate skills of Victorian craftsmanship and design.

1
THE WORKSHOP

Many people want to know about the workshop requirements necessary to bring a complex working model to completion. Nowadays, it is the miniature tooling available which allows amateurs to achieve standards that some few years ago were only attainable by professional model builders, and this is where the answer lies to the question of how it is possible to build ship models to 'glass case' standards that are also fully-working miniature vessels. In addition, new techniques of construction and new model equipment make such models feasible.

Glass case models take to the sea

No young child visiting a museum to gaze on ship models will leave all those wonderfully crafted objects in their glass cases without an inner desire to know what they would look like if put on the water, and indeed whether or not they would *work*.

Two major advances in technology do now mean that under exceptional circumstances (mainly for film-making purposes) glass case scale models can take to the water. The introduction of fibreglass as a material for making large model hulls which are impervious to water, and strong enough to withstand the racking forces of machinery aboard, make it quite feasible to produce large-scale, stable, waterproof

hulls, unaffected even by salt water. There is a striking historic parallel here between the inherent weakness of the old wooden-walled hulls, and those built with greater strength from the new material of iron, easily able to sustain the extra weight imposed by the demands of a heavy engine and boilers.

The other great technological advance is the introduction of proportional radio control, making it possible to replicate the movement of human fingers at a remote distance. This was a dream of my childhood, and such things do allow the operator to become master of his or her own ship, albeit on a small scale. There is nothing in terms of switching items on and off which the modern multi-channelled transmitter cannot effect. These transmitters also have the ability, *via* joysticks, to control certain items proportionally, just as in an aircraft cockpit. Thus anything from a steam valve wheel to a fully automatic winch can be controlled by radio transmission. This includes steering, reversing the engine, controlling the sails and yards, aiming guns (and even on some models firing them), activating the ship's hooter, or an electronic simulator, providing lighting and navigational signals, lowering boats with separate receivers and servos in them for individual control: the list is as far-reaching as the human imagination.

The result of all this is that models

cannot only be launched, but they can also be operated on water, as well as being safely retrieved in a totally realistic fashion. It is difficult for me to comprehend, but model submarines can also be fully controlled using the same equipment as surface vessels. It puts into the hands of the ship-modeller the means to turn childhood dreams into reality, and on occasions to release the ship model from the glass case into the freedom of the water where it properly belongs. What satisfaction it is to be able to say, 'Yes, it does work', rather than to say, 'No, it is simply for display purposes.' It is the difference between an animal roaming in the wild, and a creature condemned to live in a cage.

Machine tools

With few exceptions, full-scale electrically-powered machine tools have their counterparts in miniature and, while it is not essential to have a shed or garage crammed full of modelmaking machinery to produce a model boat, there are machine tools which are essential for serious ship-modellers.

First, I would like to make a point about machines in general. Underpowered machines are worse than useless; this single statement comes with a prejudice against those power tools that are dependent on DC transformers as their power source. These tools lack the necessary vigour to machine timber and metal, and are therefore ultimately disappointing. Only mains electricity delivers the necessary power.

A maxim for all machine tools is that each should recover its purchase price in a year. For instance, if you purchase a small circular saw, you would expect to recoup the cost of the machine by avoiding having to buy pre-sawn bundles of timber, cut to small sizes. This will not only save a great deal of money, travel and postage, but it will also enable you to use pieces of discarded offcuts, old furniture, or even your

own seasoned timber. If the machine tool in question will not fulfil this condition, then think carefully about your rationale for buying it, if all it is going to do is to occupy scarce shelf space.

A second, and equally important, rule of thumb is that you should always buy the biggest that you can possibly afford. Machine tools depend on rigidity for their accuracy, and the heavier the castings are, the more accurate the machine is likely to be. A good machine will last you a working lifetime; what better investment could there be?

Bandsaw

From the outset, and predating my enthusiasm for model shipwrighting, I had a small bandsaw in my workshop, a tool that is an essential item for the scratch builder of boats. The cutting action of this machine tool is a constant downward movement, and its rate of feed is controllable by sound and feel, no matter what the material being cut. It will also machine non-ferrous metal, such as brass, aluminium, copper or bronze, and will tackle mild steel with the aid of modern cutting fluids. It will cut bevel angles; it will cut rounded shapes, or long thin strips; it will even cut small branches in half, and is one of the safest machine tools in the workshop because of its gentle downward sawing action. And as a bonus, it creates very little dust.

Vibrosaw

The first specialist machine tool which I bought for model shipwrighting was the Italian Aeropiccola Vibrosaw. It is now twenty years old and still doing excellent work. This saw uses a jeweller's piercing blade, and enables the operator to do very fine filigree work in almost any material you care to name. The blade is demountable, thus it can cut internal work, and you can twist the blade so finely that it is pos-

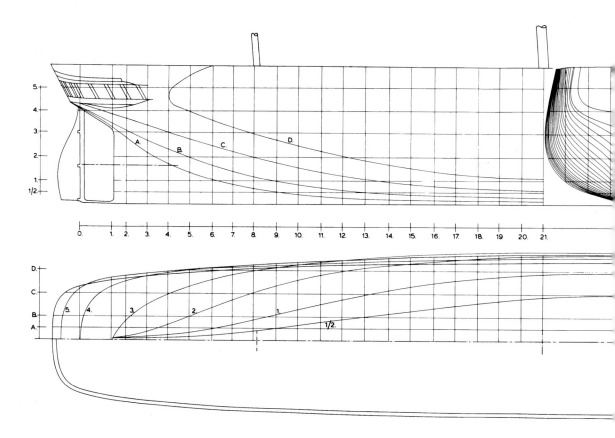

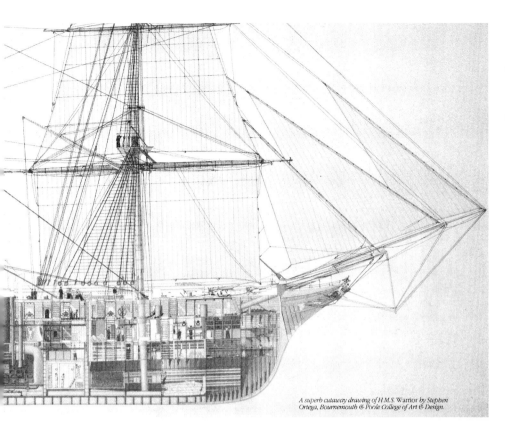

Cutaway illustration of
Warrior.
(Stephen Ortega,
Bournemouth and Poole
College)

*A superb cutaway drawing of H.M.S. Warrior by Stephen
Ortega, Bournemouth & Poole College of Art & Design.*

Hull lines.
(Author & D J Metcalf)

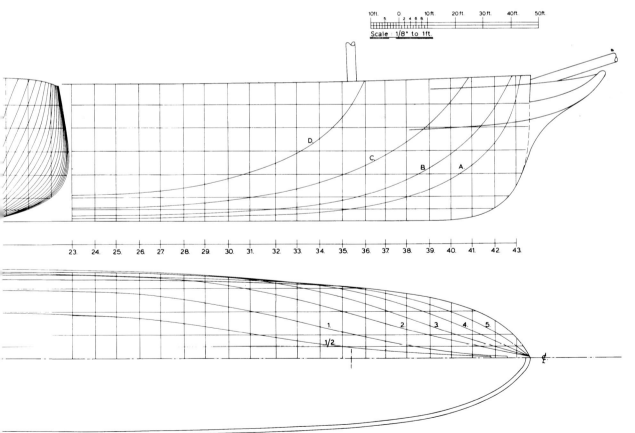

10ft.   0   10ft.   20ft.   30ft.   40ft.   50ft.
Scale : 1/8" to 1ft.

D.

C.

B.   A.

23.   24.   25.   26.   27.   28.   29.   30.   31.   32.   33.   34.   35.   36.   37.   38.   39.   40.   41.   42.   43.

1.   2.   3.   4.   5.

1/2.

sible to cut square corners in one pass without breaking the blade.

Pillar drill

All electric drills can be converted to a vertical pillar drill with a stand, faceplate and fine feed lever on the spindle. Many of these are now quite sophisticated and work with great accuracy, but an integrated machine in constant readiness is a great boon, and it can also be used as a light milling machine when used in conjunction with a cross vice.

Mains-powered miniaturisation

No workshop dealing with miniature fabrication could pass by the Dremel precision power tool products. This American company produces a number of machines. Admittedly, their machine tools and accessories are more expensive than their rivals, but each of them is an outstanding product in its field. The Multi Tool is a mains-powered drill, about half the size of a standard unit but very powerful, with revs to 30,000rpm, making it ideal for routing and other high speed applications; it can also get into the most awkward places with the use of a Robart angled head attachment. Their second product of note is a table saw with rise, fall and tilt. It can carry out all the operations one would expect of a machine twice its size, including cutting non-ferrous metal with a tungsten blade. This machine is not perfect, but no-one else has taken so seriously the

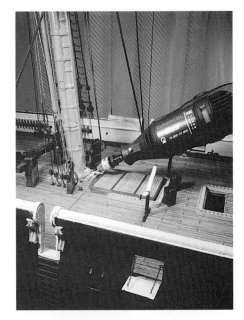

need for modelmakers to have a miniature, mains-powered table saw.

Universal sharpening

The most useful machine tool in the workshop, that is to say, the one which is most often in use, is the disc and belt sander. This is an innocuous-looking machine, which for many years I dismissed as a toy not worthy of serious consideration. What I had failed to appreciate was that, because abrasive belts are so advanced in their cut-

(Below)
Dremel router.

(Opposite top)
Dremel Multi Tool.

(Opposite lower)
Dremel saw.

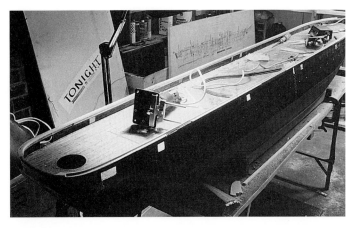

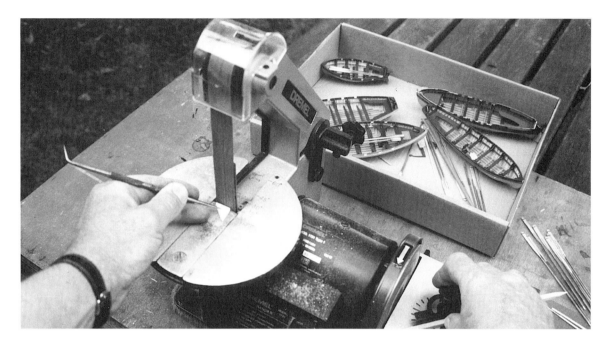

Dremel linisher.

ting ability, this machine is the most versatile sharpening device yet invented for
general workshop use. It will put an edge
on cutting tools of all kinds without drawing the temper of the metal because the
running belt stays cool, unlike an electric
bench grinder which builds up a spiral of
heat at the point of contact. The action is
very gentle, and complicated form tools
can be ground out using the edge of the
belt, something that it is almost impossible to do with stones. Knife blades, chisels, screwdrivers, gouges, scalpels, needles, drill points, scissors, snips and so
forth, can all be sharpened and dressed on
the revolving belt with relative ease. To
this list must be added the notion that
when you are dealing with very small
items they can be offered up to the
machine without having to clamp them in
a vice. It is possible to sand down minuscule parts by controlling them at needle
point against the abrasive strap, with maximum visibility over the marked line.

The lathe

Now for the question considered sooner or
later by every ship modeller with high
hopes: whether or not to invest in a lathe.
For many years I convinced myself that I
neither needed nor wanted one. (To be
truthful, I did always want one, but the
cost was way beyond what I felt I could
justify.) I was also concerned that I might
not have the necessary skills to operate a
screw-cutting lathe to good effect.

The purchase of a second-hand
British-built (Myford) screw-cutting lathe
was a dream come true, but it also represented the largest investment I have ever
made in a machine tool. It was a well-
loved and well-used thirty-year-old
machine which came with all the tooling.
Roughly speaking, if purchased from new,
you might expect to spend the same
amount again as you pay for the basic
piece of equipment on all the essential
pieces of tooling which make it into the
immensely versatile machine it is.

Thinking back to those days, ownership of a lathe taught me what precision
meant, and it brought a discipline into my
work which had not been there before; it
also taught me to think processes through
in a logical way before embarking on the
machining process. Measurement became
very important, and I also discovered that

the lathe itself is a wonderful piece of measuring equipment for marking out datum lines and divisions of circles, as well as making an item perfectly square. Any initial feelings of inadequacy soon disappear as skills with the lathe quickly develop, and your work will be elevated into a completely new realm. A lathe is not an essential piece of equipment unless engineering is involved, but those who are fortunate enough to own one have the capability of making not only a finished item, but also of carrying out the intermediate tooling and jigmaking required in any engineered item that you would expect to see in a full-scale professional machine shop.

Forgework: the uses of propane gas

Heat is essential for four processes in modelling, which means that a propane torch is a requirement. These processes are: softening and tempering metal; silver-soldering; heating the crucible; and heating the copper bending tube.

Softening and tempering the metal

The fierce heat produced by a propane torch can be used for softening metal of all kinds, and tempering it for sharpening. One cannot deal with metal fabrication without a source of intense heat, and propane gas provides this in a quick and instant fashion; I use a Swedish Sievert torch, accompanied by a series of nozzles.

Fire bricks are important companions to the process of silver-soldering, in reflecting conducted heat around the metal. This means that a small forge is called for, although this can be quite simply wired together.

Silver-soldering

This process has almost no relation to soft-soldering, depending as it does on heating the whole item to red-heat and applying the solder in that state. It makes an extremely strong joint which will put up with a great deal of punishment, being harder than the metal it joins, and is good for both non-ferrous and steel jointing, with appropriate fluxing. (The flux allows the silver to flow into the joint.) Surprisingly, silver-soldering is much easier to do than soft-soldering, in that it is possible to regulate and control the flow of the solder stick, but it does require the heat of propane to effect it.

Heating the crucible

You also need to be able to heat up the ladle for metal casting; butane gas will do this adequately, but propane saves time. Finally, the torch is useful for putting inside copper tubing for steaming and plank-bending purposes, although only a low setting is required for this.

Most of this can be seen as black-smithing on a small scale, apart from the plank-bending, but this is really what scratch building turns out to be; every scratch builder is fascinated by the age-old skills of the smithy, partly because the skilled modelmaker knows that what goes on over the forge can be emulated provided there is an equivalent heat source in the workshop. The taming of metal is just as fascinating as the mastery of timber, and there are times and places where it is much easier to fabricate an item in metal, rather than reproducing it in hardwood. Metal can be persuaded in a way which timber will not allow, and timber likewise can be dressed up to look like metal, at less than half the weight.

Victorian craftsmen had bandsaws, table saws, pillar drills, shapers, lathes, screw-cutting and boring machines, forges, casting facilities, as well as a whole array of hand tools. If the modelmaker is to emulate in miniature what the Victorians did, but bearing in mind that they used steam power, rather than electricity, it is likely that we will end up with a similar array of bits and pieces, if only

Illustration of forge and alligator clips. (Author)

we have the room to house such things. It is nearly always true that it is space, not money, that is the final arbiter on how far we can tool up for the job.

Adhesives

Apart from machinery and tooling, the other great leap forward for modelmakers has to do with the myriad of adhesives now available. It is quite possible to glue pieces of metal together, without having to resort to either soldering practices or mechanical joints. Epoxy resins of all sorts, if they are properly applied, have great inherent strength, as well as water-inhibiting properties, far superior to the animal glues of which ancient models were built. The use of resin paste fillers makes possible the repair of some very ugly mistakes without trace. Glass-reinforced polyester (GRP), in conjunction with glass mat strand, allows for the waterproofing of boat hulls from the inside, or the construction of complete hulls in the form of GRP moulding.

As far as timber adhesives are concerned, proprietary brands abound, but it should be remembered that only the two-part glues can be said to be truly water-tight, although a one-shot water-miscible resin glue, for example Cascamite, can be relied upon to give long service. Instant glues of the cyanoacrylate variety have a proven record of longevity, provided they are used in the right circumstances. Contact glues, where both surfaces are covered before the two parts are brought together, also work well, and allow non-permeable material, as well as cloth, to be stuck to a dissimilar surface.

Raw materials

Depending on the modelmaker's ability to machine wood and metal, a huge variety of raw material is available from everyday sources, and items regarded as junk by most people can be as gold-dust to the inventive modelmaker. Seasoned timber comes in abundance from old furniture; a hardwood plank can provide a basic source of stock for a complete model, or a sheet of resin-bonded ply can become the beginnings of a ribbed structure for a plank-on-frame hull. GRP, and all its resinous relations, provides another way of tackling the production demands of a difficult shape which must also be water-proof. It is an excellent material in many ways apart, that is, from the smell.

Non-ferrous metals, such as aluminium, brass and copper, are much easier to cope with than they used to be. Aluminium can now be soldered to itself quite easily, and is more readily available than brass. Such advances have come about because of improvements in fluxes, which were previously rather crude in their chemical composition. The machining of copper and brass has been advanced by cutting fluids which cool the tips of blade teeth and tool bits. Tungsten carbide lessens the need for constant sharpening, and high-speed steel drills are relatively cheap and easy to obtain in minuscule sizes. Aluminium, copper and brass can all be cut with appropriate blades in a bandsaw, jigsaw, or even a table (circular) saw, so that all are potential modelling materials. Brass tube, bar and flat stock are all made in miniature sizes, although they may be more difficult to obtain than their plastic equivalents. Plasticard is yet another medium on the ascendancy, because it is clean and easy to deal with, requires no priming before finishing, and comes in many different thicknesses. Miniature plastic extrusions in the profiles of all the standard stocks are also readily available, as are the adhesives to join (or chemically weld) the material together.

Chemical engineering with acid is discussed in the text, and is a fascinating way of producing very fine work, in either brass or copper sheet, without a saw or file being involved. Model shipbuilding also requires the use of glass, leather, thread, felt, rubber, stainless steel and copper wire: almost any raw material or compound that one cares to name. Silicone rubber used with low-melt metals also means that modellers can now make master patterns of high quality for casting purposes, which has advanced the cause of realism no end, as well as removing some of the tedium of producing many identical small parts. The final link in this chain is the low-temperature solder now available, which means that the modeller can solder parts to low-melt castings, for example sights onto a gun barrel, and build up detail in this way, without the use of adhesives.

Paints and finishes

Fashions change enormously with regard to final presentation. Time was when scale models at the pond side were painted in bright, glossy colours, often displaying gleaming brass fittings. These days modelmakers are aware that if they wish to emulate the full-size ship or craft, any sort of shine apart from a dull haze will look unrealistic. The arrival of satin finishes and matt shine varnishes have greatly improved the realism of presentation of model ships and boats, although it is a hard lesson for those who can produce a magnificent mirror finish on timber to learn to resist this. The truth about shiny surfaces is that in full scale the gleam fades away the moment any distance is put between the vessel and the shore: the shine disappears into the atmosphere.

Colour

The other lesson, which has still to be learned by many modellers in all disciplines, is to paint the subject one shade lighter than the prototype. If true realism is sought, you have to consider the density in an object which is a diminution of the original. Some modelmakers believe that if they can obtain a pot of paint in the identical colour of the prototype then the model will look exactly as it should, but this does not take into account the effect of light on pigment. Tonally speaking, if the model is painted with prototype paint, it will appear denser than it should; the model is a diminutive of the full-scale object and as the size of the object is reduced, so also should be the tonal value of the paint. If you cannot believe this, there is a simple way of proving it: shake a light mist of talcum powder over a black hull, and note how it appears more realistic. Mix talcum powder with any gloss paint and it will turn into matt, and matted paint is the first great advance towards accurate representation. Film-makers, and artists in their paintings, demonstrate an understanding of the interactions between light and colour; modellers cannot afford to disregard this knowledge, which has been acquired over many years of observing and considering the effects of light and shade.

One last piece of advice: beware the colour white when dealing with anything predating the 1930s. The white paint of previous generations was what we would now call cream, and on older ships this was the colour which one associates with tobacco stains. A mid-brown varnish over cream will give you a nautical white; never use white straight from the pot - in fact, never use any colour straight from the pot. No artist ever paints without first mixing on the palette, and this is preceded by a great deal of consideration as to how the object is lit. In real life the effects of colour are more complex and nothing is a single colour, thus models painted straight from the pot will look clinical and lifeless. The more that you study paintings of ships, and look at the way that artists handle what we actually see, so much the more will your finishes authenticate themselves.

The substance of this book is about working with all the above raw materials: fabricating them, joining them together and making sure that they not only work, but also look right. These days there are almost no excuses that modelmakers can offer in terms of the deficiencies in equipment available for producing a crafted piece of work; the fascination is in how many individual interpretations there are in the finished product, whereby no two models of a prototype will ever look the same, despite being built from the same plan.

Benchmark philosophy

Modelmaking is an adventure, so be adventurous and experimental in your work. There is no 'right way' of doing things and everyone must at times eat the humble pie of failure, but the only way to remove that taste from your mouth is to succeed next time by improving on the original mistake. Each and every small component that you make must be a model in its own right and one which can stand close scrutiny; think of yourself as being on a factory production line where each of your offerings must pass through quality control before it is accepted for fitting. This way you will not regret at the conclusion what you did at the outset because it will have been your very best effort at the time - and this is vital because, as your work improves, you do not want to rue the early stages of the model which have become unalterable.

Deadlines can be both good and bad. In the early stages, do not set them if you are not obliged to. Much more important is to keep a log of what you have done, and what you propose to do; this will give you a more realistic idea of the length of time it will take to bring the model to completion. It also acts as an *aide memoire* for the different ways you tackled jobs, as well as a notebook in which to jot down your thoughts at the end of a session, so that you do not waste time when you come back into the workshop, and can pick up straight away at the point where you left off. This saves a huge amount of time and is a discipline worth adopting.

The last piece of advice is not to be isolationist in your modelmaking. Talk to people who use their hands - plumbers, mechanics, boatbuilders in full scale, people who machine timber for a living, panelbeaters, welders, turners, saddlers, patternmakers, foundrymen, glaziers. The list is endless, but they all have advice to give which is worth hearing and which will impinge on your work in miniature and the way that you go about it. Although you may complete a model, you never reach a point where you have perfected all the skills. There will always be a belief that you can do better next time, and that is the hook, line and sinker of scratch building.

2
BUILDING THE HULL

Dimensions of Warrior

Source: Admiral G A Ballard, *The Black Battlefleet* (London: Society for Nautical Research, 1980)

Hull
Tonnage: Burden 6109; Displ 9137
Weights: Hull 6072; Equipment 3034
Length: BP 380ft 2in
Beam: 58ft 4in
Draught: Fwd 26ft 2in; Aft 26ft 9in

Armour
Thickness: Sides 4$\frac{1}{2}$in
Weight: 975 tons
Depth below designed load water line: 5ft
Timber backing: Teak 18in

Armament
Main deck: 8-110pdr RBL; 26-68pdr SB
Upper deck: 2-110pdr RBL; 4-40pdr RBL;
2-20pdr RBL; 1-6pdr RBL

Engine
Engine builder: Penn
Type: Trunk
No of cylinders: 2
Nominal HP: 1250
Diameter of cylinder: 104.23in
Stroke: 48in
Pressure: 20lbs
Coal: 700 tons

Screw
Diameter: 24ft 6in
Pitch: 30ft

It is a remarkable stroke of good fortune that no natural disasters have destroyed the two prime examples of Victorian iron shipbuilding in this country. The concept of manufacturing iron ships rather than wooden ones was the product of a new breed of ship designers and builders in early and mid-Victorian times: in their training and outlook they were primarily engineers and scientists rather than shipwrights. Foremost amongst these was Brunel. The SS *Great Britain* (1843) was his second transatlantic ship, and one whose clincher-built hull was fabricated solely from iron, and double-riveted throughout. She was so strong that she survived a hazardous beaching on the northeast coast of Ireland for almost a year in 1846, punishment which no wooden ship could possibly have endured, and proved to the world the innate strength of wrought iron ships. Over one hundred and fifty years later she is still extant and back in Bristol where she was built. The other example is *Warrior*, now fully restored and afloat at Portsmouth.

The prototype

HMS *Warrior* 1860 was the first major all-iron warship ordered by the Royal Navy, and her purpose was in part to restore prestige and national pride after the adverse criticism of the fleet's perfor-

mance in the Crimean War. The launch of
this vessel was hastened by the decree in
1857 of the French *Genie Maritime*, under
the direction of Napoleon III, that there
would be no further timber ships built in
France.[1] The world's first ironclad battleship *La Gloire* came down the slipway in
1859, accompanied by a rumour that she
was made from polished steel. The truth
was that she was built from oak, with an
armoured belt and top deck of iron, and
capable of a top speed of 12 knots. The
plans for three more similar vessels were
in hand to keep up the momentum generated by France's success in the Crimea.

It must be understood that the French
Navy at this time was better organised
than the British, although it did not have
the capacity to manufacture ships made
totally from iron, whereas the British were
several years ahead in technological terms,
due to their experience gained with building merchant ships and transatlantic lin-
ers. This also applied to the excellence of
the engine-producing firms such as
Maudslay's and Penn's, whose expertise in
the manufacture of steam plant was
revered throughout the world.

HMS *Warrior* was laid down at the
Thames Iron Works and Shipbuilding
Company in May 1859 as HM Naval
Dockyards were at this time unable to
build iron ships. *Warrior* was built to a
design by the ageing Sir Isaac Watts, the
Navy's Chief Constructor, and the whole
project masterminded by Rear Admiral
Sir Baldwin Walker, Controller of the
Navy. Launched eighteen months later,
and commissioned by Captain the Hon
Arthur Cochrane with seven hundred officers and men, *Warrior* started her career
on 1 August 1861. John Scott Russell had
submitted a model and drawing to Sir
Baldwin Walker in late 1855, and since
then there has been an ongoing dispute
regarding the extent of John Scott
Russell's contribution to the design, with
the Admiralty formally rejecting Russell's
claim to be co-designer in June 1859.[2]

According to George Emmerson, Russell's
1855 design was:

of a completely iron ship constructed on the
longitudinal system with an outer skin of
thick iron armour plate backed by wood.
The lines and proportions ... were based on
his wave-line theory. Sir Baldwin Walker ...
was reasonably impressed. The time was not
auspicious, he feared for placing a revolutionary idea of the kind before the Admiralty,
but he would take the first opportunity to do
so. Russell enquired after the fate of his
design on each occasion he met Sir Baldwin
over the next three years and submitted further proposals until, late in 1858, Sir Baldwin
asked him to prepare a larger version of his
design while at the same time the Surveyor's

Stern view of *Warrior*
under construction.
(Mary Evans Picture
Library)

1. Ropp, Theodore,
*The Development of a
Modern Navy: French
Naval Policy 1871-1904*
(Annapolis, Maryland:
Naval Institute Press,
1987), p9.
2. Emmerson, George S,
*John Scott Russell: A
Great Victorian Engineer
and Naval Architect*
(London, 1977), pp160-
61; Brown, D K, and
John Wells, 'HMS
Warrior', Paper No 2,
Royal Institute of Naval
Architects, Spring
Meeting 1986; letter to
author from Captain John
Wells.

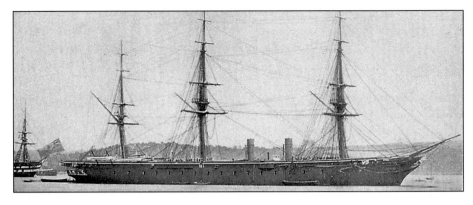

department under Isaac Watts prepared a similar design and invited some other shipbuilders to do likewise.[3]

In spite of these contributions, Russell's tender for constructing *Warrior* was refused because of its cost and its timescale. He felt that his efforts so far warranted some acknowledgement, but the Admiralty response was that many of *Warrior*'s innovative features were not original to Russell, being part of the general language of contemporary ship design. Emmerson puts it thus:

> Russell's pioneering contributions were not protected by patent and the Admiralty felt no sense of obligation to one of its most valuable and imaginative advisers. Russell, over a period of years, had submitted a whole range of designs of armoured ships embracing all the various sizes. In conducting this campaign in secret he unfortunately committed his advanced and original designs to sterility, and, in the end, to plagiarism.[4]

Whatever the extent of the different contributions, the brilliance of the design for this totally new breed of iron warship was undeniable; overnight the sailing wooden warship had become obsolete. *Warrior* was not an iron-*clad* ship, but a vessel built from stem to stern of wrought iron: pure puddled metal.

Put simply, the design of the new ship was quite revolutionary: this was an invincible floating engine of war, with a low

profile, 120ft longer than any other warship afloat, and destined to have a displacement of 9137 tons, three times that of Brunel's *Great Britain*. The central battery of the ship was built on the principle of an armoured fortress, with 4.5in armoured plating backed with 18in of teak acting as a buffer to absorb the shock of gunfire. Her armament consisted of twenty-six 68pdr muzzle-loaders, ten 110pdr breech-loaders, and four 40pdr breech-loaders, placed on the upper deck. Her sleek, all-black 380ft hull, with its single gun deck, was crammed with other innovations which will be described later. She was nicknamed the 'Black Snake of the Channel' on account of her serpentine profile, so different from the wooden three-deckers with which the Navy had been associated for the previous one hundred years.

Having only a single gun deck, she was launched as a frigate, but with such firepower as to cause this new class of vessel to be renamed and officially referred to as a battleship. The weight of broadside shot was five times greater than that of *Victory*. *Warrior* took her place in 1861, the year of her first commission, at Portsmouth. She was the first of a fleet which was designed to maintain the *Pax Britannica*. This Victorian attempt at multilateral peace depended ultimately on the deterrent which *Warrior* and other ships of the 'Black Battlefleet' represented.

This ship had everything: steam and

3. Emmerson, *ibid.*
4. *Ibid*, pp162-63.
5. Mowll, William, SS Great Britain: *The Model Ship* (Watford: MAP/Argus, 1982).

sail, a hoisting propeller, and funnels which could be raised and lowered; a mass of ordnance, the conventional being mixed with the very latest rifle breech-loading, shell-firing guns; a figurehead and gilded galleries, and all the complex details for the quarters of 705 seamen whose courage and daring worked this vessel in fair weather and foul. There was no other living ship which so wholly embraced both the old ways and the new. This warship encapsulated all that had gone before, and was to be the model for all that has followed since.

* * *

In July 1981, I completed and launched a large model of Brunel's *Great Britain* in live steam and sail, built on a scale of 1:48. It took over four years to construct and won a Gold Medal at the Model Engineer Exhibition at Wembley in 1982, which gave me the courage to entertain the idea that I could bring to completion another vessel of a similar period in shipping his-

tory.[5] The question of which ship this might be was answered by the fortuitous sight of an almost completed illustration by Stephen Ortega, a remarkably gifted student at Bournemouth and Poole College of Art and Design. Ship-modellers are easily seduced by plans, and one glimpse of this highly detailed illustration was enough to set my head spinning, challenging me to a mental and physical duel that eventually lasted for sixteen years. For me, this cutaway illustration was a roaring lion which could not be ignored.

Having resolved to dedicate a large portion of my off-duty hours to this project, the big technical questions flooded into my mind. From what material ought it to be made? On what scale should I build? What method of propulsion should I use? Where was the money coming from to build this monster? Did I have the space in which to construct it? What should I do with it when complete? For seven months I chewed over these issues, whilst simply enjoying the fact that I was building nothing and had no deadlines to

The author launching his fully working model of SS *Great Britain* 1843 in July 1981.

6. Plans for HMS *Warrior* 1860 are available from Nexus (see list of suppliers).

7. If you need to improve your expertise in this area, much has been written in magazine form (see Robert Gardiner's article in *Model Shipwright* No 13, and David Antscherl in No 22), and even more in model shipwrighting books. Should you wish to go to full size, you cannot do better than Sir Westcott Abell's *The Shipwright's Trade* (1948) (London, Conway Maritime edn, 1981), where virtually nothing is left unsaid.

keep. Then something happened which quite abruptly ended this watershed period. Entirely by accident I met a man called Keith Lines, whose professional life had taken him into the highly specialised world of designing and constructing full-sized sculling boats from glass reinforced polyester (GRP). From what was going on in his workshop, I could see immediately that the large hull which I had in mind for a model of *Warrior* at 1:48, over 8ft in length, would best be made in GRP, and not out of timber, as all my previous models had been. It was time to investigate the techniques of mouldmaking.

Critical to my perception of how the hull ought to appear was the question of whether or not details of the plating lines could be included, in that these were an important factor in the way that the original vessel was constructed. My concern was also for the texturing of the outward appearance of the hull to simulate iron, but Keith Lines was able to reassure me that not only the plating lines, but also the plates and rivets, could be simulated as well. GRP would allow for every kind of detail and decoration, provided that there was no undercut which would prevent a two-part mould being split. It was agreed that I should make the plug, which is the technical term for the shape which has the mould built around it, whilst Keith Lines

would do the laying up of the laminations of glassfibre. I had been lucky enough to find as instructor someone who shared my enthusiasm both for the full-sized vessel, and for the plans to make a working miniature as near to the original as was humanly possible.

Choosing a scale

To begin a building programme of any size means much preparatory work on the drawing board. The first major consideration is scale. The original Admiralty plans are on a scale of $1/8$in to 1ft, so that the body plan of the ship needed to be scaled to twice this size for the model to finish at 1:48. There were several reasons for choosing this large size. Most importantly, it is the traditional standard scale of shipbuilder's models, and allows for a great deal of detail to be included. It is also the scale on which the builder's model, displayed in the London Science Museum, is built. This famous model used to be housed in the boardroom of the Thames Iron Works & Shipbuilding Company, and from close scrutiny it was possible to determine whether or not a steam plant could be successfully operated amidships. The final reason for choosing this relatively large scale was the future hope that, if all went well, both models could take to the water simultaneously and be used for comparative purposes.

Basic draughting skills

You may well be asking yourself at this stage whether or not you have to be a draughtsman before tackling a model of this nature. Certainly you need to have in your possession a T-square or an integral A3-size drawing board. A full-sized drawing board with parallel motion is, of course, the most desirable, but they are expensive on the pocket and on space. An inexpensive implement is a drawing device called a Flexicurve, which is a snakelike

Using the drawing board to transfer the body plan lines onto carbon paper.

flexible rule used to assist in drawing smoothly round such shapes as the body line plans. The curve remains in the shape to which it is contoured, and therefore has many applications in transposing from paper plan to timber. A dressmaker's curve is also part of the recommended kit for this initial work, as is squared paper, which will be found useful time and time again. If you are working from plans,[6] as a scratch builder you will also require the basic draughting tools of compass, rule, and dividers. These are all essentials for turning two-dimensional plans into a three-dimensional model, and it is cheaper to make a mistake on paper than it is to have to start again in raw material - so always think of draughtsmen's implements as cost savers which will help you to think before you cut.

It is important to learn how to read ships' plans and to be able to transfer the lines into the scale you require. The three contours with which you will be presented are the sheer plan (the side view), the half breadth plan (the overhead view), and the body plan (the end view). With these three elevations it is possible to begin work on any hull. The longitudinal lines along the length of the hull are known as buttock lines, and reveal the form and shape of the hull at the intersections of the ship's frames. It is not my intention here to enter into a discussion about draughting ship's plans, although this is unquestionably a very important subject, because the ground has been covered thoroughly in numerous other publications.[7]

Possible methods of construction

The published modelmakers' plans (see suppliers appendix) for this vessel outline two methods of hull construction: plank-on-frame and bread-and-butter. These are traditional methods of hull construction using wood and the vast majority of ship models, both working and static, have been made using these methods. GRP

hulls offer two bonuses, however, the first of which is the inclusion of exterior plating details without having to apply plates, and the second is a guarantee of water-tightness. The disadvantage is the high cost of making first a plug, followed by the split mould, and, last, the laying-up of the moulding inside the mould. Until these three processes are complete, the fitting-out stage cannot begin. For a one-off model, GRP construction is costly in every way.

Lath and plaster plug

My original thoughts concentrated on the idea of cladding the hull with lath strips recessed into the frames, but further brooding told me that this would mean

(Left)
Half frames pasted onto *two* layers of 4mm ply, stapled together with the template uprights abutting the sawn edge of the planks. All the faces of the planks are pasted back and front to prevent warping. When the frames are finally separated, this produces mirror imaging, or bookleafing.

(Below)
Finishing the outer profiles of the frames with a spokeshave.

Six illustrations of hull
construction technique.
(Bournemouth and
Poole College)

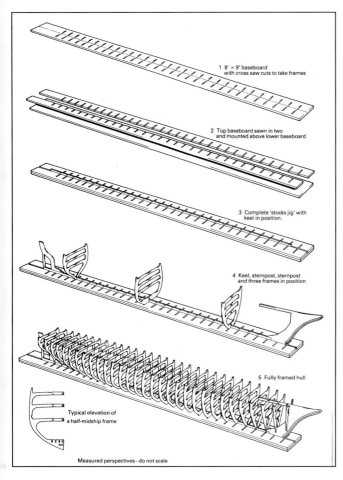

1 8' × 9" baseboard
with cross saw cuts to take frames

2 Top baseboard sawn in two
and mounted above lower baseboard

3 Complete 'stocks jig' with
keel in position.

4 Keel, sternpost, sternpost
and three frames in position

5 Fully framed hull

Typical elevation of
a half-midship frame

Measured perspectives – do not scale

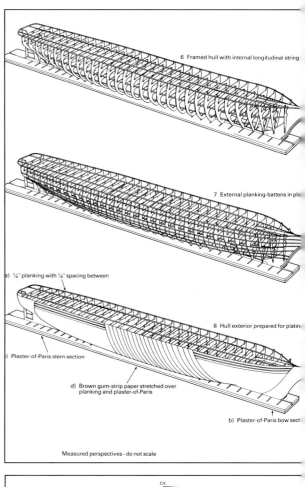

6 Framed hull with internal longitudinal string

7 External planking-battens in pla

a) ¼" planking with ¼" spacing between

8 Hull exterior prepared for platin

c) Plaster-of-Paris stern section

d) Brown gum-strip paper stretched over
planking and plaster-of-Paris

b) Plaster-of-Paris bow sect

Measured perspectives – do not scale

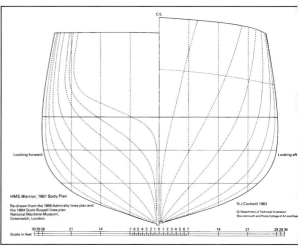

C/L

Looking forward   Looking aft

HMS Warrior, 1861 Body Plan

Re-drawn from the 1859 Admiralty lines plan and
the 1864 Scott-Russell lines plan
National Maritime Museum,
Greenwich, London.

N J Cockwill 1983

© Department of Technical Illustration
Bournemouth and Poole College of Art and Desi

Scale in feet   30 29 28   21   14   7 6 5 4 3 2 1 0 1 2 3 4 5 6 7   14   21   28 29 30

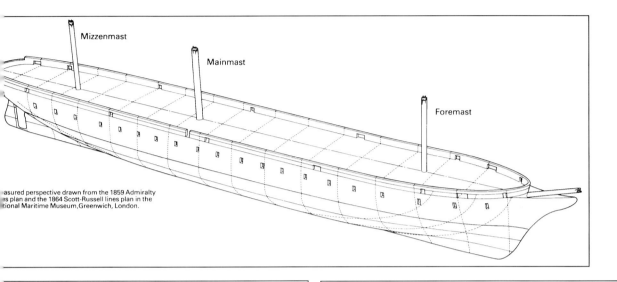

Mizzenmast

Mainmast

Foremast

Measured perspective drawn from the 1859 Admiralty lines plan and the 1864 Scott-Russell lines plan in the National Maritime Museum, Greenwich, London.

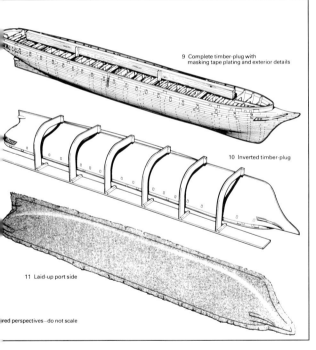

9 Complete timber-plug with masking tape plating and exterior details

10 Inverted timber-plug

11 Laid-up port side

Measured perspectives – do not scale

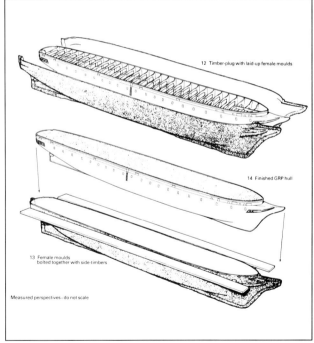

12 Timber-plug with laid-up female moulds

14 Finished GRP hull

13 Female moulds bolted together with side-timbers

Measured perspectives – do not scale

(Right)
The sorcerer's apprentice: the author's son, Josh, aged 12, removing the paper template after a good soak in the baby bath

(Below left)
Thirty-two frames, showing forward, mid and aft sections

(Below right)
Midship section.
(*Shipbuilding Theoretical and Practical*)

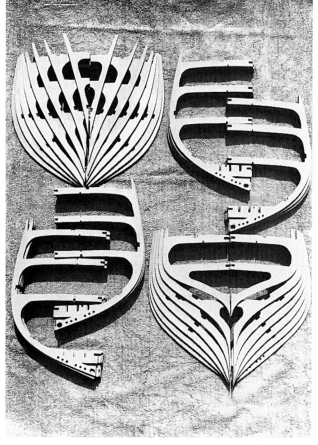

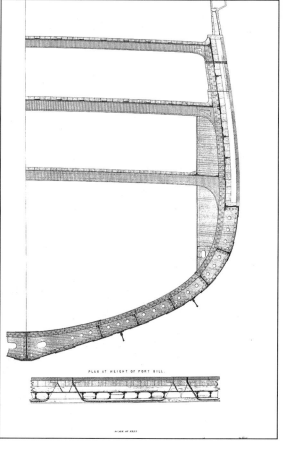

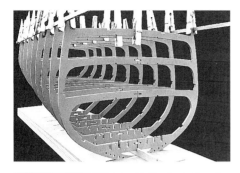

not only extra calculations and sawing, but also the likelihood of the frames showing on the final GRP skin. The photographic enlargement therefore allows for the extra thickness of the ply and eventual GRP lay-up without any recesses, except for the slots cut out on the inside of the frames to allow for the bilge and side stringers, along the interior lines of the ship's skeleton, as found in a prototype iron vessel. These combine with the keel and floors to hold together the earliest structure of the ship model plug. Thereafter it is possible to fix the lath strips with sausage sticks, which are finished very reliably to $^5/_{64}$ (0.078) in. Each position must be drilled and fixed mechanically. The sausage stick,

which is no more than a miniature wooden dowel, allows for a small amount of vertical adjustment against the frames which is very useful, and when glued into position makes a sound mechanical fixing.

Studying the prototype

With my building of *Warrior* it was inevitable that before any more serious work could begin, the proud old lady herself would have to be thoroughly investigated. In 1982 she was still afloat on her own bottom and berthed at the Coal Dock Wharf, West Hartlepool, where she was undergoing a complete refit and restoration programme. For years she had been an oil pontoon at Milford Haven, whilst still remaining under the watchful eye of the Admiralty, who ordered the occasional

(Upper left)
Frames showing aft section. Note the friction fitting grooves on centreline for lateral adjustment.

(Centre left)
The author checking the alignment of the keel.

(Below)
Warrior in profile at West Hartlepool under restoration: the first and last iron battleship.

(Bottom)
Eye to eye with the 'Black Snake of the Channel'. *Warrior* at the coal dock wharf.

(Above)
Remnants of the quarter and stern galleries in 1982.

(Right)
Quarter gallery windows: the framing being made up with three layers of masking tape.

(Below)
Creating the bulge which supports the stern galleries with wire mesh.

took to effect her complete restoration. The immediate need as far as the model was concerned was to see how the restoration of the stern galleries had been tackled, but at this time they were almost impossible to recognise. The lack of the 'bulge' on the quarter and stern galleries of the full-sized *Warrior* was a concern. What exactly supported this sizeable piece of decoration? It must have been fire-welded onto the exterior plating of the ship, as it housed the Captain's bathroom on the starboard side, and the Commander's on the port, allowing for the natural escapement of drainage below. Before starting to model this section, I would have liked to have seen more evidence of it, as it is clearly depicted on all the plans, but quite complex in shape. The problem was that it was not possible to make a complete moulding of the hull without this area being included, so mine has followed as closely as possible the shape of the builder's model in the Science Museum. A solid block of wood should be bandsawn and carved into shape and fitted at the stern using plaster and wire mesh of the sort used by car body repair shops. Expanded aluminium wire mesh in its *bona fide* role is much used in the motor trade for the repair of difficult holes in awkward places, and has the ability of holding resin or plaster. After application, it may be sanded back to whatever odd shape is required. Moulding plaster is used for infilling the stem and beakhead.

Modelling the quarter galleries

It was clear that the majority of the windows on the prototype were mock-ups, even to the extent of hawse outlets piercing the middle of the window frames. The clearest indication of how the original galleries looked comes from an early etching of the stern of the *Warrior* when on the stocks which, despite the distortion and deliberately falsified miniature figures, nevertheless shows all the details which a

visit for dry docking and basic maintenance to the hull bottom.

It took two days to photograph and record as much of the external and internal detail as was humanly possible. The ship still looked as if she were a hulk, and certain parts of her were only possible to investigate by torchlight. Only those who visited her at this time in her life will really appreciate the courage and energy it

modeller requires to execute the work. For the first time, masking tape comes firmly into the picture. With three layers of masking tape stuck directly onto the carved shape of the galleries, the main window frames can be defined by using thin strips which gives them the effect of being built-up, rather than cut out.

Skinning the plug

Water-based gummed strip has a magic all its own in terms of covering the complex shape of a model ship's hull, which has both concave and convex contours. The special property associated with this material is that it shrinks and tightens as it dries out and it can even be lightly sanded back. A raw material derived from wood, when it is bonded to wood the strength is one of a blood relationship. What no-one would believe until they have handled and worked this humble material is the fantastic strength it possesses when it reaches its fully cured state. Under normal conditions, to dry out properly takes about three days, after which it can be considered to be at maximum tautness. It appears dry after half an hour or so, but the process contin-

ues for much longer. Laying it onto the ship's hull is not at all difficult if one uses the natural lie of the strip, just overlapping the leading edge of the strip to its neighbour. The process of application involves a quick dipping into a bucket of water to moisten the glue and immediately afterwards laying it over the lath strips. Do not be over-concerned about the extra thickness of the join, as the natural process of shrinkage makes this join almost disappear when cut back with a fine grade of sandpaper. Initially, it looked as if it would be necessary to apply a second layer, but that proved to be unnecessary in terms of the job it had to do in the formation of a simple plug.

The disappearance of the bones under the covering of brown paper is a big step forward in visual terms. For the first time, one can actually see the smooth hull form and check it for aberrations of one sort or another. Where faults occur, the brown paper can be cut and repaired very easily, which is another big bonus. Fortunately, not too much of that had to happen on my model and, of all the operations undertaken so far, applying the gummed paper strip has been the simplest.

Plating the hull plug

In contrast, plating the hull plug is agonisingly slow. Masking tape is used to simulate the rough iron texture of the prototype hull, sticking the masking tape plates to the model hull to match the original. This is a difficult task because the elastic nature of masking tape is simultaneously both friend and foe. Some of the curvature which is demanded is well served by the ability to turn the tape without crinkles appearing, but in order to mark it with imitation rivets, it is necessary to be able to keep the material fixed and steady.

The rivet impressions

The rivet markings must be made from

(Left)
Gummed paper strip forming a skin over the hull.

8. Corlett, Ewan, *The Iron Ship* (Bradford-on-Avon: Moonraker Press, 1975), Ch 4.
9. *Ibid*, p29.
10. *Ibid*, p38.

the sticky side of the tape, in double rows very close to its edge. The problem can be solved using two jigs and the dressmaker's wheel in the following way. The template jigs are made from Perspex, which has two features in its favour: the first is that masking tape adheres to it very well without damaging the adhesive and second, it is possible to see what you are doing from both sides. The kerf width of the circular saw blade used to cut the Perspex is enough to allow the tailor's wheel to make a pass on either edge and produce the double line of staggered rivets.

On the full-sized vessel, years of paint and rust have combined to hide the original rivet lines behind the general encrustations which iron encourages, but in the 'as-launched' state of the ship, the flush rivet lines would have been apparent, if not pronounced. The aesthetic problem is to resist modelling them in too pronounced a fashion, yet including them in the texture of the iron plating.

In his classic book on the SS *Great Britain, The Iron Ship*, the Reverend Dr Ewan Corlett mentions that, at the time that the *Great Eastern* was built, the largest plates which could be economically rolled were 10ft long by about 2ft 9in wide by $^3/_4$in thick.[8] This means that masking tape, in scale with the width of a 3ft plate, needs to be on a roll $^3/_4$in wide at 1:48 scale, which, mercifully, is readily available. In the same chapter, Corlett also details the fact that John Scott Russell was a great advocate of the conical rivet hole, giving the rivets a degree of countersink in a punched hole which increased their strength.[9] After reading the detailed account of how full-sized vessels were riveted together, the model shipwright, who may occasionally have a mental moan about drudgery and repetition, is put firmly into his or her place. The tailor's wheel can produce a line of three plates, double-riveted, spliced and ready for application, in under a minute. When one considers that it took a gang of four rivet-

ers to drive between 100-140 rivets a day, the modelling equivalent pales into insignificance.[10]

Modelling the plating

The next item to be considered when applying the plates is to appreciate that iron ship construction depended on a system called shifting butts. Unlike a conventional brick wall, the stagger of the butt ends of iron plates were deviated from one another by two or three of the ship's frames, giving a kind of staircase effect, spreading the torsional loads along the length of the hull rather than in a specific localised area. The butt ends were joined by butt straps on the inside of the hull. These were lengths of angle bar, at least the thickness of the plate connected. The joins took place *between* the ship's frames and not to them, as might be imagined at first glance.

With all this in mind it can be seen that plating a model hull, like painting a portrait, requires that you first understand the anatomy of the body, and what is going on underneath the surface of the skin. Failure to do this can result in serious mistakes. For example, a scuttle should not appear in the middle of a butt strap, and likewise, deck levels must marry up with the plating lines, and gun ports appear *between* frames and not *through* them. The complexity of this structure, and the need to scale the plating to the hull, means that it is not possible for this part of the job to be finished quickly.

In company with many Victorian hybrid ships, there is a sample of a little bit of everything in terms of the ship's plating. You must look hard for the beginning of the armoured section and the end of the shell plating on the exterior of the prototype. There is no question of the plates cladding this hull in a clumsy fashion; the section which comprises the citadel is integrated with the inside profile of the ship's hull, as reference to the plans

Jig for making the vertical rivet lines on masking tape, with tailor's wheels.

will show, with all four edges of the armoured plates being joined by a system of tongue and groove, cold-chiselled by hand. It was an unbelievably laborious task, but that is how it was done, and it has never come apart.

Below the waterline

The hull bottom gives us the prime example of Scott Russell's 'in and out' plating. This modern system was a huge stride forward from the SS *Great Britain*, built in clincher fashion just twenty years before. As far as is known at present, there is no official plan of *Warrior*'s plating lines, although there is an illustration of how the armouring was applied in *Shipbuilding Theoretical and Practical*.[11]

When the underwater section of the model hull is tackled, it will be necessary to make more Perspex guides, with diminishing lines for the stem and stern plating to be accommodated. The calculations should be made from the midship section of the hull, using a calculator to establish the reduced area to be covered at the stem and stern. These calculations must be transferred onto separate pieces of masking tape, so that data marks can be established equally on both sides of the hull. Pleasurable donkey work is the phrase which best describes this part of the proceedings, which took me two months to complete.

Before the vessel is ready for the mouldmaking process, the plug must have various detailed items added to it, such as the guttering rigols above the gun ports, and the scuttles. The first of these items

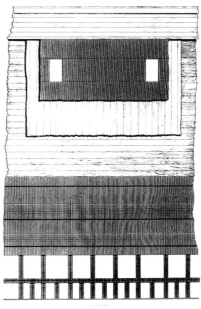

(Far left)
Replication on the model of the 'in-and-out' plating lines in masking tape: three layers of tape for the 'out' strake, a single one for the 'in'.

(Left)
Structure of plating on the prototype.

should be cut out of six layers of tape, but the half rounds of the scuttles' guttering can be made from flattened copper wire glued onto the exterior of the plug. There will also be a good deal of finishing to do on the quarter galleries at the stern, as well as marking out with lines of rivets the lifting-propeller well and the boss of stern tube.

Split mouldmaking[12]

You are now ready to make the mould from which the final hull will be formed. The first task is to invert the hull, and at the same time ensure that there is some clearance left between the hull and the baseboard (approximately 2in). All GRP moulds must be made slightly oversize on their open edges, in order to maintain an envelope of stability and to provide a point of leverage for parting the moulding from the mould. This also ensures that the resin is well wetted through, up to the trim line and beyond it. The length of solid straight timber, attached to the deck beams, suitably mounts the hull above the baseboard. The second job is to fix a false flange on the centreline of the ship. GRP will be laid

11. Macquorn Rankine, W J, (ed), *Shipbuilding Theoretical and Practical* (London: Wm Mackenzie, 1863), Plate B4.
12. The next six weeks' work really fell on the shoulders of Keith Lines alone, whilst I adopted the role of cameraman and journalist. Up to this point in my life, I had never witnessed the professional way to lay up a GRP hull from start to finish, and Keith has taught me most of what I know, for which I am very grateful.

(Above)
The inverted hull, completely covered with masking tape 'plating'.

(Centre right)
The false flange being fixed in place on the centreline of the keel. The banana-shaped timbers hold the flange in place. The model is screwed to the baseboard so that it cannot move.

(Below)
The false flange (also taped up) can be seen along the inverted keel line and follows the profile of the bow and stern as well. The hull plug is waxed for six days before any gelcoating takes place. The slip wax is the parting agent which eventually allows the plug to separate from the mould.

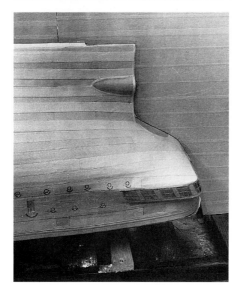

up against this flange, the purpose of which is to provide both the split line of the mould, and a point of leverage for parting one side of the mould from the other.

The first half of the mould is made with this rim/flange in place. The joint between the flange and the hull is sealed with a silicone rubber seal (Plasticine is just as good), so that the gel coat will be prevented from bleeding across to the other side of the hull. The gel coat is the outer layer of the resin, which normally provides the super shine associated with GRP. It finds every nook and cranny, and faithfully reproduces all the fine detail and any small mistake as well. To prevent the gel coat sticking to the plug, release wax must first be applied to the hull and the flange which surrounds it. This application cannot be hurried, and the world contains a number of laminators who cursed the moment of thinking that two applications of wax would be enough. It takes a week, and six applications of wax applied once every twenty-four hours, thoroughly polishing between each coat.

Release waxes come in different forms from GRP merchants; it so happens that in the photograph a liquid one is being used which suits the detail already fixed onto the hull. The wax is applied with a cloth, which is carefully dabbed into all the recesses, and gently rubbed onto the hull surface. The transom detail and the quarter galleries appear to be able to withstand this treatment, helped by the fact that masking tape is itself finished with what feels like a waxy surface, presumably because it requires a low tack-level on the reel. One side only is laid up. When that is complete, the elaborate support flange can be removed, along with the banana-shaped timbers which hold it all in place.

The gel coat

As mentioned, the gel coat is the first layer to be applied to the plug after the waxing.

It is painted on with a brush and left to cure until the outside is tacky to the touch. You ought to be able to leave a thumbprint on its surface without any of the mixture transferring to your thumb. Depending on the ambient temperature this can take anything from one to three hours, and then the second gel coat can be applied. Gel coats are designed to remain chemically active for about six hours. They harden first on the inside face, rather than the exposed one, in order to act not only as a hard exterior of the eventual mould, but also as a key to the glass which is to be laid on top of the skin they create. A well-controlled environment helps but most people have to make do with whatever weather Saturday afternoon brings, working in a non-insulated concrete garage, gently praying that the rain will stop for long enough to bring the model indoors when the job is done. Cold damp weather is the worst enemy of gel-coating. It may blister, though blisters can be cut out and more resin stippled in.

The message is that if you are going to try this method of using masking tape to depict plating lines on a hull, use only a single gel coat, making sure that you cover all the surface of the hull. The idea of two gel coats is really to ensure complete coverage, as it is very easy to miss a small area when using a colourless coating on a white background. A good idea is to add a small amount of pigment to the gel coat, so that you can see the total area covered.

Laying-down the lay-up

Resins cure very quickly, so preparation is the key to avoiding a horrible sticky mess. The items needed are:

A bucket with thinners for rinsing the brush

White can containing the pigmented resin

Catalyst bottle with calibrated spout for accurate quantity measurement

Roll of glassfibre tape

Large and small brush, plus small roller

Assortment of small containers with large scissors and knife

Pair of rubberised gloves and weighing machine for the amount of catalyst required

Stirring sticks

General purpose kitchen roll

Bulldog clips

Application

You will now lay up four layers of glassfibre matting – the first $3/4$oz to adhere to the details in the gel coat: the others of $1^1/_2$oz to add strength to the hull – over the gel coat. At those locations of the model where the turns are too tight for chopped strand straight off the roll, some preliminary work has to be done with small offcuts of chopped mat strand. There is no problem with joining glass cloth, and this patchwork approach is entirely undetectable as one layer is stippled to another. Once the pigmented resin and catalyst have been poured and thoroughly stirred together, the neat resin is applied to the details at the bow and stern, followed by the small offcuts of glass cloth being thoroughly wetted out with a brush. In other words, there is a layer of neat resin under the glass mat strands, and a layer which is stippled on top of the glass that soaks through the strands until the two coats become one. I am labouring this point rather, because I have learned that allowing this soaking action to take place is extremely important when it comes to areas with a complex shape, such as the quarter galleries at the stern, and the sharp beakhead on this vessel. In this situation, if you try to force the glassfibre to adhere as you move along it (initially with the brush), the strands will not lie down with any obedience until the fibres have had a chance to soak up the resin. This takes about a minute. So the technique is to daub the resin on, but not

(Right)
The detail is laid up first in the finer $^3/_4$oz glass mat; the resin must be allowed to harden first before the main body of lay-up is applied.

(Far right)
The first lay-up of glass-fibre cloth being applied to the plug.

(Below)
Second half of the hull being gel-coated. Use one coat only – see text.

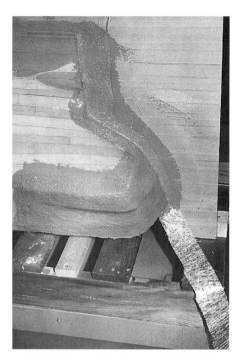

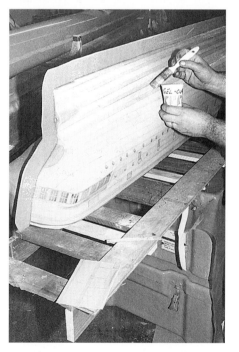

to try to make it adhere around the shape until it is truly wetted out. At this point the ribbed roller is used to eliminate any air bubbles. The rolling action is best done by starting in the middle and rolling

out to the edges, exactly as in the application of vinyl wallpaper, but this is only used when two layers of glass are down.

The major area of the hull is tackled in exactly the same way as the detail except that, because of the large size of this hull, the initial coat of neat resin is only taken to the midship section. It will take three to four minutes to stipple the resin through the glass to the midship section, by which time the coat underneath will be starting to cure. If the whole hull were to be tackled in one go, there is a chance that the glass would not be wet through from the underside to the top side, and it would make a poor lamination as a result. There is a slight difference in the weight of glassfibre cloth used for the first two layers: the finer $^3/_4$oz strand is used initially in order to pick up the detail, followed by the $1^1/_2$oz for strength.

With these two layers applied, it is necessary to stop and allow the exothermic, or heat-producing, chemical reaction in the catalyst to take place and thus to cure. Within the next half hour or so, the hull will warm up over its total surface –

and it really does get hot. Any more than two layers laid up at the same time would produce such a high temperature that one of two things might happen: either the gel coat surface could be spoiled, or the plug be distorted by fierce shrinkage. When the two initial layers have cooled (under normal conditions it takes about one hour), the two following layers of $1^1/_2$oz can be laid. Before the third and fourth layers are put down, it is a good policy to 'green trim' the edges; this should be done in the short time before the resin has gone really hard, and the use of a sharp knife means that you can cut and trim away the two layers, leaving a neat freehand line around the outer edges. The third and fourth layers are likewise trimmed. To make a really tidy job, a fifth layer of glass tissue can be laid up; this is not strictly necessary, but it does mean that future handling of the mould is a more pleasant experience, and for the small amount of extra trouble it is well worth doing.

With half the hull laid up, it is necessary to wait for a week before parting the flange along the trim line. There seems to be a great deal of waiting for a material which appears to cure pretty quickly. As with the brown paper, however, the shrinkage process continues for a long while after it is apparently dry, and it is particularly important to be patient if subsequent distortions are to be avoided. The flange is parted along the trim line by tweaking at the stem and stern, rather than by plunging a screwdriver into the centre of the keel. The false flange can now be jettisoned along with the banana-shaped supporting timbers. As may be seen from the photographs, half the ship is laid up, with a GRP flange travelling the total length of the centreline.

The second half of the hull must now be as thoroughly waxed as the first half, including the recently created GRP flange. As before, this takes a further week of waxing and polishing before the gel coat can be brushed on, and the whole proce-

dure repeated until the plug is totally enclosed. From this moment, a further three weeks must be allowed for the mould to stabilise out completely.

The only job to be done during this long wait is to drill out four holes for the locating pins, and the holes for bolting the eventual split mould together. This can be done after about a week. With such a large mould, it is advisable to create some extra support along the topside of the mould by surrounding it with some wooden blocks, rather in the manner of stitch-welding.

Releasing the mould

The mould will not easily part from the plug. The best solution is to fill the hull with warm water and allow this to penetrate through, until the two sides fall apart. This method has the added benefit of giving an early indication of the displacement of the hull to the waterline level. It took eight buckets full of carefully measured water, topping just over 146lb, to displace the hull to the low waterline. It came as a delight to see that all the tiny pieces of detail such as the guttering above

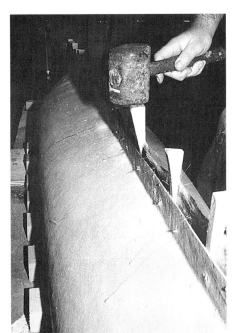

Wooden parting wedges being hammered along the split line.

The emergence of the split mould and the destruction of the sacrificial lath and plaster plug.

the scuttles, and all the rivet lines and plating had reproduced faultlessly. The plug was now in a state of soggy collapse and it had been too much to hope that this relatively flimsy structure would survive intact from such a vigorous operation. It is worth noting, however, that the structure withstood all the earlier impacting forces of shrinkage without distortion and that, had it been anything other than a hollow frame work, it is doubtful whether the resin would have cured satisfactorily on top of the masking tape, or that it would have been possible to part the mould from the plug.

The cautionary tale would therefore seem to be that, if you are considering adopting this method of construction, use paper, and not plaster, to cover the lath strips with as limited an area of solid as possible. The port side mould is nearly perfect in terms of the impressions from the plug to the mould. By picking away at the tape, the details, which are of course at this stage all in relief, were winkled out. The rigols of the scuttles (the flattened copper fuse wire) had to be dug out with a scriber but nevertheless, once loosened, came away cleanly and easily, as did all the taped detail. The final task then must be to bolt together the two halves to prevent

any untoward warping or damage.

Laying up the moulding

The inside of the mould must be thoroughly waxed and polished each day for a week, and finally finished with a coat of polyvinyl alcohol (PVA), used as an accompanying release agent on top of the wax coatings; note that this PVA must not be confused with PVA glue – the first is *alcohol*, the second *acetate*. The PVA provides a total single film over the wax, and leaves a slightly rough surface which could be described as a frosted mirror finish. For glossy mirror surfaces, wax on its own must be used. The PVA coating adheres to the moulding when released but, as it is miscible, it washes off, along with the wax, with a good scrub with warm water. A PVA coat should have been used on the original plug to help the parting process but, under test conditions, PVA attacked the adhesive on the masking tape and therefore could not be used.

The details at stem and stern should first be laid up on the inside of the mould. It is possible to lay up the two halves separately, and then join them on the centre-line with a thin layer of glass but, provided the areas of tight access are tackled first, it is not necessary to do this; once again, a demonstration of the notion of patchwork, so unfamiliar to conventional construction techniques. With the hull bolted together once again and placed on trestles, a black pigmented gel coat, mixed with its correct proportion of catalyst, should be applied with a brush. It is not exactly painted on: that is too delicate a notion, the action is more one of daubing it on. Gel coat is a thixotropic mixture which has to be applied thickly and quickly, rather like hot tar application in road construction. As soon as the mixture has started to cure (about fifteen minutes), aided by some wafting of the air above the open hull, it has to be inverted, in order that the styrene gas may be literally poured out. Styrene gas is heavier than air, and within an almost closed area or receptacle like a boat hull, it cannot escape of its own accord. If left, the gel coat would not cure for a very long time, whereas under reasonable conditions of heat, two hours is sufficient. Do not use a fan heater to waft away the styrene gas and help to cure the gel coat. This would lead to a condition known as 'forced rapid styrene loss' or 'undercuring'. Although the first coat may appear to be dry, when

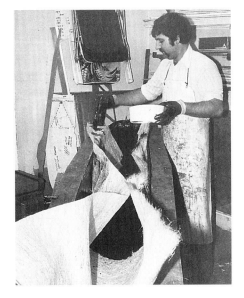

The interior of the split mould has been prepared with thorough waxing and polishing and finished with a brushed coat of poly vinyl alcohol for the purposes of the future release of the moulding. PVA puts a whole skin over the wax, and acts as a parting agent. The interior of the mould has been painted and wetted out with a layer of black pigmented resin and the glass cloth is being thoroughly wetted through from the topside with the stiff brush.

neat resin is painted on top of it, it will wrinkle horribly. This can also happen if the gel coat is too thin: 16-20 thou is about the right thickness for a gel coat; anything under 10 thou will almost certainly end up in a wavy wrinkle because the loss of styrene is too rapid.

The glass mat for the moulding is applied in exactly the same way as for the mould but in two layers only, with the addition of tissue just to make the interior look and feel tidy. With the thinner layer of the moulding the process is not exothermic and is simply a matter of stippling the resin well into the glass mat, and rolling out the air between the two layers of $1\frac{1}{2}$oz as previously described. A professional makes all this look deceptively easy, but my observations would lead me to believe that the expertise has much to do with good preparation and working quickly and efficiently. The chemical smell is overpowering and, unless you are extremely fortunate in your premises, this can only be regarded as a summer job to be carried out in the open air, preferably downwind from your neighbour.

Releasing the moulding

An interval of forty-eight hours is a suffi-

In the areas of tight access at the bow and stern, where it would be impossible to lay up the glassfibre cloth satisfactorily (with the mould bolted together), these areas are tackled *before* the two halves come together for the internal lay-up.

The finished moulding with the two halves joined together.

of the mould will finally part from the hull, at long last revealing the results of your hard labour.

On my own model, apart from one gun port rigol, I found every single detail was perfectly reproduced behind the covering of wax and PVA, with the galleries offering a particular pleasure. This method of construction allows remarkable detail to be achieved. For me, the iron texturing on the plates gave cause for real delight, because the graining on the tape looks and feels extremely effective.

Bilge keels

The bilge, or docking, keels have little or nothing to do with the science, first understood by William Froude in 1872, of counteracting the rolling characteristics of a large hull. Nevertheless, those who put to sea in *Warrior* on the long tow from Milford Haven to West Hartlepool in 1979 will tell you that in spite of the rough weather encountered on that trip the hull was stabilised by the four substantial keels which undergird the ship. For model shipwrights, bilge keels present difficulties at a number of levels. The problems have to do with the correct stock material, the strength of the material and the eventual mechanical fixing of the keels themselves. Even on a model, the relatively thin sectioned strips must be tough, but not so unforgiving that they distort the curvature of the hull bottom to which they must be aligned. The problems are further compounded by *Warrior* being fitted with the now obsolete bulb section keel. Later iron ships of the fleet had a straightforward T-section, but as *Warrior* lay chocked up on the slipway of the Orchard Yard on the Thames at Blackwall, she was fitted out with bulbs between frames 46-82 for the inner keels and 54-75 on the outer ones.

cient one before opening up the mould and finally releasing the moulding which will be used as the model hull. Anything which appears in the twinkling of an eye is completely alien to conventional model-making. Yet at this moment, when the mould leaves its husk in the manner of a snake shedding its skin, the hull makes a sudden appearance with a quite frightening series of cracking sounds as the wooden wedges force the split mould apart but, as with the parting of the plug from the mould, this process is slow and painful, too. The open edges along the gunwale can be tackled with a running wedge, and the hull tapped gently all over with the wooden mallet. Wooden wedges can also be driven in along the keel line. One side

After a long search, the stock for these keels was found in the backyard of our brothers in steam, the loco men. Severn Lamb Ltd, professional modelmakers in

Stratford-on-Avon, have developed some anodised aluminium 3in gauge bulkhead rail track, sold in metre lengths. The rail has a flat 'T' at the bottom and is bull-headed at the top. It is in near scale for 1:48, rounded at the top and giving all the right look for the job in hand, as well as being flexible, strong, and relatively cheap.

It is not really good enough to rely totally on adhesives for long thin strips of material which could receive a shock or impacted blow. Epoxy resins tend to be rather brittle and it is the sort of job which is very difficult to rectify later. So, after predrilling the rail, genuine aluminium rivets (not poppers) should be fitted and, in conjunction with the slow-curing Araldite adhesive, the miniature girders can be secured in place. With the assistance of clothes pegs, localised pressure can be brought to bear using tourniquets of string around the midship section of the hull as the epoxy resin glue cures off, giving a permanent fixing to the docking keels.

A watertight hull

Being more and more convinced that a model ship such as this must eventually have a taste of sea water when finally she comes to be launched, it is necessary to make the hull completely watertight. When visiting the full-size ship and seeing her safely at rest on her moorings in calm conditions, it is difficult to imagine why it was so important to her initial constructors to find the right compound to seal off the gun port lids and make them watertight. Various compounds were tried, including an early form of rubber and a tar-like mixture, in their efforts to form a watertight gasket between the rifle-proofed lids and the hull of the ship.

It is only when the hull is observed in motion that one comes to realise how often the gun port lids were awash with sea water, as were also the stern and quarter

gallery lights. These gilded windows also received a regular dousing when the beak of the ship was diving porpoise-like into swollen seas, with a reciprocal plunging action taking place at the stern. Small wonder that only essential window frames were pierced and glazed, leaving the rest of the stern decoration in solid form with mock decoration.

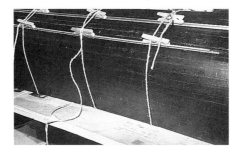

Fixing the bilge keels with clothes pegs and tourniquets.

On the model hull, sealing out the sea included the preparation of the sidelights (or scuttles) as follows. The scuttles, or portholes, are easily dealt with by the use of spent cartridge cases from a .22 rifle. Despite the damage that a rifle firing-pin causes to the edge of the brass casing, it is still perfectly possible to file them down, pop out the centre, fill them with casting resin and fit them as sidelights in 1:48 scale. Lathe owners will know that it is easier still to bore out the centre (with a $^{13}/_{64}$in drill bit) and trim the edge of the cartridge case with the parting-off tool, but I would emphasise that a lathe is not strictly necessary for this job. If cartridge cases are not available, brass tubing will suffice.

Glazing the lights: .22 shell cases filled with resin.

13. Advice from Ewan
Corlett in letter to author.

Run a thin film of casting resin onto a sheet of smooth polythene and sit the cartridge cases inboard sides down on this sheet. When the resin has polymerised, fill the cases completely with clear casting resin so that the surface protrudes in a crescent-shaped figure, well above the rim of the sidelight. When this has cured into a hardened state, take it down with fine wet-and-dry paper, flush to the surface, and buff it up by rubbing hard on a board with metal-finishing polish.[13]

Planning ahead for the boiler room

Before we move onto the decks in the next chapter we need to consider the placement of machinery and deal with the propeller and shaft. Compromise always brings with it a sense of frustration; there is often an inbuilt resentment that there has to be any such thing as making-do, and hesitation can continue for a long time before admitting that some compromise is unavoidable. Two questions to be considered are access for the stokehold, and the scale at which the boiler room ought to be shown in model form. Unlike the engine room, the stokehold cannot be built in scale if it is to be a coal- or gas-fired model. Because of the demands of live steam, it must be built on a larger scale than the rest of the model.

All of this preamble is leading up to the subject of access, which has to be so carefully planned from the outset, and not left to chance in a haphazard way. Access to working parts is an absolute requirement with all machinery, therefore nothing can be installed without some way of reaching it, either for regular maintenance or possible failure. There is also the matter of internal detail which can be seen through the weather deck, and on the level of the gun deck when the engine room hatches are removed. So you must consider how the gun deck, also known as the main deck, may best be viewed, at the same time as incorporating access to the stokehold and boiler room. Add to these thoughts the desirability of showing the teak buffering behind the armour plating on the hull interior, and you will begin to appreciate why it is necessary to move so cautiously at this stage in the proceedings.

Stern frame, rudder and solepiece

Before a start can be made on the propeller or the decking, the stern frame, rudder and solepiece must be tackled. Taking these in reverse order, the moulded hull already has the appropriate 'flat' to accommodate the solepiece, so this item can be duly bandsawn from brass 0.135in thick. Onto this must be silver-soldered the rudder post, previously machined on the miller with a groove for the banjo to slide in vertically and, on the opposite side, slots for the rudder braces. The lower half of the rudder post and the sternpost should then be built up with the aperture strengthened by gussets, as indicated on Scott Russell's plan. The rudder itself is made from brass, with a tease of a problem as to how the rudder pintles may be fitted in true alignment. The trick is to use a single piece of brass wire, and solder it in one pass. It can then be sawn away appropriately to accommodate the rudder braces on the rudder frame. In full-sized practice, the original banjo frame was also made of brass, presumably to avoid any

The heat sink and aluminium shield. This prototype was later slightly modified to vertical side walls.

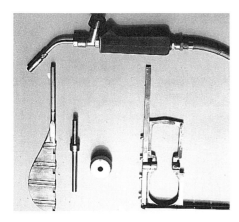

(Far left)
The stern gear, rudder and banjo frame, silver-soldered with propane torch.

(Left)
Silver-soldering the rudder stock.

corrosion in an area exposed to oxygenated seawater, which makes for a high rate of decay. On the model the banjo frame must be sawn out and the shaft bearings machined and silver-soldered to the ends of the frame. The outer bearings are made from brass with phosphor bronze inserts. The upper half of the rudder assembly should then be silver-soldered to the lower half, to make a single rigid unit, eventually to be screwed and taped into position using GRP. The cradle bearing, which housed the cheese coupling on the prototype, is false on the model in that it has no real part to play. And so, after the preliminaries, we go onto the main task - the propeller itself.

The propeller

On the model, the driveshaft and propeller feature at such an early stage of the construction process because the hull must be tested for watertightness at this point – whilst it is still easy to gain access to the area of the deadrise and propeller boss. On the prototype, though, the boring out of the stern frame in order to take the propeller shaft was one of the final jobs completed by the engineering contractors before caulking and painting prior to the launch.[14]

Turning the screw

Robert Griffiths was the inventor who

noticed that there was something basically wrong with early experimental propellers and he devoted his working life to the study of ships' propulsion with varying shapes and pitches of blades. The problems were complex but, in layman's terms, the tips of the blades were too broad in what was known as 'the common screw' and the surface area relatively remote from the axis of revolution. This caused bad vibration and inefficiency. Cavitation was also experienced by making the blades too narrow, although a less broad blade was a desirable feature for a vessel with auxiliary steam power when under sail alone. This was because propeller blades caused significant drag to the underside of a hull, even when allowed to rotate when disengaged: thus came about the invention popular with auxiliary steam vessels, the lifting screw.

Hoisting propeller

The launch of *Warrior* coincided with Griffiths' 1860 patent adjustable blade propeller, although earlier Griffiths propellers with fixed blades had already

14. Wells, Capt John, *The Immortal Warrior* (Emsworth, Hants: Kenneth Mason, 1987), p48.

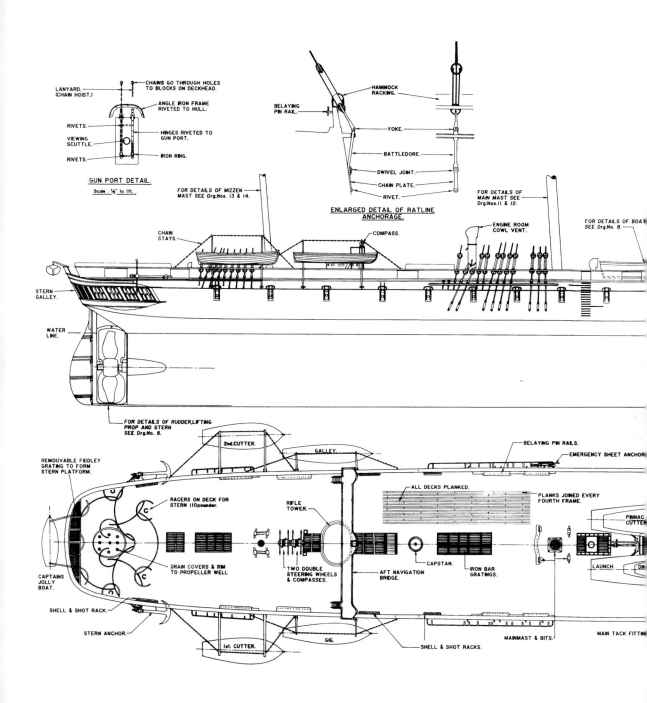

GUN PORT DETAIL.

LANYARD. (CHAIN HOIST.)

CHAINS GO THROUGH HOLES TO BLOCKS ON DECKHEAD.

ANGLE IRON FRAME RIVETED TO HULL.

RIVETS.

VIEWING SCUTTLE.

RIVETS.

HINGES RIVETED TO GUN PORT.

IRON RING.

Scale : ¼" to 1ft.

ENLARGED DETAIL OF RATLINE ANCHORAGE.

BELAYING PIN RAIL.

HAMMOCK RACKING.

YOKE.

BATTLEDORE.

SWIVEL JOINT.

CHAIN PLATE.

RIVET.

FOR DETAILS OF MIZZEN MAST SEE Drg.Nos. 13 & 14.

FOR DETAILS OF MAIN MAST SEE Drg.Nos.11 & 12.

FOR DETAILS OF BOAT SEE Drg.No. 8.

CHAIN STAYS.

COMPASS.

ENGINE ROOM COWL VENT.

STERN GALLEY.

WATER LINE.

FOR DETAILS OF RUDDER, LIFTING PROP AND STERN SEE Drg.No. 8.

REMOUVABLE FIDDLEY GRATING TO FORM STERN PLATFORM.

2nd.CUTTER.

GALLEY.

BELAYING PIN RAILS.

EMERGENCY SHEET ANCHOR

ALL DECKS PLANKED.

PLANKS JOINED EVERY FOURTH FRAME.

RACERS ON DECK FOR STERN 110pounder.

RIFLE TOWER.

CAPTAINS JOLLY BOAT.

DRAIN COVERS & RIM TO PROPELLER WELL

TWO DOUBLE STEERING WHEELS & COMPASSES.

AFT NAVIGATION BRIDGE.

CAPSTAN.

IRON BAR GRATINGS.

PINNAC CUTTE

LAUNCH.

SHELL & SHOT RACK.

STERN ANCHOR.

1st. CUTTER.

GIG.

SHELL & SHOT RACKS.

MAINMAST & BITS.

MAIN TACK FITTIN

Profile and deck layout
(Author & J.D. Metcalf)

SPECIFICATION.

Length O.A.   :   420ft.0ins.
Length P.P.   :   380ft.0ins.
Beam.   :   58ft.3ins.
Draught.   :   26ft.10ins.
Displacement.   :   9,180tons.
Speed.   :   14.358knots. (max.)
Engines.   :   5,469.I.H.P.
Sail Area.   :   48,400.sqr.ft. (max.)
Boilers.   :   10No.147". PENN Type.
Pressure.   :   22.p.s.i.
Complement.   :   705 Officers & Men.
Armament.   :   10No. 110pounders. B.L. Rifled Bore.
                        26No. 68 "   . M.L. Smooth Bore.
                        4No. 40 "   . B.L. Rifled Bore.

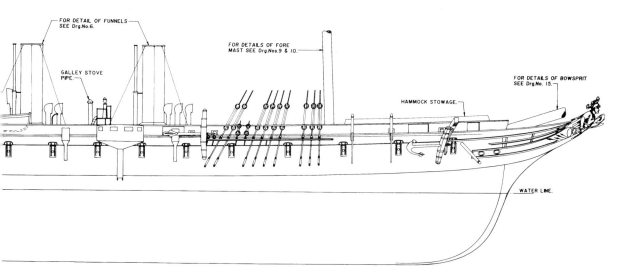

FOR DETAIL OF FUNNELS
SEE Drg.No.6.

GALLEY STOVE
PIPE.

FOR DETAILS OF FORE
MAST SEE Drg.Nos.9 & 10.

FOR DETAILS OF BOWSPRIT
SEE Drg.No. 15.

HAMMOCK STOWAGE.

WATER LINE.

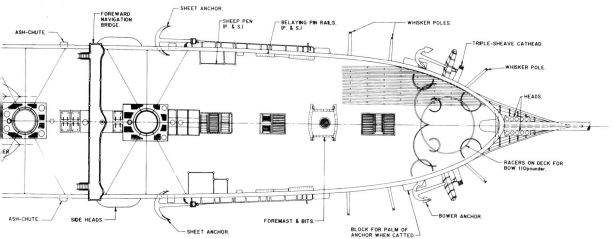

ASH-CHUTE.

FOREWARD
NAVIGATION
BRIDGE.

SHEET ANCHOR.

SHEEP PEN
(P. & S.)

BELAYING PIN RAILS.
(P. & S.)

WHISKER POLES.

TRIPLE-SHEAVE CATHEAD.

WHISKER POLE.

HEADS.

RACERS ON DECK FOR
BOW 110pounder.

ASH-CHUTE.

SIDE HEADS.

SHEET ANCHOR.

FOREMAST & BITS.

BLOCK FOR PALM OF
ANCHOR WHEN CATTED.

BOWER ANCHOR.

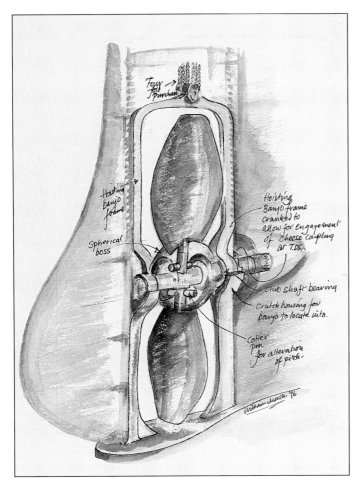

proved themselves most effective and reliable. The *Great Britain* had been fitted with one for the Australian run in 1857; it was ideal for the work, in that much of the journey to Australia was conducted under sail with the propeller clear of the water.[15] The striking feature about the Griffiths propeller is the spherical boss, which is almost one-third of the diameter of the screw. The blade has a tapering form, with the leading edge cut away more than the trailing edge; the forward rake reduced vibration. In the interior of the boss, a cotter through the stem of the blade rested in a sector-shaped recess in the boss, and alteration of pitch was made by varying the packing pieces on its sides. The one fitted to *Warrior* had the following vital statistics: two blades 24ft 6in in diameter and weighing 10 tons. It was, apart from that in her sistership, *Black Prince*, the largest hoisting propeller ever fitted to any ship.[16]

'Down funnels, up screw!'

The 1860 propeller was supported in a brass banjo frame, which could be raised or lowered in guides set between the stern

(Above)
Illustration of propeller.
(Author)

(Right)
The screw propeller.
(A E Seaton, 1909)

(Far right)
Stern gear with propeller boss and paper templates for the propeller blades.

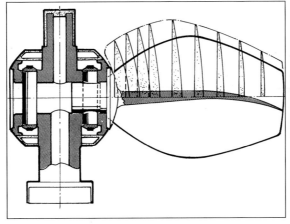

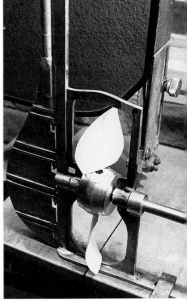

frame and the sternpost. It needed the whole ship's company to haul the propeller up when proceeding under sail alone, which was most of the time. It is sometimes forgotten that the Black Battlefleet was engined in order to be an effective fighting force. It was under battle conditions that the mobility of steam propulsion came into its own. When the Griffiths propeller was lowered through the propeller well, the shaft would engage at top dead centre into a cheese coupling located at the end of the tailshaft bearing. A diver was not required for this operation, which was as simple as it was arduous, but doubtless welcomed wholeheartedly by the stokers when the classic orders were given, 'Down funnels - up screw!'.[17]

Machining the propeller

Some good close-up photographs of the stern gear and propeller as fitted to the Science Museum's model were used for general reference purposes, and the Museum has also been good enough to produce the original patent of the Griffiths 1855 propeller. The propeller boss was turned from 3in brass bar, and transferred to the four jaw chuck for marking out the angle of the blade pitch at the root, which is set at an extremely coarse angle of 37 degrees, something that one would expect from a power source using low revolutions (53rpm maximum). An engineer's protractor placed on the lathe bed produces the necessary reading to do this.

Propeller blades can be drawn, but as any draughtsman will tell you, it is very difficult to indicate what exactly is happening in three dimensions. Trying to understand the sweep of the blades, their pitch and rake, required much staring at the photographs, but it was only when a start was made on cutting out bits of paper and card, working it between the fingers, that fear began to change into fascination with the nature of the double helix. The

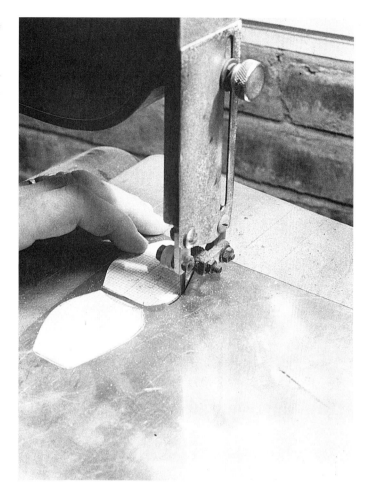

The propeller blades being bandsawn out of a sheet of brass.

back of your thumb is actually a wonderfully soft anvil on which to work paper. All you have to do is to be able to repeat this action with hot metal and grips, with a well-aimed kiss or two of the soft-headed hammer.

Paper to metal

The same piece of squared (graph) paper, used for the experiment in three dimensions between thumb and forefinger, should be glued onto the sheet of 100 thou brass to act as a cutting template, and then bandsawn. The flat surfaces of the blades can be softened up by annealing them with the propane gas torch, and they should then be hammered, filed, smoothed and polished until they match each other in

15. Corlett, *op cit*, p156.
16. Ballard, Admiral G A, *The Black Battlefleet* (London: Society for Nautical Research, 1980), p246.
17. Wells, *op cit*, pp60-61.

The author feathering the blade tips with forward rake.

The stern gear assembly fitted to the hull and glassed into place.

shape and form. A point to watch is that they are an *opposite* pair for cutting out purposes, having leading edges and trailing edges, yet they are *identical* for fitting purposes. After the blades are tapered and shaped, the abrasive flapwheel being an extremely useful item for thinning the blades, two slots for the blades should then be milled out on the top and bottom of the boss. No-one would normally silver-solder in situ on the lathe, as the flux and fumes are very destructive in terms of rust to the delicate nature of the 'queen of tools', but in order to ensure that all was set fair and square it does seem the obvious thing to do. The lathe should therefore be temporarily veiled to avoid any spillage. It can prove quite difficult to

provide sufficient heat on what is a mass of conductive metal, and it is necessary to be careful not to create distortion in the work which has already had its final machining.

After a good polish has been applied, the pitch of the blades must be feathered slightly to imitate the form of the prototype, which was set at 30ft. When this is done the magic look of the prototype will be reborn. It is a very beautiful object in its own right, a true example of the demands which science makes upon art when science goes beneath the waves. It is a fact that some of the most beautiful parts of ships of this period lie hidden below the waterline. The propeller is secured by a keyway, milled into the tailshaft, so that the assembly may be withdrawn. This is in accordance with full-sized practice, as are the pedestal and plummer blocks, which support the intermediate shaft and tailshaft bearings. With a certain amount of metal finishing and polishing, the whole assembly turns in a relatively smooth fashion, given that the model propeller is a weighty item ($10^3/_4$oz).

In order to take out any misalignment in the shafts, universal couplings should be fitted between each stage. At this stage, the unit has yet to be proven as watertight, and will require the insertion of two O-seals in the area of the bossplate, machined into the tailshaft (see Chapter 12).

3
BUILDING THE DECKS

The question of decking on model ships and boats is a paradise for critics. Any exhibition of models will show ingenious varieties of approach to the several artistic issues which decking presents to model shipwrighting. Over the many hundreds of years that ship models have been made, a style of planking has been presented and accepted which really bears no resemblance to reality. The problem in the first instance has to do with colour. Now the truth about real ships' decks is that they very quickly suffer exposure to the elements and assume a silvery-grey hue as part of the ageing process. If realism is genuinely sought, then it would mean leaving timber ex-posed to salt sea air, wind, sunlight and frost for a year or so, already cut to size and thickness, and subsequently applying it to the deck beams without any traces of adhesive to spoil the effect.

What modelmakers have done for centuries is to follow the irresistible urge to make their decks look 'pretty' (and why not?). Decking is a dramatic piece of mosaic, which really does show and reflect all the effort entailed, in a way that much that has gone on before does not. Laying decks involves sanding and finishing which naturally beautifies the surface, and the first coat of varnish applied after the matting down is a rewarding moment to be savoured. Techniques for decklaying vary considerably. Even with properly laid decks, it is unusual to see deck planks which are anything other than thin strips of veneer wood. Real deck planking is nearly square in section, typically 6in x 5in, although planking on the original *Warrior* shows nearer 9in width; translated into scale this means a mere $1/8$in square. The second concern has to do with the length of miniature planks and their relationship to the deck beams. Following full-sized practice, deck planking spans four deck beams only, so that in 1:48 scale, one ought not to see any deck planks over 4in long before looking for a change in the grain. Museum models most often show a drawn deck, done with an old-fashioned pen and Indian ink, on previously varnished timber, but this lacks the character imparted in individually laying planks.

Whether full-sized or scale model, a great deal of timber is involved in the laying of a complete ship's weather deck. It might seem unbelievable, but it was necessary for me to rip-saw 6400ft of plywood to cover both the main deck and the upper deck, without any wastage – and cutting $1/8$in strips with a 9in circular sawblade is not easy. In fact, a new sawblade had to be purchased specifically to do the job and it took me a fortnight to machine the whole bundle.

For particular reasons, my model of the *Great Britain* had her deck laid onto a

(Above)
De-Walt Radial arm saw employed to machine the lengths of scale planking.

(Right)
Teak buffering fixed behind the armoured section of the citadel and lower deck beams fitted. Note the use of the plumbline wire along the centre of the hull and the spirit level used in conjunction with the engineer's square.

subdeck of ply, with the addition of aluminium shielding on the underside. This worked quite well, but the decking does move in extremes of temperature, particularly in dry atmospheric conditions. This is an important issue with working mod-els, which are likely to spend much of their lives out of the water and lose all their natural moisture content; it is particularly a problem with warping hatch covers and a source of some anxiety for modellers who may not have appreciated the alarming effects this atmospheric change can cause.

Teak buffering and deck beams

The first job to be done on the interior of the hull is to line the inner walls with a buffer of teak, into which the deck beams will be set. This might seem a waste of time, but depth is always a serious consideration in modelmaking, and it does show in the most surprising ways, giving a look of brute strength which is so characteristic of this vessel. Into the kerfed slots cut partially in the teak buffering must be fitted over two hundred deck beams, so a decent template made from steel is called for. The camber of the gun deck and the weather deck are the same, so a single template will serve for both. It is much easier to mark up the centreline and other data before the camber is applied and, as a general principle in shipbuilding, never place any part anywhere in the ship without first marking the centres, where the item is to be placed, and the centre of the item you are placing. You will bless yourself later - sometimes years later.

The simple labour of fitting all these separate members has to be preceded by a great deal of measuring, because the deck beams, like the gun ports, are not equidistant from one another, even in the central citadel. They are influenced by the position of the gun ports, and in every case there is a full deck beam fitted on either side of the arc of the gun mountings, and a half beam directly aligned with the gun. Between each gun port, there are two more full beams fitted athwartships, and this is the pattern followed throughout the ship from stem to stern. The deck ties travel the full length of the virtually-uninterrupted flooring and, together with the reinforcement of teak and the smithed-down ends of the deck beams, the combined structure gives the ship the strength required for a floating iron fortress.

Because the model hull is made from GRP, it is necessary to use pure resin as the adhesive to join the miniature teak cladding to the walls of the citadel. It is worth pausing to consider why this relatively new timber was used on the prototype as the buffering behind the 4.7in of armour plating. Scott Russell chose teak for the sandwich between the outer and inner skins of the ship because he knew it was the only timber which could resist the triple onslaught of seawater, rainwater and condensation. Teak is also lighter in weight than oak and, once dry, noted for its stability and durability. Perhaps the most influential factor of all was that engineers had a great respect for this timber due to its innumerable uses on the railways dating from the early 1800s.

There is doubt whether or not the teak used for the model would be recog-nised as the same timber used on HMS *Warrior*, which was almost certainly *Tectona grandis* imported from Indochina, whereas that used for the model might have come from almost anywhere in the world where it is hot and wet; nevertheless, it does have that distinctive greasy feel and leathery smell associated with this impervious timber. To achieve this imperviousness, one of the age-old tricks of Chinese shipbuilders was to bury teak underground; when it was then removed from its temporary grave, it had become as hard as iron, and could not only resist all sorts of water, as Russell had recognised, but it was also immune to insect attack.[1] Despite all of its technical advantages, teak was hated by sailors under battle conditions because its splinters festered in the flesh, unlike oak splinters which were much more benign.

Imitation caulking

Technology has improved in the area of the permanent waterproof felt tip marker pen. A giant felt tip pen (I used an Edding 850) can be used as a very effective miniature caulker, just by dragging the black felt tip marker along the edge of the deck plank. These jumbo pens even have a refill option for a long job like this, for which they were not of course designed. Experiment has showed that it is more effective just to mark one side of each plank only.

Laying down the model deck

The decision to try a new type of timber adhesive for laying the decks came about because it is so much easier to use a one-shot glue for decking. Aliphatic adhesive possesses all the virtues of a quick-grab waterproof glue with a single-shot application, but sands down more satisfactorily than previous PVA glues, and it does not suffer from the brittleness of the traditional resin glues used for many years.

1. Bramwell, Martyn, *The International Book of Wood* (London: Mitchell Beazley, 1979), p182.

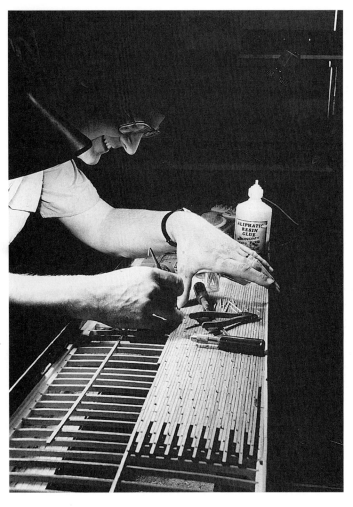

Scale planking on the model.

As with the laying of any sort of flooring, the wisest approach is to start at the centre and work out towards the edges. Now this is not easy: you are dealing with very thin strips of timber and the drilling has to be accurate, or 'snakes' appear. You also have to watch how much adhesive is applied along the edge of the plank, because any slight variation along the glued edge can produce a fit of the squiggles. It must be appreciated that, with laying planks side by side, any error or variation from the truly straight line will be exaggerated fifty times when it reaches the waterways along the side of the ship. After a day or two at it, you will begin to get the feel of it all, and one of the tips on offer is *not* to try and press the planks together too firmly, even though a little repair work may be necessary later where seams have not been totally closed. Ironically, it is the little deviations and indiscretions which make it all look real and interesting. This is not an excuse for bad workmanship, simply an observation that a perfectly-drawn deck, so often seen on showcase models, has none of the life of a truly planked deck. The monks involved in making stained glass windows centuries ago deliberately made the decorative effects around the picture stories told by these windows uneven and asymmetrical; the thinking behind this was that anything too perfect was bland. There is an important lesson in that for modelmakers.

Joggling in the margin plank

Normally, the margin plank, which is also sometimes called the plank sheer, or covering board, is laid first, and the deck planks fitted to it. In full-sized practice this requires the use of the adze, possibly the most primitive and dangerous hand tool known to man; the axe-like handle is just visible in the restoration picture from West Hartlepool.

When laying ship's decks, the ends of the planks are never allowed to take a

Before any decking is laid across the deck beams on the model, the plywood should be brushed with a coat of tinted pine varnish. This will give an ageing effect to the raw timber and will also seal it from penetration by any stray glue spots. The planks can be mechanically fixed, by using a $5/_{64}$in drill bit, through the plank and the deck beam, followed by a sausage stick which acts as a trenail. Following a strict pattern of drilling a hole at the point of the third deck beam out of four, the miniature dowel should be glued and pressed home through the plank and deck beam. The butt end of the plank can then be trimmed off to share the deck beam with the start of the new plank, and so the sequence continued. No sub deck is necessary.

sharp wedge shape. Where such a demand becomes necessary, as with the curve of the deck following the line of the sheer at stem and stern, a snipe has to be faired off at the end of the plank. The rules governing this are that the reduction on the plank must not be allowed to be less than half its width at the butt end. The margin plank itself is wider than the standard planking, so that it can accept the butt end of the snipe without being weakened overmuch, and this is where the adze comes in to play. The resulting effect of the snipe as it fades and diminishes is very alluring, but represents one of the hardest fitting jobs in shipbuilding, and goes by the charming name of joggling. The difficulties also transfer themselves into model ship-wrighting, particularly as 4mm ply cannot be knifed, but must be sawn. This means fitting it all together dry and then taking it all apart again before reassembling with

adhesive. Through the long months it took me to bring the deck to completion there was much wastage and trial and error, but as the upper deck is a major feature of this ship, the work is well rewarded, although it took me nearly ten months to bring about.

The planks must also be joggled around the propeller well. This has been beautifully done by the shipwrights on the prototype and is well worth studying as an object lesson in completing the circle. It is made doubly difficult on the model by the requirement of access through the deck to the steering yoke below. This involves staggered cutting of plank lengths, which is a good way to hide a hatch cover which is not often in use; the caulking effectively hides the joints, making it almost impossible to detect. One could do all hatch covers like this, but they are a fiddle if in constant use.

On board *Warrior*, late summer 1983. Note the adze, the margin plank and the care being taken to keep the planking level. (Photo courtesy of the *Warrior* Preservation Trust)

4

THE FIGUREHEAD,
THE SIDEHEADS AND
OUTBOARD FITTINGS

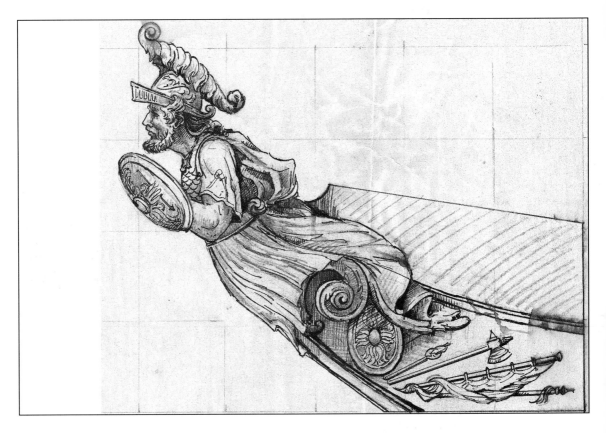

*W*arrior was unusual in that she had one of the clearest operational decks of any warship to date, but she nevertheless made full practical use of the defensive walls along the full length of the upper deck, both on the inside and on the outside. No space was either lost or wasted; this could be said to add a distinct dimension to the total undertaking of modelling her, and it is important not to underestimate how much detail is carried on the inner and outer walls of the ship. The furnishing of such detail will add considerably to the length of time needed for the construction of the model, and where better to start than with the figurehead?

The figurehead

It is perhaps not always appreciated that, throughout the centuries, ships' figure-heads were more than mere carvings by shipwrights: for the sailors whose ships were adorned with these often beautifully-crafted objects they were items of venera-tion. The ship's figurehead carried with it the powerful magic necessary to appease the sea gods, securing for the ship a safe passage through the waters which the ship must necessarily disturb. The figurehead at the prow of the ship acted as the media-tor for this disturbance of the sea gods, chief of whom was King Neptune himself. Religious superstition was not confined within the bounds of Christianity, and has its roots in ancient beliefs in the way in which the natural world was governed, a world full of myth and magic. For this reason sailors treated figureheads with great reverence. As early as 1703 the Admiralty had decreed that all figureheads should be of lions but, despite this ruling, full fig-ures and figureheads kept creeping back until such time as the shape of naval ships' bows disallowed such features, a critical moment that had almost been reached by the early 1860s.[1]

The restoration figurehead

The massive undertaking of carving the new 3-ton figurehead for the restored *Warrior* is the largest commission on which Norman Gaches and Jack White-head have ever worked, either individually or jointly. Jack Whitehead has for many years been involved with the restoration of the world's finest collection of figure-heads, housed within the hull of *Cutty Sark*, while Norman Gaches' work may be found gracing ships in such exotic loca-tions as Tasmania, Alaska, and the West

$1/_{12}$th scale figure-head, carved in lime by Norman Gaches to demonstrate the full-sized version, and used for reference purposes throughout the carving of the full-sized replica.

(Below)
Prototype figurehead at West Hartlepool, August 1985.

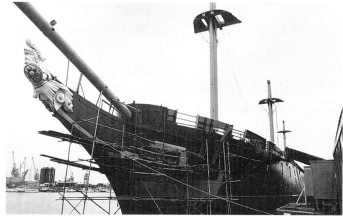

Indies.

As with the trip to West Hartlepool in 1982 to see the ship in full size and to speak to the men who were repairing her, a pilgrimage to meet these two gifted men on the Isle of Wight became an absolute priority, before attempting any reproduc-tion of a figurehead at 1:48 scale. One can-not over-emphasise the importance for a serious scale modelmaker of going to speak to those responsible for producing work in full scale. Very often it only re-quires a simple telephone call, but the result can be far-reaching in the extreme. You will learn the story behind the story,

1. Kemp, Peter (ed), *The Oxford Companion to Ships and the Sea* (Oxford: Oxford University Press, 1976), pp302-304; see also Stammer, M K, *Ships' Figureheads* (Prince's Risborough, Bucks: Shire Publications, 1983).

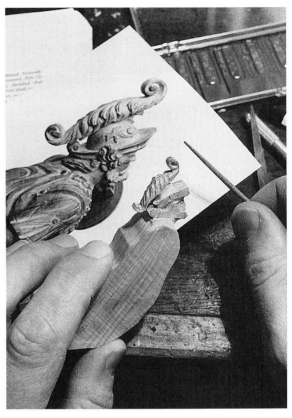

(Above left)
Bandsawing the block
of yew.

(Above right)
The plumed helmet
appearing using the
round needle file.

2. The gouges I used are
called Micro Carving
Tools, available from the
Dockyard Model
Company (see list of sup-
pliers).

and be warned of the many pitfalls for the unwary. My trip was fascinating; friendships were formed, and scale sketches, photographs and drawings all resulted from this journey. Even a beautiful carving in limewood at 1:12 scale, originally done to convince the restoration team at West Hartlepool, was offered to assist in the work which lay ahead.

Figure-carving is very seldom, if ever, required of the jobbing hobbyist, and I had a distinct feeling of being under-rehearsed for the task in hand. Added to this hesitation was the certain knowledge that the full-sized carved *Warrior* figurehead represented one of the best examples of lifelike sculpturing ever to adorn any ship anywhere.

The scaled-down photocopy of the elevation of the figure's port side reduced the mighty *Warrior* to an object smaller than a fieldmouse. How was it going to be possible to portray a feeling of importance

and grandeur in something so minuscule? The photocopied outline was glued down onto a block of yew, which had a wonderful sweeping grain, ideally suited to the flowing toga which melted away from the figurehead into the beak and trailboards of the ship. In an experimental and over-casual way, the preliminary sawing and roughing out took place, reducing the torso to a block shape (on the original this preliminary work was done with a chainsaw, cutting away half a ton of timber). Yew wood is so hard that the bandsaw, normally a plucky beast, could barely cope with ripsawing a mere 3in thickness. Just to get the feel of knocking off the corners, I made a start on the plume of the helmet using a set of miniature gouges.[2] Having gained a little confidence with carving the plume, I then moved onto gouging out the facial features in the area of nose and forehead, using a shape of file called a cutter. There is no doubt that really hard,

The torso plus left and right arm, set in the Plasticine ready for casting in bronze resin.

matured timber carves beautifully; quite a different experience from gouging away at softwood, and the smaller the item being tackled, the sharper the carved line needs to be in order to produce good definition. Some six hours' work was required before the head and helmet emerged from the solid block of yew.

The second major session started with a freehand drawing of the arm on the starboard side. This arm holds the Roman sword erect, and the major anatomical feature in need of accurate replication is the muscular portrayal of the forearm. I selected a piece of timber for its swirling grain to complement the sinuous effect captured by the replica. Attention must be given to the clenched hand, which draws the muscles of the forearm into a bowed shape. His left arm adopts an entirely different pose as he holds the double-thonged Roman shield across his chest; had the shield only a single handle, the grip would have changed through 90 degrees. This is a stance of defiance, which makes him look a fighter as he flexes his biceps convincingly.

The fixing of the arms to the torso requires shallow sockets to be cut at the end of the shoulder blades, almost in the style of a ball and socket joint, a depth of a mere $1/16$in or so, but this makes a surprising difference in terms of realism, making the arms look as though they are a working part of the whole torso, rather than extraneous fixtures to it. His Roman toga, flowing away from his torso around the beakhead of the ship, finishes up in a flourish, around what architects call a volute. This is the point where the carving converges into the ship's side, with a spiral scroll reminiscent of classical architecture, and much loved by the Victorian sculptors. The rest of the trailboard carving, that is to say, spears, axes, colour flags and all the other paraphernalia of war, can be carved from a sheet of lead.

Casting the figurehead

It was necessary, as much from a point of view about vulnerability, as well as from a desire to see how the miniature figurehead would reproduce, to consider casting the figurehead in resin from the carved pattern. The GRP experts were keen on a technique known as block moulding which means quite simply that you drown the whole figure upside down in a box of liquid silicone, and when the silicone has cured, rescue the original by literally pulling it out, relying on the flexibility of the silicone rubber for release. You then pour resin into the mould for a result.

Despite assurances from the experts, I did not heed their advice and would recommend the following method. Prepare a mould box in the traditional manner, making a box with a removable bottom. This box needs to be reasonably strong to be able to withstand having Plasticine smoothed to its edges. Ideally the box ought to be made of metal, so that the Plasticine can be heated up to a fluid state, in order that a clean horizontal joint line may be obtained more easily.

Separate the model figurehead and the two arms, and then press into the Plasticine to the halfway point, paying extra attention to the joint line around the original, allowing no gaps. This job is best done with something like the flat back of a cutting blade, judging by eye where the thickest portions of the carvings are at the joint line. White spirits are a solvent to Plasticine, and the use of a small paint brush produces a really clean line. A pouring funnel must be created out of a half-cone of Plasticine and the locators put in with the blunt end of a ballpoint pen.

Four suitable locations must be indented to a depth of approximately $1/4$in (no more).

Quick checklist of items required

Silicone rubber ($1/2$kg)
Hardener (24 hr cure) 25g
Pigment, if required
Waxed paper cups (not plastic) for mixing
Metal spatula (not wood)
Plasticine
Box with removable bottom
Knife
White spirits (Turps substitute)
Small paint brush
Talcum powder
Warming device for Plasticine
Pencil for making locators

The procedure

Mix and pour the silicone resin. As a guide, a full beaker should be just enough, filling half the box. If more is needed, it can be added without any problems, because it is slow curing. Silicone de-gases itself pretty well, and is one of the reasons

Pouring the silicone rubber into the mould.

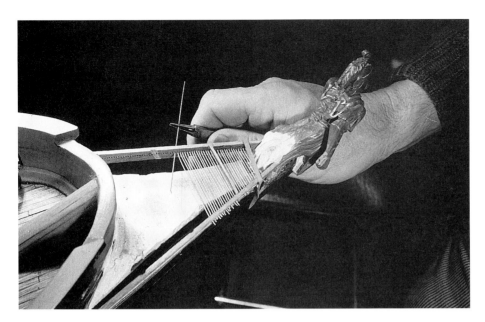

Beakhead grating. Note the bronze finish to the figurehead casting.

for allowing such a slow rate of cure, as bubbles keep coming to the surface long after it has been poured. The pouring operation must be preceded by very thoroughly mixing with a metal spatula (a wooden spatula should not be used because it may contain harmful moisture). It also helps to let the mixture stand for five minutes after stirring and before pouring into the mould box. A full twenty-four hours at house temperature has now to be endured patiently; silicone stays sticky right up until the last few hours, so do not panic when it all still appears tacky when you wake up in the morning.

It is now a question of digging away the Plasticine from the underside of the mould box, being careful not to damage the original. The Plasticine goes hard and cold and keys itself to the box but, when the bulk of it is removed, it will be possible to press the whole block of silicone and Plasticine out of the box in one go. Silicone does not readily adhere to anything, so there is really no need at any point to use a parting agent, but old habits die hard and I personally dusted down the wooden figurehead with talcum powder before replacing it into the silicone half mould, prior to the second pouring.

Before the final pouring, the second half of the pouring funnel must be made out of Plasticine. The cunning bit of the whole operation is that by virtue of the locators being impregnated on the first side, the second pouring automatically produces the exact relief moulding and the perfect contacts of the two halves. Retrieving my original carving back out of the silicone caused a certain amount of relief on my part, and I repaired and reassembled the original carving after some cleaning and polishing.

The local experts were full of doubts as to whether or not the resin, mixed with a heavy dose of bronze pigment, would pour successfully down the mould and into all the detail, as resin behaves differently from hot metal, where the air is pushed out as the metal runs into the mould. This seemed rather gloomy, but it was suggested that the thickish resin pigment could be poured into the two halves and slapped together like a bread sandwich, which is what did happen, and by the following day the figurehead had a twin brother in pigmented resin of an impressively bold shade of bronze; this, when buffed up on the highlights, made him look very important indeed. For those who have not come across resin pigments,[3] they are truly deceptive, even to the point that the pigment will grow its own verdigris if painted with vinegar or other dilute acid. The figure should be painted in white and then gilded. Resin flash lines, etc, clean up well with a dentist's burr.

Beakhead

There were a number of research issues associated with this area, in that the beakhead belongs more properly to the fifteenth century rather than the nineteenth, and from the point of view of photographic evidence it is a place obscured by shadow, quite literally shrouded from view. The Science Museum builder's model depicts no details, showing it as a flat area with no heads or gratings to copy, unlike the plan view of the ship which details both. An end-on glance at Nelson's *Victory*, built almost exactly one hundred years before *Warrior*, shows the bluff-ended bow of this famous old flagship to be a shape redolent of a traditional Christmas pudding.[4] Stripped of all the timbering at the forepeak she would make a very ugly vessel indeed when viewed from the sheer. Likewise *Warrior*, with her shapely cutwater and clipper bow, is also dependent on the iron knee for her good looks and sharp entry, topped off with the rails and head timbers which lie near the heel of the bowsprit. It was necessary to delve into this area in some depth, this research enabling me to sort out one item from another, and I will attempt to condense my discoveries into a short description of the correct terminology, the jobs these items have to do, and how they fit together, for a clear understanding of this area is important from the point of view of accurate modelling.

In very basic terms, the beakhead is essentially a triangular and self-flushing lavatory. There are only two places aboard any ship which offer natural and simple

escapement for man's necessary needs, and the beak of a ship has provided the first of these two options since time immemorial. The stern of a ship has likewise been a reserved quarter for the Captain and Commander, with the privileges of privacy which accompany their high office: thus ships' plans show the accommodation for private heads and baths in the tuck of the stern counter at the swell of the quarter galleries. At the bows of the ship, people today view the exposed latrine troughs and urine dales with varying degrees of horror, finding it almost impossible to believe that over five hundred seamen would be expected to relieve themselves every day in an environment so exposed to rain and sea spray, to mention nothing of ice and snow. These men had no more than a canvas dodger for side protection, and as they sat side by side, they were open to the heavens above and the spuming seas below. Worse still, when the seas were so bad that the heads were dangerously unusable, the whole area had to be abandoned in favour of a makeshift, rigged up in the lee forechains by hitching ropes along the sheer pole. From this precarious point, hanging on for dear life, the desperate call of nature could be answered.[5] The beakhead had a secondary, but equally important, function as a platform which gave support to the bowsprit, and in vessels predating *Warrior*, the lashing of the bowsprit, called the gammoning, was fixed to the head rail, or upper cheek.

There were five main components to the beakhead deck.[6] Working down rail by rail from the top there was firstly the stanchion rail, which surrounded the exposed two sides of the decking and to which the canvas dodger was lashed. Next down was the head rail, which supported the iron gratings and carlings (fiddley grating); underneath this came the triangular head timbers which supported the athwartship cross beams; down one more level and faired into the skirt of the figurehead was

3. Resin pigments are available from glassfibre merchants.
4. Longridge, C Nepean, *The Anatomy of Nelson's Ships*, revised by E Bowness (Watford: MAP/Argus, 1977), Plate 45.
5. Ballard, Admiral G A, *The Black Battlefleet* (London: Society for Nautical Research, 1980), p64.
6. Longridge, *op cit*, Ch 5.
7. Ballard, *op cit*, p52.

the lower head rail supporting the three head timbers. Below that comes the upper and lower cheeks (also known as trail-boards), edged with what is called the hair bracket, leading down to the double hawse outlets. Together these flying bulwarks, outboard of the main structure of the hull, provided the function and character of early warships until the disappearance of the bowsprit and of sail itself. The only surprise, perhaps, was that with a ship so modern in concept and design, building techniques in iron were following the exact pattern of vessels built solely from timber four centuries before. There was a price to pay for this piece of naval tradition, in that the heavy cast iron knee, the beakhead, the figurehead and the supporting iron rails gave this ship's bow 7in of forward draught, and in swollen seas made her dip her beak, which considerably slowed her down in a head sea.[7]

As far as the model is concerned, the only difficulty is that of drilling out the holes for the iron gratings. This should be done in a drill press fitted with a cross vice, so that close drilling does not present the accuracy issue it otherwise might. The two head rails can be taped together and drilled through as one. The acute angle can be overcome by use of annealed brass wire, rolled out and fed through the holes, with a small angle put onto the fed end of the wire. (Coiled brass wire can be made straight by rolling it on a hard flat surface, using a flat steel rule like a rolling pin.) Both the head rail and the lower head rail should be milled out in order to add to a look of lightness, and in the case of the lower head rail, to allow it slight curvature. The head rail was absolutely straight, though it is often depicted with a slight bag to it, which is incorrect.

The sideheads

At first sight these might appear to be armoured balconies, or even rifle turrets, but were in fact sheltered seating for four

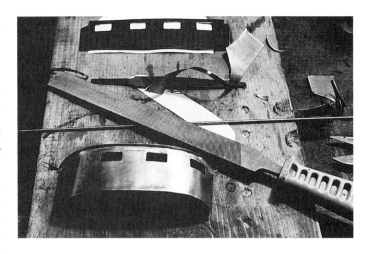

Sideheads constructed from brass shim.

persons, port and starboard, and an opportunity for great relief on the curved interior of this huge latrine. The fact that crew members no longer had to walk the length of the ship to relieve themselves must have contributed greatly to the efficiency of this fighting machine. The sidehead, with its demi-lune design, is no more than a giant, airy sluice. There are four opening ports on the side walls, and the plans also detail a skylight port through which, possibly, a fire hose could be used to flush down the walls thoroughly. Although the structure of these sideheads looked like an afterthought, they featured on all the upper deck plans and were added to the ship in the 1862 refit. The restorers of the ship have not included them in the programme, partly because the forward gangplank for visitors is positioned at their exact site (port side). In that they were part of the prototype, it is therefore all the more important that they should be included on the model. The Science Museum model politely omits them, neither have I seen them recorded anywhere else but in contemporary photographs of the ship.

The miniature construction of these latrines is, in my mind, like cutting an old-fashioned petrol can funnel in half, appreciating at the same time that the top is not semi-circular, but a stretched arc to which the top and bottom would have to be silver-soldered. A start should be made by giving the metal a thorough taste of the annealing process to reduce it to an amenable state. With the soft-headed hammer, only the lightest touch is required to stretch brass sheet and, when in this malleable state, it is as easy to work as silver paper.

The photograph details what happens next. The flattened sewage outlet pipe, which I detected from a very old photograph of a ship, is made from copper. This oval shape presumably provided a greater surface area against the side of the ship to which it was attached, the pipe acting as the anchorage for the sluice floor. The domestic-style window openings in the swell of the curved sides of the latrines are a logical detail, since this is the only way in which the hinges could work. One simply cannot have a flat opening port on a rounded curve, or it would jam the hinges. The roof is not flat, but designed to drain off both rain and sea water. On the model this can be achieved by soft-hammering and smoothing with the back end of a chisel handle. It just gives it that slight bellying which makes it look one degree better than a tin can with a downspout.

These sideheads must have been a welcome addition to this ship which had a reputation for 'pushing up the green Atlantic'.[8] The beakhead was totally inaccessible in rough weather, and almost anything was an improvement on the makeshift, of which more will be said later.

Handmade chain

Studded link cable chain, to give it its full title, dates back in history to the days of the 'dark satanic mills' of the early nineteenth century where the hammer welding techniques associated with the Black Country were used in the production of South Staffordshire bar for chainmaking.[9] The famous photograph of Brunel standing by the chains of the stern checking

drum, shortly before the launch of the *Great Eastern*, serves as inspiration and evidence of man's boldness in the forging of iron links, each one of which weighed 60lb, making it the largest nautical chain available to the Admiralty in 1857.

Captain Wells' book informs us that the studded cable for the bower and sheet anchors was made up from $2^3/_8$in bar, with the exception of the second sheet anchor which was attached to 100 fathoms of hemp ($18^1/_2$in).[10] Each stern anchor was provided with $1^5/_8$in iron cable, whilst the stream and kedge anchors relied on hemp. Because the studded chain link cable was too cumbersome to be worked around a ship's capstan, the cables had to be hove in by means of a messenger, an endless chain with studless links to which the main cable was attached with nippers, as shown in the diagram in Admiral Ballard's book.[11]

Massive as these weights and diameters of chain were in full size, miniaturisation reduces them down to the techniques and tooling of the jewellery trade. Links are $^1/_4$in long, and soft copper wire of 0.040in can be used as the bar stock. The tools required are a sharp- or snipe-nosed pair of pliers and a pair of Maun parallel pliers. They are cantilevered, and wonderfully powerful - a lovely tool, but you could use a plain-jawed vice, or an adapted pair of gas pliers (anything in fact where the jaws work in parallel). Further requirements are a pair of side-cutters; a second pair of pliers to twist the link open; and a soldering iron, some soft-solder and killed salts (Baker's) fluxing fluid.

The method

Mark the sharp-nosed pliers with tape or paint at the point which gives you the desired length of the link. Unless you are working in a big scale, this will be pretty close to the tips. Flatten the stud of the link by squeezing in the upper jaws of the pliers. This is done for two reasons; first-

8. Ballard, *op cit*, p52.
9. Cossons, Neil, *Industrial Archaeology* (Newton Abbot: David & Charles, 1987), p125.
10. Wells, Capt John, *The Immortal Warrior* Appendix 8, p234.
11. Ballard, *op cit*, p53.

ly, for appearance: the studded link in full-sized practice is smaller than the bar used for the outer link, so that in miniature it needs to be crushed into a narrower width and filed off later on the top edge when the link has been completed; secondly, it provides a tighter and more distinct turn at the beginning of the inner link.

With the sharp-nosed pliers gripping the squeezed part of the stud, make a 360-degree turn of the pliers until you meet the exit of the stud, still gripped in the jaws of the pliers, and then cut the link level with the stud at the jaw line of the pliers. Now squeeze with the parallel jaws to make the shape uniform, but do not let go. With the second pair of pliers, twist the link sideways. Do not open it outwards or you will spoil the preforming. Join the links uniformly, with each link closed the same way up as its predecessor, and finally soft-solder as below.

Place the tip of the iron on the outer part of the link, opposite the start point of the stud. Do not touch the solder to the iron tip at all, but let it feed by capillary action towards the heat source, across the stud. That way you keep the solder from getting anywhere near the crowns of the links, where it can be a nuisance. Should that happen, and you perhaps have not heard of the product, there is something called de-soldering braid, which is used by electronic technicians. This metal braid soaks up molten solder like blotting paper and is useful to have around.

How long does it take?

Approximately 12in of chain can be made in an hour, on the basis of each link taking approximately $1^1/_2$ minutes to fabricate. It is indoor work, and surprisingly satisfying as the chain lengthens. Approximately 6ft is needed for the bower and sheet anchors, and because the sheet anchors were fished opposite the fore funnel, the studded cable trails back from the aft hawse pipes along

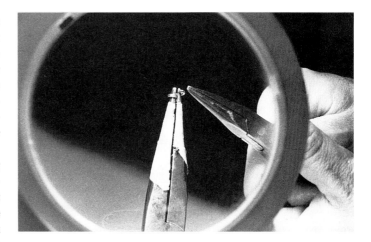

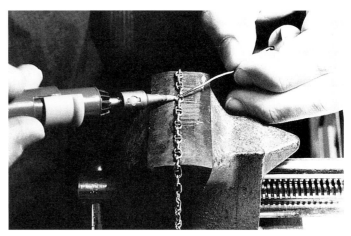

the fore chains in full view.

Ordinary studless chain can also be produced by hand techniques. Soft wire wrapped around an oval shank of suitable diameter, and snipped or sawn off in a straight line whilst still on the former, works well. Other techniques include slipping it off the former and cutting down its length with tin snips or endcutters. Unless it has to be loadbearing, you will probably not need to solder chain made like this,

(Top)
A studded link being formed at the tip of the long-nosed pliers. The pliers held in the right hand are opening the link so that it may be joined to the chain.

(Above)
Handmade studded link chain; the joins are being sweated with soft solder.

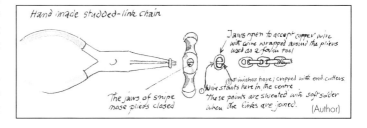

Hand made studded-link chain
Jaws open to accept copper wire with wire wrapped around the pliers used as a forming tool
Finishes here; cropped with end cutters.
Wire starts here in the centre
These points are sweated with soft solder when the links are joined.
The jaws of snipe nose pliers closed   (Author)

particularly if the wire is not too soft. Either way, it is a good feeling to be able to say that you make your own chain, even if the reason for doing so is simply that no-one else produces such an item in proper scale. It is a classic case of 'You want it – you make it', which is not far from where many people started off in their hobby of craft work.

Anchors

In the world of merchant shipping, by the 1860s Mr Trotman's new patent anchor, with its yoked crown and bird beak flukes, was much in evidence and favour. Nevertheless, *Warrior* was to stick with the traditional Admiralty pattern in the matter of her main ground tackle. Both the bower and sheet anchors (5.6 tons apiece) were of this order, with their massive timber stocks and crescent-shaped castings. *Warrior*'s four main anchors were the largest and heaviest ever to be manhandled aboard a naval vessel,[12] and must have contributed considerably to her tendency to be stem heavy, adding as they did 22 tons of top weight, exclusive of the cabling. It is no surprise that with a ship of this size the old traditions were adhered to. At a fairly mundane level, any alteration to the anchor drill normally carried out by the marines would have meant new practice,[13] an idea that was always unpop-

ular with those who had practised the old arts to perfection, and saw no reason for change.

Nevertheless, changes were permeating through, and when it came to the two stern anchors ($2^1/_2$ tons apiece), there were some concessions shown to the new innovations. Patented by Rodgers, they had the niceties of a removable iron stock, and more interestingly, flukes which were attached to the outside of the anchor's arms.[14] This is the kind of detail which is all-important to those who are looking for historical accuracy. The seventh anchor, stowed amidships between the ship's main launches, was a light stream anchor of just under $1^1/_2$ tons. This was used either for temporary anchoring in deep water or assisting in getting the vessel afloat when grounded. The stream anchor was slung under a ship's boat and then let go some distance from the ship. This provided a haul for the capstan, and a means to the end of temporary embarrassment. This left anchors eight and nine (0.4 and 0.8 ton), known as the kedge anchors, stowed port and starboard abaft the mainmast. As with the stream anchor they could be used for warping ship and other like purposes.[15]

As to the anchors themselves, it is perhaps worth pausing to catalogue their different component parts, in order to appreciate fully their separate functions. The Admiralty Pattern anchor is really a common bower anchor, and it consists of the anchor ring (technically known at this stage of development as the shackle); the wooden stock (two sliced baulks of oak); the shoulder (which prevents the stock slipping down the shank); the shank or shaft; the trend (the flare at the bottom of the shank); the crown (the outer edge of the crescent); the arms (the continuation of the flare towards the flukes); the palms or flukes (the spade ends); the bills or peas (the final tip of the arms, thus the term billboard, which is the ledge on the external walls of the ship from which the anchor fluke hung when catted).[16]

Anchor rigging: note the anchor release gear atop the cathead.

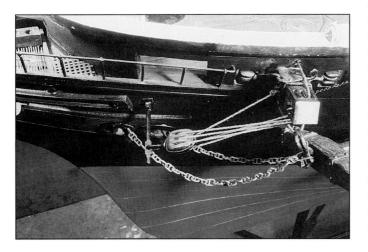

As one might expect, anchors were built to certain established specifications; thus the square section of the bottom of the shank tapers to two-thirds of its diameter at the stock. The outside circumference of the crescent shape is equal to the length of the shank; the palms should be as broad as they are long. The bill is half the size of the arms in section. Dr Longridge also details in his *Anatomy of Nelson's Ships* that the anchor stock is

> square in section and is 1in in width to every foot in length. Thus an 8ft stock is 8in square in section at the middle. Towards the ends, it tapers to half its diameter. The top is straight along its entire length, the taper being confined to the sides and under surface of the stock.[17]

The method

When it comes to the assembly of the stock in miniature, these instructions made good sense. The iron bands on the prototype were put on red-hot from the forge, with the action of shrinkage clenching the sliced timbers together. As they were cooling, the blacksmiths knocked the squared section up the taper of the timber, tightening the timber around the shank, making a very permanent cross joint. Everything except the heating of the bands can be followed in miniature, the workshop tip being that the mark made for the final location of the hoop is made undersized by one width of the band, which allows for the stretching of the hoops which the knocking-up process causes. On my model, the four heaviest anchors were cast up to the base of the

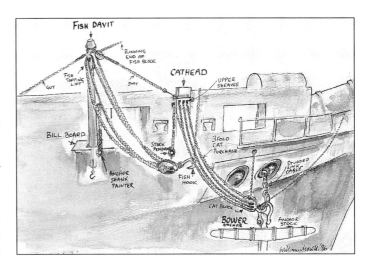

shank; this was done because the flask (sandcasting box) was not long enough to take in the shank as well. There were also doubts in my mind that the crucible was large enough to take enough lead mix for a single pouring.

Dust the wooden pattern with talc and centre into the sand in the lower flask, sunken to its halfway point. Then fill the upper flask and tamp down, having first dusted down the surface of the parting point between the two flasks. Runner and riser holes should then be pricked into the top flask and the wooden pattern removed. The pouring can then take place, and after a few minutes for the cooling down process, the anchor will be complete.

The shanks of the four main anchors are best made from a dense hardwood; fix the whole object to the crown and 'ironise' with a coagulant paint to give the roughened texture reminiscent of cast iron.

The Rodgers' patent anchors can be sandcast with the shank in total, and as well as their strange flukes, they also have a removable stock, which is an oval-shaped bar. This can be constructed by flattening brass tube in the engineer's vice, and soft-soldering the nut rings to their extremities. They also have a hole bored through them at the crown, possibly for purposes of underslinging them to a ship's boat in full scale, in the manner of

(Above)
Sketch of fish falls.
(Author)

(Lower left)
Anchor stock being banded. The stock ought to show a split line along its length, as they were traditionally made in two halves.

12. Wells, *op cit*, p53
13. *Ibid*, p235; Nares, Lieut George S, *Seamanship* (1862), first published in 1860 as *The Naval Cadet's Guide: Seaman's Companion*), facsimile of second edition, introduced by David R Macgregor (Woking: Gresham Books, 1979), p122.
14. Wells, *op cit*, p234.
15. *Ibid*.
16. Kemp, *op cit*, p22; Nares, *op cit*, p120.
17. Longridge, *op cit*, p134.

the stream anchor as described above. The Science Museum model corroborates all this *prima facie* evidence.

The cat block sheave

The cat block is the most handsome of the reeving devices, having a triple sheave and a hook of a very fetching shape, which attaches to the anchor shackle. In general terms, rigging blocks consist of four main parts: the shell, which is the outside wooden part; the sheaves, which are the wheels on which the rigging lines run; the strop, which can be made of rope, wire, or in the case of a cat block, with metal banding; the eye, on which the purchase is made at the top (not necessary on a cat block). Nearly all the original ship's blocks were made of *lignum vitae*, because of that timber's very special qualities of

Illustration of cathead. (Author)

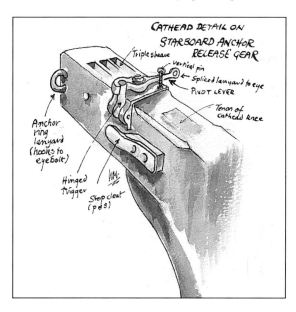

self-lubrication. An almost equally exotic timber called wenge was used on the model.

The process

This is rather lengthy considering how small the item is, but it is definitely worth

the trouble. Take a square section of timber, and cut off the end, leaving approximately $1/4$in and keep it safely. Mark off and cut the three slots for the sheaves to run in; open up the slots with a pillar needle file (the flat one), and then replace the sawn-off end and glue it back on. Now drill the axle for the sheaves. Make the sheaves to fit the slot, but remember to make them undersized in diameter because ropes swell. The shell must then be sanded into the round. Use a round needle file to give a seating to the strop, particularly on the corners.

Spin up some three-stranded copper wire in the hand-held drill brace, and twist some copper wire around the block, leaving some strands to which the hook may be soft-soldered. This captivates the sheaves and axle. Manufacture the hook by using $1/16$in solid brass wire, softened by heat treatment, and then sharpened on the lip hook end. The lip is made by twisting with sharp-nosed pliers, starting from the sharpened end, and once shaped, hammered cold on the anvil. This process more than restores the hardness of the brass, and makes a very strong scale hook.

The anchor release gear

The cathead has several more details to be included, even after the completion of the two cat blocks. The most obvious of these is the anchor release gear, which does what the title promises. It is basically a T-bolt, which is held captive by a parrot beak hook on the end of a pivoted iron bar, and secured with a locking pin. It is definitely not a piece of engineering, but an item straight out of the blacksmith's forge. Even so, in miniature it is all very visible, so that it must be carefully made. As with the cat block, the interesting bit is the hook, made this time by sharpening both ends of $1/16$in brass rod/wire, softening with heat, shaping round with sharp-nosed pliers, and then hammering cold on the anvil. This process, even at 1:48 scale, gives the blacksmith's hammered finish in miniature, and there is nothing to touch it for realism.

Rigging the anchors

The bower anchor rigging is best tackled first, preceded by making the collars around the hawse outlets. They have the look of the dilated nostrils of a wild boar, and on the model were made from lead. Their sharply oviductal shape is a study in itself of the way in which light falls, and is a distinctive feature of this ship, and the effort put into the production of the hand-made studded cabling will pay off handsomely. Chain, in whatever size it is produced, has two very attractive properties, one of which is the way it hangs, and the other the way in which it shivers when there is any ambient movement. This all adds to the life and vibrancy of the model, both in and out of the water. The bower and stern anchors are rigged in the 'ready for letting go' position, as depicted in Nares' *Seamanship*.[18]

The stream, or waist, anchors amidships were swung clear of the ship by use of a purchase between the fore yard and main yard. As these anchors weighed over $5^1/_2$ tons, it must have been a very difficult evolution to carry out when one considers the pendulum effect which a heavy seaway would have caused. The lower stunsail booms were lashed to them.

The stern anchors, as can be seen on the restoration, rest in crutches which pivot outwards from the walls of the ship, ensuring that the anchor is thrown clear of the quarter galleries. It is an awkward installation, emphasising that there is very little spare space around the exterior of this vessel. The restoration does not quite match up with the builder's model, but the builder's model does not include the details of the crutches, showing the anchor as merely being lashed, with no side hawse outlet. A compromise can be reached between the two, that does at least make

sense, and it is possible to let go. The Rodgers' patent anchors at the stern weighed approximately 3 tons and required smaller cabling (in full scale, $1^5/_8$in, as opposed to $2^3/_8$in for the bowers).[19]

Anchor buoys

The switch from round anchor buoys to pyramidal ones came about as the result of the new age of iron. The excellent illustration in Nares' *Seamanship* of 1862 shows that this style of floating buoy was the standard issue of the time.[20] Robust and riveted, it is an easy item to reproduce, requiring only the angle of 60 degrees to be sanded off the four sides of a piece of square timber stock. By cutting the ends off on the bases and sticking them together, the basic object can be made ready for the application of riveting detail and a ring bolt at either end. Note that one must only rivet up one edge: the metal was obviously turned and overlapped at the edge, requiring only a single line of rivets. When each one must be caulked to make it watertight, a double row of rivets would not be wanted.

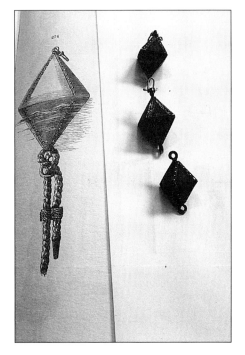

Anchor buoys: pyramid pattern.

18. Nares, *op cit*, illus no 271.
19. Wells, *op cit*, p234.
20. Nares, *op cit*, illustration no 274, p124.

(Above)
Fixing the half-round beading with cocktail sticks and epoxy resin adhesive.

(Right)
The entry ports and ladderway. Note the extra wide tread at the passing points.

On the model, the line of rivets was made by using a tailor's wheel to impress on pewter sheet, then cutting and gluing along one edge.

Gilding the galleries

There ought to be a modelmaker's caution about making things look over-pretty. Nevertheless, because handling gold leaf is an ancient technique, I made the decision to try the technique out on what really constitutes a statement of sheer flamboy-

ance at the stern of this ship.

The mystique of gilding ought not to cause too much trepidation; the gold leaf is backed on a piece of what seems a bit like greaseproof paper, which is really just to facilitate the handling of the leaf, and makes the whole business a good deal easier. The glue-size needs to be carefully painted on for, wherever there is even a trace of this application, gold leaf will cling to it. However, it must be said that gold leaf is initially easier to repair than misplaced paint, and can be scratched off with a kebab stick, or whatever sharp wooden implement comes readily to hand. The painting can be done freehand, mainly because the gallery surrounds all stand proud from the original moulding and it is therefore easy to do. When the glue-size (also called gesso) has become tacky, but not dry, simply overlay the gold leaf with either very light finger pressure or with a brush. It breaks away from the backing paper and transfers to the painted gesso, initially looking rather messy until the line is cleaned up with a very soft brush, removing all the excess gold leaf. It is at this moment one understands why all the old masters used gold leaf: it does look special. Gold leaf can also be burnished, although it will stay bright of its own accord for a few hundred years.

Stern quarters

On my part, delay in tackling the decoration of the stern quarters was associated with the difficulties of making the half-round strakes which surround the window galleries. The track which they have to take is tortuous, given that they sweep through compound angles, and a simple reliance on adhesives or clamping would be misplaced. Kebab sticks are made from a cane-like timber (technically a creeper), which is very hard and flexible, like boxwood in that regard. All one needs to do in preparation is to plane the stick into a half-round shape, immerse it in a bucket of water (it is so dense that it sinks after an hour or so), and then use the hot copper tube to steam it into shape. The fixings are made with cocktail sticks.

The entry ports

I also felt a reluctance to cut the two amidships entry ports, which appear at the summit of the steps on the outer plating of the hull sides. These rather grandiose gilded portals replaced the canopies of wooden ships of the line, but retained the ornamental carved brackets which apparently, but not actually, supported the hammock rack channels. Because of the thickness of the walls of the ship, extra decoration in the style of the memorabilia of war, as depicted on the trailboards, also finds its way to block up the end grain and add to the general feeling of luxury; these carvings were done in lead and then gilded. One fear was that cutting through the wall of the top plating might upset the fair line of the hull, but this was unfounded, and nothing moved out of alignment. The near catastrophe which befell the full-sized SS *Great Britain* in the Falklands was caused when someone had cut through the sheerstrake in order to gain access to the hull, and started a fearsome split which, over the years, ran almost to the bottom plating. This probably innocent act almost made an end of that piece of nautical history, so even in miniature the entry ports were cut with some trepidation.[21] The brackets on the model can be carved in hardwood, cast in metal, and gilded. This is on the basis that if you have more than two pieces of detail like this to make it is quicker to make up a mould.

Gun port lids

Although the gun port lids are a small detail compared to the total hamper which surrounds the hull topping of this ship,

the gun ports themselves are the ultimate distinctive mark of the armoured ships of the Black Battlefleet. The piercings are more widely spaced than their predecessors for reasons of safety and strength, and are also pinched up from their traditional square shape into rectangles 2ft x 4ft, a return to the archer's slit, rather than the battlement crenellations, of their land-based counterparts. These distinctive port openings are the sure signs of the citadel, the concept around which these battleships were designed.

The narrow openings of these gun ports were made possible by anchoring the guns to the gun port reveals on a pivot, which in the case of *Warrior* allowed a 26-degree arc of fire to each gun. Without this pivotal anchorage, any misalignment of the gun would have gravely endangered the lives of the gun crew, because the muzzle of the gun only just protruded through the thickness of the armoured walls, and no more. In full scale, the port lids were only proofed against rifle fire because under battle conditions they would in any case be raised.[22] To have had them armour-plated would have greatly increased their weight, and made them very difficult to raise and lower, already an awkward manoeuvre by virtue of the fact that the chain running tackle was not secured outboard to the sheerstrake of the ship, but piped back inboard to the under-

21. Corlett, Ewan, *The Iron Ship*, (Bradford-on-Avon: Moonraker Press, 1975), p185.
22. Brownlee, Walter, *Warrior: The First Modern Battleship* (Cambridge: Cambridge University Press, 1985), p12.

Gun port lids being fitted.

side of the upper deck through two sides of a triangle, which made for poor leverage. The port lids of *Warrior*'s rival, *La Gloire*,[23] were armoured but split $2/3:1/3$, with a double hinge top and bottom, which seems a more practical solution, and was indeed adopted for one or two later British ships. Both *Warrior* and *La Gloire* had the small port scuttle in their gun port lid, which allowed a minimal amount of light to penetrate through to the gun deck.

As to the model, I attach a good deal of importance to making such items work. Making your own hinges is not as alarming as it sounds, in that any hinge is basically only a strip of metal with a piece of pipework attached to the end of it, and a pin running through it. On the model the pipe is best silver-brazed, but soft-soldering can also make a mighty strong hinge. A flat piece of metal, with piping soldered to it, can then be cut into strips, to make butt-strap or whatever shape of hinge is required. Brass tubing, which solders so beautifully, is available quite readily at $1/16$in (outside diameter), and brass wire (0.045in) can act as the pivot. To me, handmade hinges are a delight, and a distinct trade-mark of the scratch builder. (A manufacturing tip: heat up the metal strip and the piping separately before soldering – they expand at different rates.)

I experimented with several different ways of approaching the task but I have come to the conclusion that really these port lids are one big hinge and look neatest when treated as such. The mock straps of the hinges above the lids have already been detailed into the original fibreglass plug, so that all that is needed to complete the effect is to mill out the central portion of the lid, leaving a mock strip on the outer edge of the metal. These should then be mock-riveted through the strip using soft-solder on brass pin heads, and at the same time the scuttle centred into the hole.

It is not really the hinge which is the

23. A wonderful model of *La Gloire* (scale 1:32) is displayed in the Musée de la Marine, Trocadero, Paris, France.

problem, but the fitting of the hinge that requires skill. The slightest error of the pilot hole means that the lid will not close and sit correctly. If the pivot pin is sharpened into a point and passed through the tubing, when turned through 90 degrees the sharpened point will exactly mark the position where the drill has to be centred. The other end of the pivot pin should then be bent round into a U-formation. Measure the distance between the sharpened points using a vernier calliper, and then mark up the holes and drill them out. The working part of the hinge thus disappears into the side of the hull, allowing you to believe that it is all happening according to full-sized practice on the upper and lower strap hinges. A slight squeeze with smooth-jawed pliers along the brass tubing means that the lids will stay put with friction: a useful detail in that port lids break off easily in transport, and are much safer in the closed position when the model is being handled.

The photographic evidence indicates that when *Warrior* was at anchor the lids were raised during the hours of daylight throughout the length of the ship; other sources confirm that they were firmly battened down when she put to sea, not least because in a swell the port lids would swing up and crash against the hull sides, putting great stress on the halyard chains.

Bulwark sheaves

These are the sheaves through which the fore/main sheets are riven, and are belayed onto cleats on the inner walls of the ship. This might be easy enough where the sides of a ship are not of the armoured thickness of *Warrior*, and where normally a single sheave would do but, so far as it is possible to tell, an inner and an outer sheave must have been necessary, running in tandem and fixed in a casting. No other system would have allowed for the lubrication of the sheave axles or kept the sheets from severe fraying. The sheave slots themselves lie in sympathy with the fall of the tack rather than horizontally. On the model, separate castings (sixteen in all) must be made and fitted to their appropriate locations.

Davits and other projections

Working from the stem, the first projection from the hull of the ship is the bumpkin, a thin pole used for hauling the foretack down. The hook of the anchor is lashed to the bumpkin on the model, as on the Science Museum model, but that is not its main purpose. Then comes the cathead, which acts as the main hoist for the anchor, and is triple-sheaved. In support of the cathead (literally) comes the fish davit, or davits in the case of *Warrior*. This was originally a removable pole, used for fishing up the fluke of an anchor once it had been hauled to the limit of the cathead purchase, and enabled the placing of the fluke onto the billboard. The billboard was a ledge on which the palm, or fluke, of the anchor rested. Such was the weight of

Warrior's anchors that she needed the extra support of two fish poles, stayed with chains.

The midship section of the vessel is then relatively clear of projections until we come to the radial davits, fixed close to the aft conning bridge. Two of the lightest of the ship's boats were attached to these: the gig on the starboard side, and the galley on the port. There is a detail on these attractive shaped davits, namely the bottom bedplate swivel, a charming piece of ironwork which the restorers have gone to much trouble to reinterpret. The reproduction of this on the model involves more metal casting. There is a difficult job to be done with low-melt solder joining the casting to some brass tubing, a job only made possible by the advent of hydrobromic acid flux, which enables one to solder brass to white-metal castings. The skill is in putting enough heat onto the object to be soldered, without melting the lead/tin mix of the casting. It takes practice!

The radiused arms of the davits are

Radial davits made from steamed beechwood and bound with thread. Note the bulwark sheave sited at an angle between the 40-pdr gun barrel and the bottom bedplate radial davit swivel.

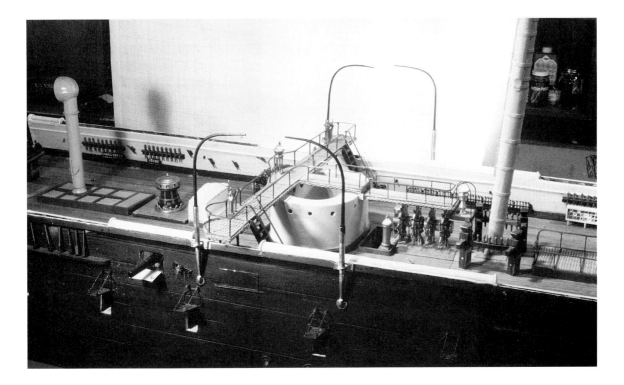

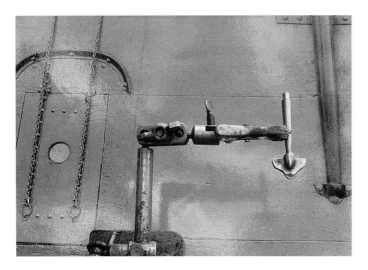

Brass pattern of the bottom bedplate swivel for the radial davits, ready for casting.

pair of stern bumpkins which act as outriggers for bracing the main yard. The last item to protrude over the stern galleries of the vessel are the Captain's jolly boat davits. These should be modelled from brass section and bolted through the ship's walls. They are extremely vulnerable, being at the absolute extreme of the vessel.

Final details

There are a few more details which can be attended to at this stage. These include ring bolts all the way round the interior of the ship; a manhole inspection cover at the breast forepeak; shell racks plus shells; ropework around the canvas covers of the hammock racks – yards of it, made from plumbline thread with one of the plies removed; a hinged metal hatch cover in the rifle tower. Three sizes of cleats must be cast, drilled and fitted; seated forestay blocks, heart blocks and billboards for the anchors must be made; the propeller well cover must not fit too precisely, and must be provided with a support rim to prevent it jamming. Chains must be fitted to the upper gun port lids; the funnel stays must be prepared; and an etched nameplate for the stern galleries depicting *Warrior*, which involves more acid etching with dry letter transfers.

not made from metal, but from wood (beech), and bound round with linen thread like the handle of a cricket bat. Meat skewers can be used: hand-plane to a tapered point, plunge into a bucket of water, and steam round a half-inch copper tube. The result is that they are flexible but firm: yet another demonstration of the versatility of hardwood steamed into unlikely service.

Immediately abaft the mizzenmast come two pairs of squared boom davits from which the first and second cutter boats were suspended. These squared baulks of tapered timber were so massive that they had to be rigged to the mizzenmast. In line with the propeller well are a

5
FIXTURES AND FITTINGS

The accumulation of accurate detail is what is so important for the scale modeller and having grappled with outboard detail we must now turn our attention to all the fixtures and fittings – the gratings, the ship's wheels, capstan, compasses, ladders to mention just a few – found around the deck of the ship.

Funnels

In 1852, eight years before the launch of *Warrior*, the 131-gun wooden First Rate, *Duke of Wellington*, sported a small retractable funnel. With *Warrior*, the two fully extended 31ft funnels stood bolt upright in a defiant attitude. *Warrior* presents an assertive image, confident in her superiority. The retractable funnels, coupled very neatly with the ability to raise the 24ft propeller, meant that under sail *Warrior* presented little extra windage and much reduced drag. Once again, we need to be reminded of the incredible inefficiency of burning coal for the propulsion of these hybrid ships; they were engined for manoeuvring in harbour, and for out-smarting the enemy in naval engagements, but not for conditions under which sail would normally be used. The engine, massive though it was, was still considered as an auxiliary to sail.

The manufacture of the two funnels will be relatively simple once some 2in diameter brass tube has been located. The only reason for offering the brass tubing up to the lathe is to mark out some plating lines to simulate a constructed funnel. The lathe makes an excellent scorer and index-er for plating work in the round, although one has to be very careful not to pierce through the metal when using a sharp cutter tip as a scorer. Once this is done, it will then be a question of annealing the lip around the top of the funnel casing. Three heatings and quenchings should be sufficient to soften the brass enough to allow the back of the ladle to force the metal into a flange. Any hard round object will suffice to bell out the mouth of the metal using this technique.

For the bases of the funnel cases, the upper deck as-built plan should be followed, because it makes the most logical

Flanging out the top of the funnel, having previously softened the brass pipe with heating and quenching. The rounded back of the ladle is forced against the rim and flares it out. Several annealings are required to achieve the effect.

sense. The stowage of the ship's launches is so tight abaft the funnels that it makes a demand for the cowls to be moved in closer to the funnel, something which must have been adapted when the final fitting out had taken place, as the earlier plans show identical bases for both funnels. An important concern is how to tackle the grating bars around the funnel bases in miniature form and, once again, for me the path to knowledge was littered with previous failures.

Acid etching

Acid etching is quite simply the finest way of dealing with non-ferrous metals, and virtually the only way of getting the detail of iron bar gratings. A source of supply for ferric chloride acid must be found: it is sometimes marketed as etchant for making electronic printed circuit boards. The principle of its use is very simple: all metallic items not to be subjected to the acid attack are screened off with acid resistant materials or paint. (Take some precautions to screen yourself off as well. Ferric chloride might not be the nastiest acid on earth but neither should it be treated as a harmless substance. Anything which attacks metal as effectively as this does will do nothing for your complexion, should you happen to splash some on yourself.)

Most sorts of sticky tapes will act as an effective screen against attack. Wax will also prevent attack, and thus dry letter transfers can be used for reproducing lettering in metal and name plates. Enamel paints will also inhibit the action, so that if you cover the surface of the metal with a good quality enamel paint, everything which has been painted out will not be subject to attack. This allows great flexibility, and careful preparation will be rewarded with an excellent result. A tip when using the dry letter transfers and/or paint is to warm the surface of the metal gently, and slightly roughen it with an abrasive paper, such as wet-and-dry grade 400.

Once the acid is in the plastic container, simply soak the metal in the etchant and the chemical reaction starts right away. Some sort of tongs will be required to handle the objects. Gentle agitation every ten minutes or so will wash away the residue of the metal which has been destroyed. Tiny particles build up on the attacked surface of the plate if it is left facing upwards, thus it is preferable to let it face downwards. The etching depth (cold) is approximately 1mm per twelve hours, and that is quite sufficient to give the effect of raised lettering or gratings.

Now for two final tips when using acid. A weak solution of ferric chloride produces an acid pickle which removes all the latent activity of silver-brazing and soft-soldering fluxes as well. Anyone who does a lot of soldering should keep a container handy for soaking soldered items which must have all the flux removed, because fluxes remain chemically active unless neutralised. As a by-product, this weaker chemical mix gives raw brass a wonderful verdigris - a green coating that looks as though you have just fished the object out of the sea after a few hundred years. Copper and brass items treated in this fashion look wonderfully authentic.

But most important of all is to remember the '*Three A's*' whenever you dilute acid. They stand for *Always Add the Acid*

Soaking the funnel base grating in ferric chloride acid etchant.

to the water. Never do it the other way round, or the result will be an explosion. The reaction of the acid on metal works in all directions, like burning a hole in the centre of a piece of paper, and you must allow for undercut once the acid is no longer protected by the tape, paint, wax or whatever. Consider also the thickness of the metal under attack, because in the heavier gauges, unprotected thin lines become thick lines, and small holes become large holes. The dangerous aspects ought not put off those who would like to try this production method. If you are careful, you are guaranteed good results for what is a minimal effort in terms of other kinds of metalwork involving saws, files and piercing blades.

Ventilation

When Captain Moses Rogers got up steam to sail the very first hybrid steamboat, *Savannah,* across the Atlantic it was rumoured that the cranked funnel, amidships with its 30-degree elbow, was supposed to deflect sparks away from the sails.[1] In fact, the comical shape of the funnel had nothing to do with the deflection of sparks, but everything to do with increasing the suction of air under the fire grates and through the boiler uptakes, and was demonstrably the first example of a rotating cowl of its kind, making the point that the later development, the bell-shaped cowl, can act as both a downdraught or an uptake, depending on whether it faces into, or away from, the prevailing wind.

Ship-modellers who confine themselves to a period of history before the mid-nineteenth century need never be faced with having to make a bell-shaped cowl at all. It would seem that the introduction of these came in the early 1850s, and persisted for a whole century with virtually no improvement. The first hard evidence of bell cowls is aboard Robert Napier's iron-hulled paddle steamer *Persia* (1854). The famous transatlantic paddlers of the 1840s show none of these ducting devices, and there is no evidence of them even on the *Great Eastern* launched in 1859, a year before *Warrior*.

One of the factors contributing to the inefficiency of boilers in these early days was an apparent lack of understanding of the need for fresh air for effective combustion. Iron hulls forced a radical rethink on such matters, particularly with the problems of condensation which the new material caused. Without sufficient fresh air, spaces for stowage in iron hulls became damp, and life for the ship's company in the lower decks uncomfortable. In this matter *Warrior* scored a triumphant first, in that she had a built-in design for both natural and forced draught. This was not primarily for the personal comfort of the crew, but for the efficiency of the fighting machine. A large steam engine amidships powered a ducting fan which brought air up from the lower deck to the citadel, *via* an ingenious piece of trunking, and expelled the clouds of gun smoke out through the gun ports. This gave the gun crew distinct advantages in terms of the aiming and firing of the gun and sighting the target. It also meant that they no longer choked on the gun smoke.[2] When the crew was not at Action Stations, the ducting was diverted to provide fresh air for the lower deck. The only place where fresh air was not welcome was in the coal bunkers: spontaneous combustion was a very real risk in these enclosed spaces, and was of constant concern to all members of the crew.

Bell cowls

The bell cowl is such a familiar sight on the superstructure of ships both great and small that it is often overlooked. The peculiarly attractive shape allows it to be used both as an air intake and as an exhaust duct, depending on which way the bell faces. The small forest of cowls clus-

1. Brinnin, John Malcolm, *The Sway of the Grand Saloon* (London: Macmillan, 1972), p28.
2. Wells, Capt John, *The Immortal Warrior* (Emsworth, Hants: Kenneth Mason, 1987), illustration p62.

(Top right)
Quartering out the bell cowl in sheet brass.

(Upper middle)
Using the punch and die on the cowl disc. Note that the cone has been silver-soldered along the joint line. Soft-soldering would split from too much stretching.

(Lower middle)
The lathe tailstock centre used as a punch to flare out the end of the copper tube; the tube is first softened with heat, cut off at the appropriate angle and flared out by use of a soft-headed hammer: this achieves the trumpeted end.

(Bottom)
The cowl will sit fairly into the flared neck of the tube, to which it is silver-soldered.

oven/stove, were responsible for feeding the whole ship's company (largely on boiled food).

The manufacture of the bell cowls

This was approached with some trepidation on my part. In *The Ventilation of Ships*, F L Bullen informs us that the Ministry of Transport's ruling in 1950 was 0.400in gauge thickness of steel for ventilators of 18in and above,[3] which translated into modelling terms means a piece of brass shim. This is the moment to put away the micrometer and remember that there is no such thing as a true scale working model.

To set about the manufacture of the bell cowls, it is necessary first to make a metal punch and die from brass in the shape of the cowl, but for me the technique required experiment. It was simply impossible to force a brass disc (0.017in) satisfactorily into the die without splitting it at the collar, despite several annealings. It seemed that there was too much metal in the disc. The only solution was to cut a quarter of the disc away and silver-solder it into a cone shape, which allowed it to go halfway down the die without any hammering. Although initially I doubted whether a silver-soldered seam would put up with the ill-treatment it had yet to endure, I derived a great deal of pleasure as the cone shape was persuaded down into the die, with much further hammering, heating and quenching, at least three times before the final depth was reached to the die bottom. At this point the metal has been stretched very thinly, and hardened by the process. This adds to the look of authenticity, and makes a serviceable product which has to do the same job as on the prototype; even small coal- or gas-fired boilers need air.

Thirteen of these cowls are required in all, plus two smaller ones at the stern of the ship. When I was fabricating these, by the tenth one the process became routine

tering around the funnel base tell the tale of the extravagant needs of the fires beneath. The only other way of dispersing heat was through the iron bar grating and the wooden fiddley hatch coverings. The galley had its own arrangements, with a tall tapering chimney appearing just abaft the forward conning tower. The fire grates, in this case at the bottom of the

3. Bullen, F L, *The Ventilation of Ships* (Liverpool, 3rd edn 1950).

but still, what lay ahead was a cause for some apprehension: namely joining the downpipe to the cowl top. A hole drilled at a steep angle through a piece of thin material very close to the edge and requiring silver-soldering is a difficult specification to fulfil. Using a miller bit, the first cowl was totally destroyed: this was obviously not the answer, so I used hand tools for the next one. A small hole first, which is increased with the use of an elongated countersink drill. It is a slow method but one I recommend.

Cowl down necks and downpipes

The anticipated difficulty with manufacturing these was in flaring the neck, but a recent discovery of mine had been the effect of flanging annealed copper tubing on the slant with a wide-angled punch (a Morse tapered centre). This is easy enough to do, and is very effective once you know how. With some experimenting, I found that a previously cut 30-degree angle, flanged out from the front lip of the cowl to the cone at the back, produced the briar-pipe effect. To the absolute purist

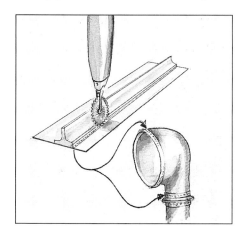

they will never be right because they are made with punches rather than pieced together, but they represent the best one can do using silver-solder and beaten brass metal. They could be produced quite easily in thermoplastic, but they

would not damage so effectively.

The final touches include simulated riveting, and levers to adjust the dampers on a quadrant. In full scale, cowl vents always show a degree of natural wear and tear, particularly where boat stowage occurs, and this will undoubtedly happen in miniature as well.

Chainwales

Around the upper strakes of the model *Warrior* there is a mass of detail, some of which it is possible to work into the original glassfibre plug, but much has yet to follow. The chainwales, or channels, are a serious piece of structural work in terms of

the forces exerted upon them, in both prototype and model form. They are not, as is sometimes supposed, the anchorages for the shrouds, but a mechanical device to lessen the load on the backstay irons (known as chainplates), spreading the base area of the whole masting rig as widely as possible.

Warrior has a belt and braces system, incorporating massive wrought iron chainplates sufficient to withstand the incalculable forces exerted upon them aboard this colossus of a ship. The only record of damage to these robust fittings was not one of storm damage at all, but rather an embarrassing account of *Warrior* shearing off the channels and chains of HMS *Royal*

(Above)
Modelling the wrought iron chainplates to the chainwales on the port side of the mainmast: note the gaps to allow for the gun ports and the pivoted joint on the knuckles of the irons, to allow for the lateral movement of the mast.

(Left)
Illustration of detail to cowl ventilator.
(Author)

Oak on Squadron manoeuvres off the Scillies, partly as a result of her 'sluggishness in answering the helm under canvas'. This was the only collision of her career, and she removed every protruding item, including the ship's boats, from the other ship's starboard side.[4] Where the tumblehome of the hull is in favour of the steep pitch of the rigging, the channels can hug the side of the vessel in a fairly streamlined fashion. This applies to both the mainmast channels and the mizzen, but the foremast shrouds are sited at the breast of the ship where the curvature of the hull is no longer in sympathy with the rigging pitch. This, in turn, means that the forechannels have to be broader on their leading edges, or the shrouds could no longer be rigged in line abreast.

Hammock racks

For more than a hundred years, hammock racking had been used in a twofold role along the top sides of a warship. The first intention was for the stowed hammocks to provide cover against enemy fire, in the same way that infantrymen used sandbags in trench warfare. The tops of the stowed hammocks were used as a steadying platform for the return of pistol and rifle fire, and as a protection against flying fragments. The hammocks also acted *in extremis* as a primitive form of life raft, providing enough buoyancy to keep a man afloat for quite some time. Each seaman had two hammocks, one slung below and one above in the numbered stowage provided.[5] As can be seen in the photograph of the racer arcs, the modelling technique used to simulate the hammock racks is to groove out the hull topping, fit the partitions and cover over with expanded aluminium mesh. For the tight turn at the stern a thick piece of electrical cabling can be used as a former over which the aluminium mesh can be formed. The racking must then be covered with shrinkwrap plastic and heat applied to make the wrap-

ping adhere to the partition and the aluminium mesh; the same technique can be used for the canvas covering of the hatchways.[6]

Although the hammock racks aboard *Warrior* were made of iron, they were nowhere near strong enough to withstand the massive strains of the backstay irons, nor could they be converted to channels. The only solution to the mechanical difficulties of dissipating the pulling strains of the shrouds was to allow them to pass *through* the gunwale capping to the hinged chains below on the sheerstrake of the ship. These chains, which are not chains at all but solid wrought iron bars, take on a square form at their knuckle ends, in order to provide a yoke which pivots on a gudgeon pin, allowing lateral movement to the mast without overstraining the channels, the latter being fixed solidly to the walls of the ship with iron brackets. Under the old system, where the deadeyes were rigged to ring-bolt chains with hemp, the movement of the mast was likewise accommodated. In common with their forebears, the chains below the channels all adopt the differing angles of the rigging pitch of the shrouds in order to distribute the strain in the most efficient way. The characteristic gaps in the splay of the shrouds are accounted for by the gun ports, which cause an interference in what would otherwise be a perfect spider's web.

Fiddley grating

Fiddley grating, with its pattern of half-lap joints, has for centuries provided positive grip to the bare feet of sailors and at the same time given degrees of light and ventilation to the decks below the hatches. Its more sinister role, that associated with naval discipline as a flogging rack, is witness to its utility, while in extreme situations, frames of fiddley grating were also used as life rafts, being an easier option than launching a

4. Ballard, Admiral G A, *The Black Battlefleet* (London: Society for Nautical Research, 1980), pp4-5.
5. Nares, Lieut George S, *Seamanship* (1862), first published in 1860 as *The Naval Cadet's Guide: Seaman's Companion*), facsimile of second edition, introduced by David R Macgregor (Woking: Gresham Books, 1979), p82.
6. Shrinkwrap is used for the covering of model aircraft wings and is available from good model shops.

boat in the general panic of abandoning ship.

At a scale of 1:48, the problem which presents itself is how to produce a uniformly square hole. The extravagant use of fiddley grating aboard *Warrior* means over 5,500 joints must be constructed, with manufacturing standards to a very precise tolerance. This kind of sawing has to be done on a lathe, with the use of graduated slitting saws ranked together. For technical reasons, Myford lathes cannot combine slitting saws with their production saw table in anything under 5in diameter blades, and all the small slitting saws which were available to me were approximately half this size; so, for me, there was nothing for it, but to build, or rather adapt, a saw table to do the job.

The critical factor with fiddley grating is to have the width of the groove which the blade cuts (the kerf) the same as the width of the sawn timber strips. Experience has shown that the ideal is to have a +0.005in width tolerance of sawcut if possible. My adapted saw table includes as a secret weapon a strip of metal attached to the underside, the exact width of the groove made by the combined saw blades, positioned so that it is precisely the same width again from the cutting tips of the blade. The guide must be set marginally lower than the tips of the sawblades' teeth. Before machining the strips, the first saw cut must be made with a freehand saw; this cut makes the first groove which can then sit in the guide; thereafter, the guide acts as the automatic width spacer between the sawblade and the guide. In its turn this means that the sawkerfs are automatically spaced equally from one another.

Ranking together some presawn strips (0.5mm x 2mm) with masking tape in bundles of twelve, I was initially optimistic that sawing the strips in a block would not prove to be too difficult. Boxwood is unique in being able to take the stresses of being sawn into a comb for-

mation, but it is inclined to be sticky enough for resin to build up between the very carefully judged slitting saws (three of them ranked together), and thereby increasing their cutting width. Much later it was pointed out that an easier way to tackle this would be to construct a sawblade of the exact width of the presawn strips out of a common steel washer. This may sound difficult, but it requires only a hacksaw to make the teeth of the blade, without the necessity of putting any set to them, as the depth of cut is so minimal.

Two more cautionary tales finish this most aptly-named foray into the world of fiddley grating. When it is being trimmed to fit within the coamings, there are two possible ways of presenting the grain, either warp or weft in weaving terminology. When sanding it all down evenly, care

(Top)
Underside of the saw table reveals the spacer saw guide for fiddley grating.

(Lower)
Fiddley grating being sawn together in a rank of strips. The strips are held together with masking tape.

has to be taken to go in one direction only with the long grain, or all the short grain teeth will tear out. The other little matter concerns gluing, which should be done from the underside, literally blowing the adhesive through the squared holes to get it into all the joints. In its finally dried form, it is like its counterpart in full size, immensely strong and really requiring no further finishing, boxwood having a particular sheen all its own.

The conning bridges

The conning bridges fore and aft are distinctive hallmarks of the Black Battlefleet.

(Below)
Bending previously wetted timber round a copper tube; the blowlamp is on a very low light, but a word of caution - the exhaust end is very hot!

(Bottom)
Illustration of plank bender.
(Author)

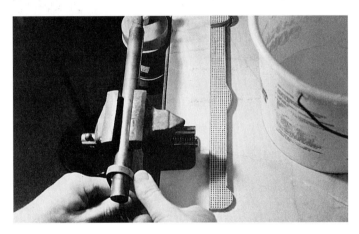

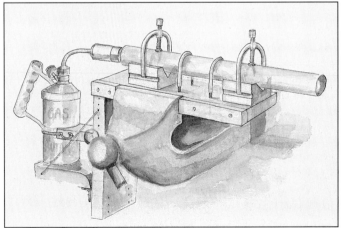

In general terms, they provided a raised platform from whence the extreme walls of the ship could be viewed and appropriate commands given. They also provided a platform for the ship's telegraph and compasses, all of which are detailed on the original building plans. The visitor to the restored ship in Portsmouth is privileged to be allowed to climb up to these exalted positions and have the mental command of the ship from this high ground. The hawser rope decoration which edges the surrounds of the walkways was originally a piece of shipwright's carving, echoed at the bases of the binnacles. The decoration served no particular purpose other than to enhance the feelings of elegance of those whose high estate made them lords over all those whom they surveyed.

Producing these grated platforms is not as easy as it appears, for they follow the gentle camber of the deck. To reproduce this camber, the stern side of the fiddley grating must first be glued to a piece of timber sufficiently wide to accommodate the curvature, and then planed off at the extreme ends. This piece of timber needs to be sufficiently tough to stabilise the camber and allow the fronts and the bays to be tackled. These swellings, which are passing points, can be created by cutting into a wider section of fiddley grating and edging off with a solid mahogany strip as follows.

The copper tube trick

This technique for bending timber has its origins in the steam chest, which was so vital a part of wooden shipbuilding for centuries past, and still reigns supreme. Persuading timber to take curvature on the long grain without losing any of its strength is best done by subjecting it to water and heat. First soak the timber thoroughly: you cannot overdo this, but allow at least half an hour; then take a small butane gas blowlamp and a suitable length of copper tube, slightly less in diameter than the radius you wish to curve the timber around. The flame of the gas burner does not need to be on fierce heat setting, as the tube needs only to be warm, not overhot. Clamp the tube up as safely as you can, remembering that you are going to exercise some pressure and force on the copper tube as the timber is bent round it. You may find it easiest to clamp the tube in a vice, so that it has an open end on which you can work, but watch out for the emerging heat: you will burn yourself if you are careless. The blowlamp nozzle is placed up the copper tube acting as the heating element, and the tube will quickly warm up. Press the soaked timber against the tube and hear the splutter and hiss of steam. Quite spontaneously, the wood will start to plasticise, in the proper sense of that word.

Keep a bucket of water handy and whenever the timber dries through, quench it in the bucket. Slowly, and I emphasise the word slowly, the timber will take the form of the copper tube's diameter, losing all its desire to be straight, and will retain the curvature with apparently increased strength. The longer the length of tube, the more adjustment there is in the heated surface, although copper does spread the heat very evenly. Virtually any species of timber or plywood up to approximately 4mm thick can be used, but the thinner the stock, the easier it is to work. Thicker pieces may be made by clamping two curves together making a plywood. So efficient is this system that with boxwood it is possible to make a wooden compression spring round the copper tubing. As always, the encouragement is that by trying the technique, one acquires the skill.

The rope decoration

This nautical motif surrounding all the conning bridges is recorded in contemporary photographs, and it is relatively easy to reproduce using an old jeweller's trick.

Three-stranded copper wire, heated to straw red, then allowed to cool. It is then ready for hammering out.

First, find an old hand brace, and then take three strands of copper wire of the same length and push them into the jaws of the chuck. Tighten the jaws and fix the other ends into a table vice. With an even tension, hold the hand brace and start turning. The strands will twist and draw the hand brace towards the static vice. The more you resist the tension, the tighter the twist will become, but either way, what happens is that you will be spinning a three-stranded metal rope.

The metal rope is then softened with heat and hammered into a flattish form, which slightly opens the twists and provides the look of the decorative carving of the original. But there is no need to stop there, as the possibilities of this process in decorative work are endless. More strands provide different patterns; harder hammering opens up the strands, producing a woven pattern. Annealed square stock which has been softened and twisted produces that wonderful barley sugar twist so characteristic of fairground carousels and showman's engines.

The handrail capping

I discovered this process by a happy accident; the handrailing around the raised

The result nailed to the forward conning bridge.

platforms is made from annealed brass tubing in $1/16$in diameter, measured whilst still in the round, like a piece of test wire for plumbing. The tubing can be bent into shape whilst still in the round, and then gently hammered flat to the required shape. Going gently with the hammering process still allows the tubing to have that slightly rounded edge of the full-sized rail capping, and another little advantage with tube, rather than bar, is that when it collapses into flat section it provides its own channelled groove into which the drill bit can centre most satisfactorily for the upright stanchions. Just why it stoves in like this has always been somewhat of a mystery to me, but the fact is that it does, and you learn to be grateful for these crumbs of good luck

Ladder making.

when they come your way.

The railings which billow out around the bays of the conning bridge are a considerable challenge to this method and end up looking satisfactorily light, as well as being strong enough to put up with a lot of handling. With a light undercoat, finished with a tinted varnish, they can quickly be made to represent an all-wood finish.

The ladders

Ladders are the first real indicators of scale aboard any model ship and they really mark a big advance in the way that detail begins to build up. They must conform to certain geometric principle: that is to say, the angle of the tread depends on the availability of space on the base angle of the triangle; thus arises the difference between a sweeping and spiralling staircase (of which *La Gloire* has a wonderful example), and the simple iron ladder which leads vertically down the propeller well aboard *Warrior*. In between these two extremes, the between-decks ladders of *Warrior* are good examples of double width gangways, with the passing observation that there are a great many of them. As to their representation in miniature, ladders look really effective when the treads are of a lesser thickness than the uprights (styles), and a point to note is that ladders must be built slightly underscaled. The finished product needs to be understated and light. This in turn means building the treads from veneer (0.020in), and using the slitting saw, accompanied by both a left- and right-handed bevel, made from ply and nailed to the correct angle. This operation can be done by hand with any small saw blade, combined with a mitre box, and a limitation on the depth of cut into the style. Even with excellent equipment, any deviation from absolute accuracy will land you in a vale of tears. My first few were disappointments and impressed upon me the problems of compounding inaccuracies. In other words, an item which is a hair's breadth out at the beginning of the run has, by the time you have machined ten of them, become easily detectable. The probability is that you will have to produce some scrappers before you produce some charmers; the eye has no difficulty whatsoever in telling the difference.

The ship's wheels

At this time the ship's wheels were certainly the crowning glory of the vessel, and *Warrior* is no exception to this statement. Gigantically handsome, the wheels stand together, open to the four winds as a marvellous example of man's handiwork and a monstrous challenge to produce, both in full size and miniature.

In the engineer's workshop, the indexer is simple to use once it is set up correctly, but it is not easy to centre onto the machine bed of the miller. 'Should be made out of wood', was the comment of one doubter, and truth to tell, this was tried, but only boxwood comes close to being machinable at less than $1/16$in diameter. This demands a woodturning lathe which can spin at several thousand rpm, whereas it can be done in metal at a much more sedate pace.

Machining the spokes

To build four identical wheels means that the first priority is to have some tool bits for the lathe, ground into appropriate shapes. Trying to make the spokes freehand is a waste of time because they cannot then be profiled identically, but one is also hampered by the fact that there is far too much whip in $1/16$in brass to be able to have a form tool which cuts each spoke in one go. It is easier to use several small form tools, each one picking up in the groove left by the former one. I do not possess a 'steady', so back support to take up the whip in the brass wire was given by

a handheld device: a grooved wooden handle. This sounds crude, but is actually easier to control and manage than a fixed steady at such a small diameter. In order to make the handles appear through the rim, it will be necessary to use the indexer in horizontal mode and cut grooves out of solid brass bar with a small milling bit. This ring of square cuts can then be centred in the lathe, bored out and parted off, leaving only the narrowest ring on the blind side. The series of 30-degree angles provides a precise location for the outer ends of the spoke handles, whilst the hub end, tapped and died, provides fine adjustment to their length. It is necessary to tap the ends in order for them to survive the silver-soldering process. The tricky part is in getting enough build-up

(Top)
Ship's wheels; rims and spokes.

(Lower)
Silver-soldering with needle flame burner (propane).

7. Wells, *op cit*, p104.

of silver-solder into the machined grooves, without burning out the turned ends of the wheel spokes. One of my early wheels did not survive, and was assigned to the bin of experience, so do not be put off by initial difficulties: this is yet another example of learning by doing.

The wheel indicators

The wheel indicators are positioned at the centre of the steering system at either end of the wheel hubs. They show the exact position of the tiller within three and a half turns from midships to full helm. This was an old convention, required by Admiralty Regulations, and sometimes survived even into the era of steam-powered steering. Each full turn of the wheel

moved the tiller approximately 10 degrees, bringing the rudder, when hard over, to an angle of 35 degrees.[7] The clock mechanism was geared internally to the movement of the indicator. Idle thoughts on my part about making this functional, along with the idea of having working compasses, were roundly dismissed, but real glass can be used on their bezels, and that seems quite enough of a labour of love for the time being.

The galley 'greenhouse'

This is a rather surprising skylight, appearing in two major sections sited between the funnels, and containing sixteen panels of glass directly over the galley. This must have been the best-lit floating kitchen the Royal Navy has ever seen. Glazing is difficult to do cleanly, particularly with Perspex, which is invariably attacked by the adhesive, making the job look messy. There is also a question of perspicacity: the clarity not only of vision through glass, but also the quality of its reflection of the objects around it. Only pure glass has this property, and a useful source of glass is that used for photographic slides. This glass is very thin and brittle, but can be cut with a standard glass cutter, or TCT wheel, and split off as one normally would a full-sized sheet. Remember though, if you are using glass which is not brand new, you will need a lubricant (paraffin or white spirits) to help the cut, because old glass case-hardens with age. Mark the glass with engineer's marker blue fluid before cutting it. This way you get a very accurate cut line, important because you cannot get the TCT wheel exactly to the edge of the rule, and judging the precise point of contact with the wheel is important for an accurate cut. Only make one pass with the cutter; you do not get a second chance.

The glass is inserted into the framework with an instant glue but screened off from the underside with masking tape in

(Right)
Finished with wheel indicator and glass bezel. Note the double-decking down the centreline of the ship.

(Below)
Detail of prototype wheel indicator as restored.

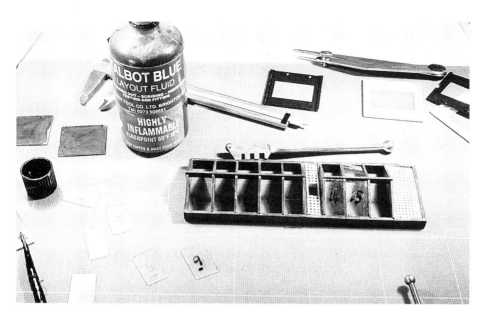

Galley lights. Note the glass-cutting tool and layout fluid.

order to avoid any bleeding of the adhesive onto the glass. The removal of the tape from the glass should be done when the adhesive is still 'green', approximately ten minutes after the initial cure has taken place, or it becomes quite a task to remove the draughtsman's tape. The great advantage of glass is that adhesive does not attack it, so that you can always polish back to the surface, but what you will find is that the clear instant glues leave a residue of white around the glass edge, where one would normally see putty in full scale. This can be dealt with by use of matt shine varnish which absorbs the white crystals as water does when added to sugar.

Compasses

If the fourfold ship's wheels represent the crown of this vessel, then the jewellery which surrounds that coronet is worth some close inspection. The compasses, the wheel dial indicators and the pedestal engine telegraphs all have in common the characteristic of being made from brass and glass in both full size and miniature form: these fittings do not have to be dulled down with paint, being the only details aboard which can be polished to a highly buffed shine.

The original compasses, of which there were eight aboard *Warrior*, were a cause of great concern, being set within so strong a magnetic field as this vast metal hull produced. Fifteen years before the launch of this ship, Brunel's pride and joy, the SS *Great Britain*, had gone aground at Dundrum Bay off the coast of Ireland on account, it was said, of the irregular magnetic field set up by the all-iron hull. This was never proven, but it lay at the heart of many an unsubstantiated rumour about metal ships. The nervousness about this was well-demonstrated, not only by the number of compasses aboard *Warrior*, but of their high positioning. The compass mounted on the fighting top of the mizzenmast was the one which needed least correction, a mere $1^3/_4$ degrees, whereas its counterpart below had a maximum deviation of 28 degrees, despite its high mounting. Captain John Wells' book records the fact that recesses were cut adjacent to the binnacles to fit magnets which reduced steering compass deviation, the steering and the standard compasses often varying by several degrees. In her first commission *Warrior* was swung

(Top)
Grinding down the
glass crystal on the car-
borundum stone.

(Lower)
The finished crystal, set
over the compass rose.
Note the refraction.

8. *Ibid*, Appendix VII, p232.

ellery, in the form of a crystal necklace. Glass crystal is extremely hard to grind down, but not impossible. The gems need steady work to reduce them to half their size on the base area. This can be done by first using the coarse grit of sharpening stone. They can then be polished down with 120 grit wet-and-dry abrasive paper, working through the range to a fine finish. The top of the crystal gemstone I used had been cut by the manufacturers on eight sides, and after some experiments with a compass card beneath the crystal, I discovered that a prismatic effect is achieved by simply drawing eight lines, which are refracted around the binnacle head. The pierced hole through which the string originally passed will provide a location for the acorn as seen on the restoration version.

The ship's telegraphs

Ship's telegraphs are clearly indicated on the plan view of the upper deck on the original Scott Russell drafts, four of them being sited on the conning bridges, dead ahead of the gangways, rather than placed in the bays where one might have expected to see them. Information on how they should look is a little scanty, as they were not illustrated in elevation, and they were a new innovation at the time. The unchanged style of this piece of ship's furniture belongs solely to the patent taken out by William Chadburn, but there is a historical snag in that his first reported Mechanical Telegraph was fitted to a little steamer called *Iona III* in 1864. Although it is too much to expect that he also got the contract to fit them to *Warrior* five years earlier, there is comfort in the thought that at least we are operating in the same decade, but one is always on the edge of provenance in such matters. The Chadburn transmitter has a circular dial marked with the seven orders: hard, port, steady, course, steady, starboard and hard; it is mounted on a pedestal and provided

six times as well as artificially heeled to $7^1/_2$ degrees to investigate compass heeling error.[8]

Modelling the compasses

As to how these compasses can be effectively modelled, one could guess that it is the glass above the compass card which presents the biggest problem. The pointed cappings are six-sided and pyramidal in form, finished off by acorns at the pinnacles. These cappings must be made from glass if they are going to look right, and added to that, they have to be made out of the solid, in the form of a kaleidoscopic prism. Modelmakers develop a magpie's eye, and the answer to the binnacle head problem lies in a piece of costume jew-

with two handles, one for transmitting and the other for receiving. The transmitter consists of a system of wires and chains. The axle of the pointer also carries a wheel with studs which actuate a lever arm and strike a bell at each order. A separate hand lever communicates with a repeat pointer on the bridge dial and thus enables receipt of an order to be acknowledged.[9]

The racer arcs

The racer arcs at both extremes of the upper deck were made from brass, and wrought iron on the main (gun) deck, of which several original ones survive. Their job was to protect the deck planking and provide accurate positioning for predetermined arcs of fire by use of pivots and slide bars. The extra-heavy 110pdrs, the bow and stern chasers, were also equipped with sliding carriages. Admiral G A Ballard, in the account contained in the book *The Black Battlefleet*, describes their operation as follows:

> To bring [the gun] into action at any port ordered the gun tackles were hooked to the front end of the slide and the front flap raised, so that the slide could be swung round pivoting on its rear till the front was over the nearest 'traversing' pivot. The front flap was then put down on this, the tackles shifted to the rear end of the slide, the rear flap raised in its turn, and the swing round repeated but with the slide turning on its front till the rear was over the next traversing pivot. By a third lateral movement in this fashion the gun was finally brought opposite the selected port with its muzzle pointed for running out. The front of the slide was then connected by a pivoting bar to the 'firing' pivot on the port sill...When so placed the tackles were shifted to the rear and both flaps raised, so as to leave the slide free to turn on the firing pivot. The gun was now ready for action...[10]

The arcs themselves are unusual, and peculiar to naval vessels fitted with rela-

tively accurate and much heavier guns, although their practical use was cumbersome and time-consuming. In swollen seas, the guns must have been near-impossible to control, and the central pivot on the king plank of the ship was the anchorage of the gun under all conditions except when the crew was called to general quarters. Historically, racer arcs disappeared from the upper deck almost as quickly as they had appeared, replaced by the revolving cupola turrets of the next decade. As with the ship herself, that which made her old before her time was the decline of the concept of broadside fire with which these circular marks are so intimately connected. No longer was the Navy concerned with general broadside fire at almost point-blank range; the new engines of war, where aim and accuracy were becoming a real and desirable possibility, meant that obsolescence was the consequence within five years of her launching, despite all her other undoubtedly advanced features.

The making of the miniature arcs on the model is a development of the flying bridge stanchion rail capping technique mentioned previously, where $1/16$in O/D brass tubing was heated and quenched, measured whilst still in the round, and subsequently hammered flat. After reheating to soften the now curved strip, a very fine drill (0.025in) can be used to pierce holes for the brass wire nails used to secure the racers to the deck.

The capstan

The capstan of a major warship had always been a focus of attention, understandably so considering the dramatic visual effect created by juxtaposing dark exotic hardwood and gleaming brass. The only visible capstan on the upper deck of *Warrior* was sited between the engine room hatchway and the armoured rifle tower. The spindle of this capstan was designed to connect with another similar

9. Spratt, H P, *Marine Engineering Descriptive Catalogue* (London: Science Museum, u/d), Cat No 404, p140.
10. Ballard, *op cit*, p165.

(Right)
Capstan being turned
on lathe.

(Below)
Capstan and pawl rim
over illustration from
Paasch's *Marine
Encyclopedia*. Note the
whelp chocks to
strengthen the whelps,
and the pawls at the
base of the capstan, to
prevent 'running back'.

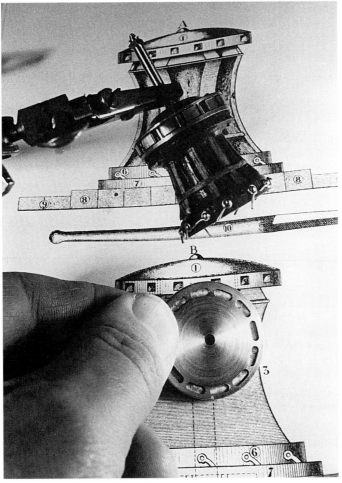

one placed directly below on the main (gun) deck. This enabled up to 120 men to hove in the heaviest cables and loads and demonstrates how vital these sturdy contrivances were to the operation of a large vessel. These two aft capstans are not to be confused with the fore capstan, sited on the main deck, between the aft funnel and the mainmast. This was a Brown's Patent Capstan, the first of its kind ever fitted to a vessel of *Warrior*'s class, and made from cast iron. Such was its massive construction that it survived all the removal of the ship's fittings throughout her long life, and has been wonderfully restored as a prize item of original Victorian ironwork.

Modelling the capstan for the upper deck poses all the usual problems of historical accuracy. The restoration capstan was built on site, as no doubt the original was, according to a functional pattern as outlined on the profile drawings. It does differ from other historical sources, particularly that of a careful engraving of *Royal Oak*, and more vitally, that of the builder's model in the Science Museum. After due consideration, I decided to work from the measured drawing of this item from Paasch's *Illustrated Marine Encyclopedia*.[11] Its component parts consist of the following items: the barrel; square stock spindle (plus acorn); the drumhead; pigeon holes (for the capstan bars), twelve in all; the whelps; the horizontal whelp chocks; the pawls; the pawl ring.

In practice, the capstan is a pivot point of the ship around which the seamen would spend much of their time and expend much energy, stomping to the rhythm of the ship's band. Unlike the merchant service, Her Majesty's Royal Navy did not sing shanties, which means that many of the old capstan songs have been lost to us for ever, although Victorian seamen knew them all by heart.[12] Another lesser known detail about ships' capstans is that, housed under their removable drumheads, were the basic needs of first aid: bandaging cloth, linen thread and bottles containing tincture of iodine. The fore capstan on *Victory* has some beautifully-made decorated drawers which fit into the pigeonholes and provide a handy repository for these essential medical items.

The inclusion of a pawl rim on the model ship's capstan is unusual because, admittedly, it is a troublesome item to make accurately, but logic dictates that no ship of *Warrior*'s size could leave harbour without a pawl rim at the base of her capstan. The consequences of a capstan running back against the crew, acting like a whipping-top, would be quite horrific. A loose pawl rim would have the potential for injury or death to the many seamen working closely together in this area.

The process

The brass drumhead is turned on the lathe. The pigeon holes, the whelp grooves and the pawl rim must all be milled out in their appropriate divisions. Using the table in a horizontal mode, the pawl bolts and whelp grooves necessitate turning the indexing table into the vertical position. Whereas an indexer is a wonder-

ful asset to any amateur workshop, it is not a necessary item for miniature shipbuilding. A system found to be most useful for jobs like this can be constructed from a simple Meccano toothed cogwheel, with an axle and detent set in a U-channel, which will allow objects like capstans and wheels to be marked off accurately in divisions.

As with all machining, there is the difficulty of gripping the item sufficiently tightly without damaging the stock. Clamping up is an art form not to be underestimated, and it requires a square-threaded mandrel through the centre of

11. Paasch, Capt H, *Illustrated Marine Encyclopedia* (1890), facsimile reprint edition with an introduction by David R Macgregor (Watford: MAP/Argus, 1977), Plate 67.
12. Kemp, Peter, (ed), *The Oxford Companion to Ships and the Sea* (Oxford: Oxford University Press, 1976), p776.

(Left)
A simple form of indexer. This is a piece of U-channel with a mandrel (axle) running through it, to which a cogwheel is attached and held captive. In the arc of the cogwheel teeth is drilled a small hole, to allow a drill bit to act as a locating pin (or detent) between the cogwheel's teeth. The capstan can then be marked and sawn accurately in any divisions which the cogwheel allows. Twelve is usual for a ship's capstan.

(Below)
Illustration of mitre box and indexer.
(Author)

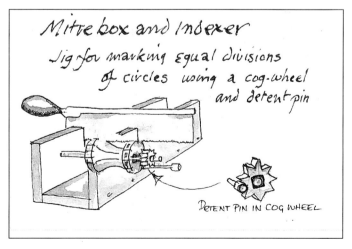

the barrel to prevent it from slipping when being turned on the lathe. One of these may be made by filing a piece of threaded studding on four sides to a point, which will act as the basis of a square file. A bored hole to the inner limits of the piece of studding is then made, and finished square by the studding as a square file working it through the bored hole. A nut at either end of the barrel will prevent the barrel from slipping.

The bitts

The rails and bitts, which are the furnishings at the bases of all three masts to which the majority of the running rigging will eventually be belayed, need to be constructed to take account of the fact that they sustain a great deal of upward haul and must therefore be capable of withstanding the considerable pull exerted upon them. Should they ever come adrift, they would be extremely difficult to deal with, and this applies to both full-scale and model forms. The restoration bitts are bolted to wedge-shaped iron anchorages which are an integral part of the base of these upright timbers. The axles on which the sheaves run are at the apex of these

(Right)
Bits shown against
Amerigo Vespucci.

(Below)
Mizzenmast bitt with
four sheaves in slots.

metal castings, and provide the necessary resistance to the stresses demanded of them. The most striking feature of the bitts are the brass plates covering the sheave slots in groups of three, four, five and six grooves. In miniature terms, milling slots out accurately at 1:48 scale makes the mouth and lips a little dry, as each plate has to match perfectly back and front. The rails and braces are all mortised and tenoned into the deck for mechanical strength and the kevel heads to which the ropes are belayed are cut out from the solid upright. The technique for this is to saw all round the head of the post as though making a tongue for a tenon, then flare the outer edges and saw out their centres.

The vessel which most readily demonstrates the working of these fittings is the Italian training vessel, the *Amerigo Vespucci*, whose falls of halyards are shown in a background photograph. She is a working sailing ship and accurately displays the full activity of belaying the halyards at deck level. By comparison, *Warrior*, as a berthed vessel out of commission, has undersubscribed rigging lines.

The brass plate along the aft side of the rails gives protection from damp cordage. It is matched by the brass capping on the end of the baulks, which prevents heat and damp from splitting and rotting the end grain of this vulnerable timber. The fact that it all looks extremely handsome as brightwork may also play a part in all this, and kept many hands from being idle in the past.

Just to forestall any thoughts of buying in belaying pins for the model, it needs to be noted that those which surround the mast are nearly twice the length of those used in fife rails, so it will be back to the lathe for making these, using the same form tool that was used for the ship's wheels.

Flag lockers

Surprisingly, the flag lockers are not shown on the plan view of the upper deck of *Warrior*, but they are included in the Science Museum builder's model from which, presumably, the restorers have gained their measurements and positioning. It is partly because they are sited beneath the mizzen fife rails and obscured by the falls of the running rigging that they tend to become hidden from sight,

but they are, nevertheless, an extremely important part of the ship's signalling system.

Stowed away in the compartments of these lockers were all the necessary flags and pendants for operating the new International Code of Signals, begun by Captain F Marryat in 1817 and internationally agreed in 1856: a single code for universal use. Marryat's first signalling code had only fifteen flags and pendants, but this developed into one flag for each letter of the alphabet and one pendant for each number between zero and nine, with three official pendants for substitutes and four for special meanings, agreed and adopted by all maritime countries for communications between ship and ship, and ship and shore.[13]

According to these calculations, pigeonholes compartmentalising the lockers must have at least forty-three spaces, and some spare capacity for various sizes of ensigns and jackstaffs. Captain Wells' book also details other items which would have been stowed for general signalling purposes, namely 'halyards for hoisting flags, signal slates to record messages received and transmitted, and pyrotechnics, eg, blue lights, long lights, rockets and night signal lights'.[14] Also mentioned are Admiral Popham's Signal Code book

Flag locker on restored ship.

13. *Ibid*, p802.

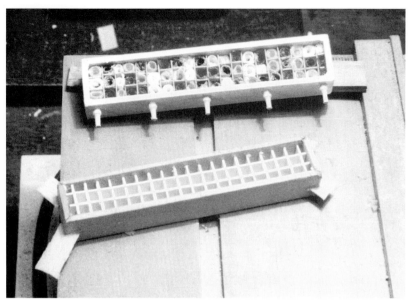

Flag locker carcass and pigeonholes. Note the veneer scraps at each of the mitred corners

calls for a bit of concentration during the sawing process. The legs, which can be added later, are sawn-off belaying pins. It is the pigeonhole compartments which pose the challenge; with the first locker, I used veneer strip of 0.011in thickness, but switched to Plasti-card for the second attempt. Veneer tends to break away like a row of broken teeth if the timber is not previously treated. The interlocking joints can be made with previously sawn strips of stock bound together with tape at either end, using the same technique as the ladders and gratings. They should be gangsawn for greater accuracy.

(1816) and the use aboard *Warrior* of the *Vocabulary Signals Book*, a publication in use as a signalling manual throughout the Channel Squadron. The model deck lockers, port and starboard, have a total capacity of 120 spaces, which seems reasonable given all the extra requirements over and above flags and pendants.

Quite apart from the technicalities, it would be a great shame to omit these lockers as they provide a wonderful splash of colour in an otherwise rather colourless quarter of the ship. There will be model shipwrights who have done the honest thing and painted each flag individually before placing them all in the compartments. Experiment has shown that, to gain the effect of a flag locker, finely woven and very brightly coloured dyes, such as are really only available in the form of coloured ribbons, must be used. This is one of those cases which breaks all the usual rules of demure colouring and restraint. Vivid specks of colour in their brightness immediately convey to the eye the need for attention.

In miniature, these flag lockers are a mere 3in long and $9/16$in high, which

Construction

The outer carcass of the locker is then constructed on the principle of mitred edges, jointed with strips of veneer and matched to the width of the sawblade kerf. This is not just to add strength to the joint, but actually allows the setup to be assembled dry to check for the internal width and squareness. Using the saw fence as a guide, the stock should be run through vertically to provide a slot which will perfectly match its neighbour. Push the scrap of veneer, which locks it all together when the adhesive is applied, into the slot on the mitred edge. This jointing system can be used on all the hatchways and the delight of it is that it leaves no end grain, cleans up well, and is a joint which will never come apart.

For my model, the ribbons were purchased in the royal colours of red, white, blue and yellow though there ought to be some black in there. Logically, there ought also to be some blank spaces for pendants already flown.

14. Wells, *op cit*, p233.

6
ARMAMENT

he 1860s marked many dramatic changes both in the design of new ships and in new forms of armament. The *Illustrated London News (ILN)* possess in their picture library a contemporary and accurate scale illustration of a vertical cross-section of the inte-

rior of *Warrior*, which depicts both the old and the new great guns together.[1] On the port side is shown the new, and still experimental, Armstrong 100/110pdr, the very latest of the rifled breech-loading guns. With its reinforced shrunken hoops of iron around the breech it was the biggest gun yet to be mounted aboard any battleship in the world. This weapon's vital statistics were as follows: overall length 12ft; bore 7in; widest diameter $27^1/_2$in; weight 86cwt. On the starboard side of the vessel is depicted in profile the 68pdr muzzle-loader, the big brother of the British Navy's old favourite, the 32pdr, but five times as powerful. There were a total of twenty-six of these 68pdrs aboard ship.

The broadside fire arrangements for this ship were in the long and low-profiled

1. Perlmutter, Tom, (ed), *War Machines at Sea* (London: Octopus Books, 1975), p69.

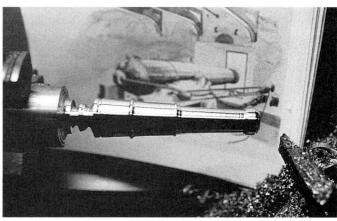

(Left)
Detail of 110pdr Armstrong Gun.
(W Milln RN)

(Below)
68pdr gun barrel pattern being turned in the lathe from brass bar.

style of the frigate, but more spaciously spread than in any other previous warship, thus adding several advantages in terms of diminishing the target area for the enemy, increasing the strength of the hull, and allowing the gun crews a greater measure of safety in the operation of these savage beasts. The ship even had ventilation tubes provided at each gun station to expel the stifling effects of the spent gunpowder. The Armstrong guns were positioned one on either side of the four citadel walls, port and starboard, making eight in all,

(Above)
The model ship's heavy ordnance.

(Right)
Restored gun deck at Portsmouth.

(Below)
Illustration of internal working of 110pdr.
(Author)

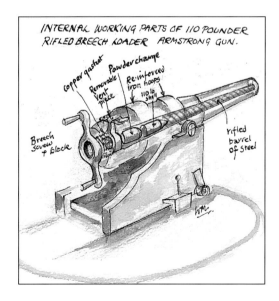

with the two remaining ones sited on the upper deck mounted on racer arcs, as bow and stern chasers.[2]

The *ILN* drawing also tells something of the new way in which the heavier guns were mounted. No longer do the gun carriages have a wheel, or truck, at each corner: the rear trucks have been replaced by a large baulk of heavy timber in which a half-lap groove has been cross cut. Another piece of timber, running directly in line under the gun carriage, acted both as aiming bar and brake. The friction between these two absorbed much of the recoil, and the aiming bar was pivoted in the reveal of the armoured gun port, assisting with both the aiming and the taming of the gun. The whole system ran on racer arcs of either brass or iron which were set into the deck and are still visible as original items today.

The ratio of old to new guns showed a hesitant approach by the Admiralty, 3:1 favour of the old muzzle-loaders: a caution in which they were proved right. Whereas the simple smooth-bored muzzle-loaders had a reputation of great reliability, the Armstrong breech-loaders gave some dangerous moments to the gun crews operating them. Not only were the vent pieces apt to fail, because of the inadequacy of copper being used as a gas-tight seal in the breech of the gun, but also because the breech mechanism was a complex item to load and unload, involving a heavy metal block and a large screw. It gave rise to a variety of mishaps so serious to the gun crews operating the 110pdrs that these guns were withdrawn altogether in 1863.

Several possible methods were considered before embarking on the production in miniature of twenty-six 68pdrs and ten 110pdrs. The replica gun barrels on board *Warrior* have all been cast in GRP resin, and extremely handsome they look. At West Hartlepool, they used as their master patterns two original guns of the type depicted in the *ILN* drawing. One might imagine that there were hundreds of them lying around to chose from: there were certainly thousands of 68pdrs cast, but it seems that, like flies in winter, they had all disappeared to unrecorded destinations. After two years of searching, in 1982 an original 68pdr was found at the Rotunda Museum at Woolwich. The fact that this example is thought to have a flaw in the original casting has meant that it was never issued for service and has no proof markings. This piece of fortuitous salvage work underlines the importance of gathering these iron relics together to provide us with the source material required for proper restoration work

The Armstrong breech-loader find was perhaps even more obscure. One can-not help wondering how it reached its destination, but it was found mounted, in perfect condition, on a fixed coastal defence carriage on the Island of Jersey.[3] The Channel Island authorities were more than happy to let it be used for the master plug of the replica guns.

Sandcasting

The method chosen for making the gun barrels is sandcasting. Sandcasting is one of the oldest methods of reproducing anything, and is a thoroughly satisfying occupation. Providing that certain basic things are watched carefully, the necessary skills are soon developed. One might imagine that sand would leave a rather rough casting, but this is not so. Proper casting sand has a consistency of rubbed flour and will pick out the smallest detail required, giving cannon barrels that primitive look, complete with the moulded joint-line.

Probably the most difficult item to acquire these days is the casting sand itself, to be had from the nearest foundry works. Proprietary sands have metallic oxides mixed in with them and contain a certain amount of clay, which gives the material its plasticity.[4] Without this the sand would fall out of the mould box, and would not replicate the pattern with any accuracy. If you cannot obtain any sand through local sources, try the model engi-

2. Wells, Capt John, *The Immortal Warrior* (Emsworth, Hants: Kenneth Mason, 1987), Appendix VI.
3. *Warrior News*, Issue No 5 (1983).
4. Aspin, B Terry, *The Backyard Foundry* (Watford: MAP/Argus, 1978), Ch 1.

Sandcasting: the lower half of the frame being filled and tamped down with casting sand.

neering magazines, or contact your nearest working museum who often know of local craftsmen still practising this art.

Apart from the sand, before you begin, you will need the following items:

A well-made, jointed wooden frame, sawn in half along its length (to be fitted with sliding fit locating pins so that it may be rejoined with accuracy)

Sand rammer - a solid piece of timber cut to the inside dimensions of the mould box

Large tray with a lipped edge to it

Bucket or a polythene bag for the sand

Fine-meshed sieve

Smoothing trowel

Twist drill bit for cleaning the sand out of the locating pin holes

A pricker for making the metal ingate (a needle file is ideal)

Talcum powder and a very soft brush

Crucible

Heat source for low melt metal (lead/tin)

Preparing the mould

The bottom frame has sand sieved into it and packed down with the rammer to produce an even surface into which the pattern of the gun barrel, or any other object, is carefully placed, and pressed home to its halfway point. There must be no undercut to the pattern, which would prevent the item from being withdrawn cleanly. The locating holes are cleaned out with a hand-held twist drill bit, and the whole of the lower box, including the pattern, lightly dusted with talcum powder and brushed over with a very soft haired brush. The powder acts as a parting agent when the two frames have to be separated. The top half of the box is located to the bottom half using the two sliding pins (dowels), which need to protrude beyond the top edge of the frame. More sand is added, sieving the sand over the pattern initially, then compressing the sand down with the rammer.

The mould is then parted with great care and with as little disturbance to the pattern as possible. The length of the locating dowels in the mould box means that this withdrawal can take place with the sides parallel to one another. The pattern has now to be withdrawn, and the runner and riser holes created by making an ingate runner at one end of the pattern, and a riser exit at the other end. These holes are made from the inside of the sand pattern at the entry and exit points.

Molten metal is then poured down the ingate until seen running out of the riser hole. The pouring from the crucible is important in that it needs to be done in one shot and at the right temperature to avoid holes in the casting. There is virtually no wastage: bad castings can always be melted down again, which is the way that the skill is acquired. The casting is left to cool down for a few minutes, during which considerable shrinkage takes place. It may then be recovered from the sand and brushed up.

As with all casting, undercut is the most familiar problem. After casting about half a dozen or so of the 68pdrs, I discovered that it was better to set these guns into the moulding box with the trunnions pointing towards the top and bottom of the box. This allowed the cascabel to be withdrawn much more cleanly. The cascabel is the knob on the back end of the barrel, through which the breeching tackle passes. The mixture in my ladle is lead and tinman's solder, at a ratio of 4:1. The solder gives it extra strength and ease of pouring. The proprietary mixes of lead-based alloys like pewter are rather expensive, but they do pour nicely. If you do not mind melting down some old carburettors, which are made of a metal called mazak, this will also do the job. Whatever you do, a good heavy ladle is a big advantage since it retains the heat whilst you are pouring the metal, and for a good casting that is essential.

Those worried about a possible health

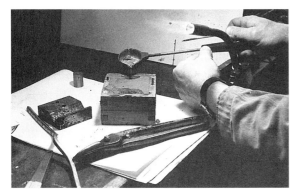

hazard can do no better than take note of the following safety precautions quoted from the Health and Safety leaflet produced by Tiranti:

Danger from lead absorption only arises from the oxide which forms on the surface of the liquid metal, whenever alloy is kept molten. The oxide is in a finely divided powder form and can easily be wafted around the workshop. Whenever dross is removed from the pot, a perforated ladle should be used to allow the metallic portion to drain back into the bath and the dross should be tipped into a container with a self-closing lid. Smoking, drinking and eating should be discouraged in the melting area, and the operator should wash thoroughly before meals. Extreme care should be exercised to ensure that ingots added to the pot of molten metal are perfect dry. A serious explosion can result if damp ingots are added to molten metal.

Similarly, all tools immersed into molten metal should be perfectly dry.[5]

Reverting back to the cannon barrels, the bores must be drilled out, and it requires a jig to centre the drill bit and paraffin wax to lubricate the tip of the drill. Unfortunately, the lathe chuck cannot grip the barrel without damaging it, because the lead is so soft and the barrel is also tapered. I personally spoilt quite a few before convincing myself that both guns would need separate jigs to effectively centre the bores. The resulting cannon

(Top left)
The gun barrel pattern being pressed into the sand to the halfway point.

(Top right)
The top frame being located to the lower frame. Note the offset dowel pins which prevent the frame being assembled the wrong way round.

(Above left)
Pouring the molten metal from the ladle into the runner hole.

(Above right)
the 68pdr casting revealed.

(Left)
Miniature gun barrel castings.

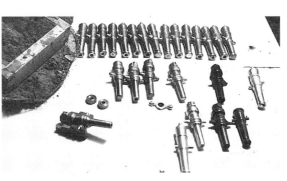

5. *Health and Safety Leaflet* (Reading: Tiranti, 1991).

6. Cantwell, Anthony, and Peter Sprack, *The Needles Defences, The Solent Papers No 2* (Ryde, IOW: Redoubt Consultancy, 1986), p9.
7. Necessary material may be had from good sculpture and modelling suppliers, Tiranti of Reading being one of the most well-known (see list of suppliers for details).
8. Available from glassfibre merchants, or from Tiranti.

barrels do look and feel right. When picked up for inspection the total gun weighs a full 90g ($2^1/_2$oz), which adds to its authenticity.

The auxiliary guns

To complement the great guns, other smaller ordnance was mounted amidships, firing broadside. These were four 40pdr rifled breech-loading guns (RBLs), on standard carriages; two 20pdr RBLs; one 12pdr, which also acted as a field gun complete with caisson; a 6pdr RBL, and, on the restored vessel, a small signal gun, formerly used aboard *Ganges*. These guns must be cast to complete the total armament of the ship.

In full scale, the Armstrong guns were constructed on the same principles as were their big brothers mounted on the bow and stern. The barrel was built up by heated wrought iron hoops, shrunk onto a tube of steel. The bore of the gun was cut along its axis with spiral grooves, so as to spin the elongated shell and make its flight more accurate. The shell was covered with a thin layer of lead in which the barrel cut the thread on the projectile. It was loaded through an opening breech at the rear of the gun, but the old problem of the unreliability of the vent piece persisted, a problem caused mainly by constant handling and the corrosion which the exhaust gases

caused. Despite all the problems, this gun was accurate to a distance of 8000 yards and was a formidable weapon, of which the Elswick Factory was very proud.[6]

Moulding the auxiliary guns

Four of the 40pdr guns must be made, but rather than using the ancient technique of sandcasting, the new technology of mouldmaking, using RTV31 low-melt casting rubber, is preferable. There are several advantages to this material, the main one being its ability to handle undercut, which sand cannot. Once the silicone rubber mould is made, it can withstand repeated use. It is expensive in terms of the initial outlay, but quiet reflection on its possibilities for the mass production of small parts like bollards, cleats, blocks, brackets and so forth, quickly reveals what a time-saving system this is.

Lego building bricks for children and Plasticard are both on the list of requirements. The shopping list also includes quick-setting dental plaster, or similar mouldmaking material - there are many to choose from.[7] You will also need stirring sticks, waxed cups and a jug of water.

Preparing the rubber mould

Prepare the base of the Lego mould by cutting a piece of Plasticard to size and placing it in the bottom of the brick mould, so that the base comes out smoothly. The plaster will stick neither to the Plasticard nor to the sides of the Lego bricks if you coat the base and sides with a parting agent, such as Freekote.[8] Make the mould as economically as you can around the master pattern. Economy with the rubber solution is important, because it is expensive, but avoid getting too close to the edge or bottom of the mould. You will also need some Plasticine to make a pouring funnel at the top end of the mould; a rough cone shape will do nicely. Although you can carve this funnel shape out of the

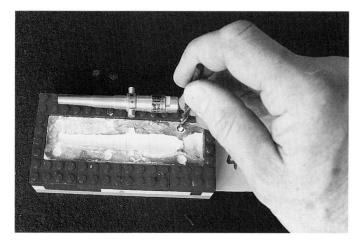

Lego mould box filled with moulding plaster, having taken the impression of the 40 pdr gun barrel. Locators pricked out with a drill bit.

mould when it has hardened off, this is rather wasteful.

Then mix and pour the plaster. Be prepared, as it goes off in roughly two minutes, and as soon as it has formed a skin over the top, gently lower the pattern to the exact halfway mark. With a gun barrel this is easy, but with more complicated patterns of multiple items, for example deadeyes or cleats, ensure that all the patterns are in line on the sprue stick. If they are out of line at this stage you are in trouble, because you cannot fool the joint line, except by even more difficult repair work to the plaster mould. Great emphasis must be placed on care in the preparation of the masters. This is a skill which will improve with experience, but it is the only really critical stage of the proceedings.

Method

The gun barrel (or any other pattern) should then be lowered into the plaster to the halfway point. This is really best done using a pair of pliers, so that you may see more easily when you have reached the critical point. The six locating pins are made using a twist drill after the plaster has hardened up. Do not drill too deeply: $1/4$in is quite sufficient, otherwise the locators break off. Note also the pouring funnel cavity.

Add layers of Lego bricks as necessary, not forgetting to spray a couple of coats of the parting agent over both the pattern and the plaster. The liquid rubber, which has the consistency of thick paint, is mixed with a catalyst hardener; basically, it is three drops to an ounce, so you will need a weighing machine to gauge the weight. Your estimation of how

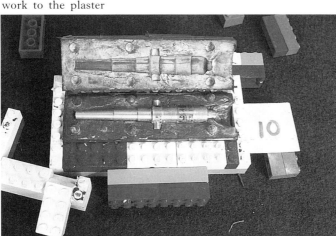

much is required to fill the mould will improve as you gain more experience, but do not mix up too much. If the solution does not reach the top of the mould, you can always mix some more and add it to that which has already been poured.

Patience is required at this point as the cure takes twenty-four hours at normal household temperature. The mould may then be demounted and the rubber separated from the plaster; the plaster mould is now redundant, and the rubber replaces it. Once again the sides should be rebuilt, the whole mould sprayed with release agent, and a second solution poured onto the first, the pattern, of course, remaining in place – and then there must be more patient waiting for another day.

(Above) Silicone rubber being poured over the built-up mould box to create the first half of the rubber mould. Beneath the pouring is the gun barrel pattern and the plaster cast. The rubber will also replicate the locators.

(Left) When the rubber has cured, the plaster cast is disposed of, the pattern replaced into the first rubber cast and the walls of the mould built up another layer so that the second pouring of silicone can take place. Thereafter, the rubber mould may be used indefinitely for pouring low temperature metal castings. A simple conical hole is cut with a scalpel to act as a pouring funnel.

Then comes the long-awaited moment: the release of the master pattern and the sight of the two halves, which ought to fit perfectly together. The two halves have now to be dusted down with talcum powder. Use a soft brush, but do not let the powder collect in the sharp corners of the mould, or definition will be lost. In common with all moulding techniques, the first casting is never the best: this is something to do with a kind of case hardening.

Now for the pouring of the metal: use Low Melt KA, which is specially designed for hand pouring. You could use any old receptacle for heating the metal up, but a proper ladle is good to have in that it retains heat during the pouring process. The metal will melt quite adequately using a small butane bottle gas fire, and it does not benefit from being overheated. Melt the sticks and pour the metal straight away; this tends to avoid air being trapped and other nasties like distortion. The picture might seem to indicate that this is an

indoor job, but this is not so: it is just that the light was right for photography, but spelter and acrylic carpet will love each other to death.

Manufacture of the gun carriages

Gun carriages are not built squarely, but follow the taper of the breech and barrel. This in turn means that none of the joints to the carriage cheeks is square, and the fitting of the cross bolts and trunnions are not square to the face either. It also means that the axle trees must have sufficient width to allow the trucks to turn freely and not bind against the carriage cheeks. In other words, this is yet another job which has to be preceded by measurement and by jigmaking.

The framework at the bottom of the carriages should be made with slot mortises to accept the two cross pieces (called the bed). This allows for sliding the cross pieces through the mortises, and setting the angle as required to the taper. The cross pieces can then be finished back when the glue is dry. This will produce a very strong and accurate carriage without too much effort. On the bed sits the pig, and on the pig sits the quoin, or wedge, which was the method by which the angle of the gun was adjusted. The trunnions are set in such a way that the point of balance of the barrel makes the adjustment with the quoin surprisingly effortless. The miniature metal model satisfactorily echoes this operational detail.

The completed 40pdr Armstrong RBL.

7
SHIP'S BOATS

The restorers of *Warrior* have built two marvellous ship's launches, placed between the grand entry ports and the outboard sides of the aft funnel. They have the athwartship windlass and trunks, which are also included in the model versions. Fitting out the two ship's launches for *Warrior* was an exceptionally satisfying task, particularly as much of it was possible to do indoors as a winter project. They are complete models in themselves, and certainly not a tiresome addition to the mother vessel. They make strong statements about their important role in the smooth running of the mother ship, and the interior fittings of these boats reflect the purposes required of them.[1]

It is not generally appreciated that ships of the line were almost always anchored offshore. This meant that everything which had to come aboard ship was

1. A most useful discussion of ship's boats and plans, to which I am indebted, may be found in Brian Lavery's book, *The Arming and Fitting of English Ships of War 1600-1815* (London: Conway Maritime Press, 1987).

(Left)
Restored pinnace launch aboard *Warrior*.

(Below)
Illustration of ship's boats being lowered.
(Author)

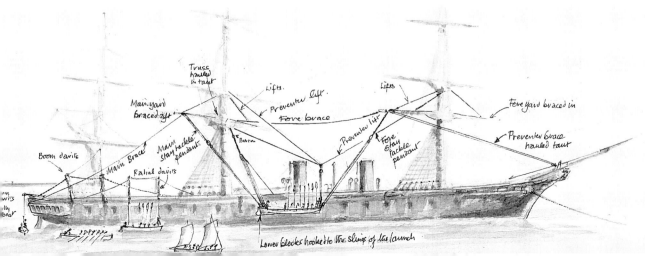

Ship's boats.
(Author &
J D Metcalf)

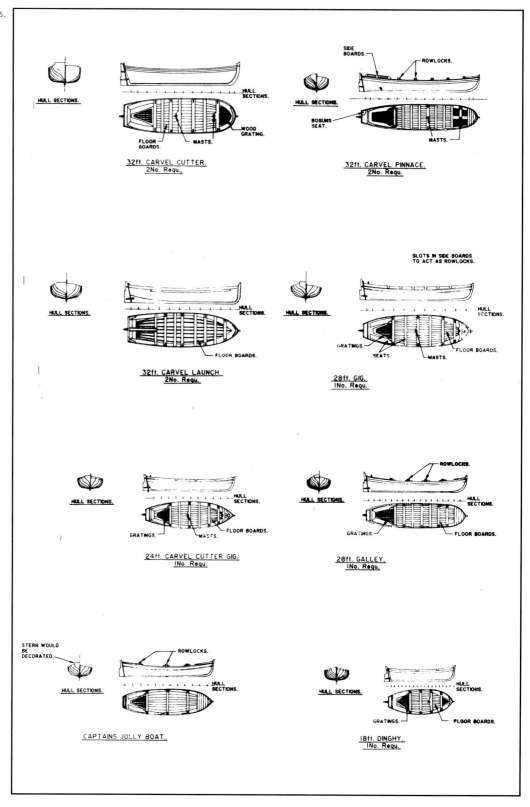

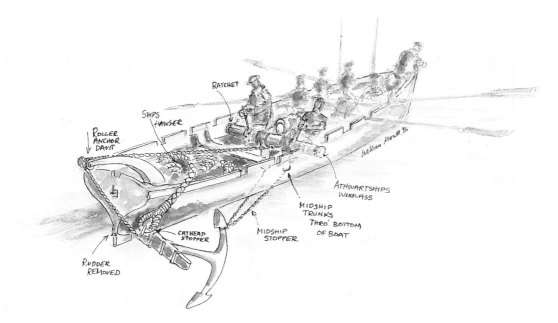

Labels on illustration: RATCHET · SHIPS HAWSER · ROLLER ANCHOR DAVIT · ATHWARTSHIPS WINDLASS · MIDSHIP TRUNKS THRO' BOTTOM OF BOAT · CATHEAD STOPPER · MIDSHIP STOPPER · RUDDER REMOVED · William Mowll 96

transported by the ship's boats. This included all the stores, the mails, fresh water, bits of machinery and gun barrels, as well as all the daily necessities for the seven hundred or more men living aboard such major warships. There can hardly have been a day at anchor when the ship's boats were not in full and active use.

Propulsion

Although the ship's boats were supplied with oars, they hoisted their sails whenever possible. In the case of the infamous mutiny on the *Bounty*, the ship's launch was sailed for 3600 miles by the commanding officer, William Bligh. Such sails were not pocket handkerchiefs: the mainmast on the *Warrior*'s launches rose 38ft into the air, as befits a vessel of over 8 tons. In conjunction with the foresail and jib, a large spread of canvas made these vessels a much speedier option than with seamen pulling on the oars.

Use as gunboats

The ship's launches were designed to carry out cutting-out operations and take part in amphibious operations; they were also essential to the day-to-day running of the ship. The size of the ship's anchors, for instance, were determined by the carrying capacity of the ship's launches, and when the ship had to be warped, or kedged, it would mean the launches being converted to their role as barges for the heaviest yet the most delicate manoeuvre in the manual, that of underslinging the anchors and using the athwartship windlass in conjunction with the anchor davit to raise and lower the cabling. Those who wonder why *Warrior* has four hawses will thus comprehend why, under certain circumstances, one anchor would secure the vessel whilst the other could be rowed out, slung beneath the hull of the launch, to make the new point of haul for the ship's main capstan.

Modelling ship's boats

Even with professionally-built models, ship's boats are often depicted in the form of solid block hulls, or canvassed over to hide the detail of construction. It is rare to see clinchering on the hulls of the lighter ship's boats such as gigs and galleys. None of this is very surprising: where people are building professional scale models in

Sketch of laying out an anchor from the ship's launch.
(Author)

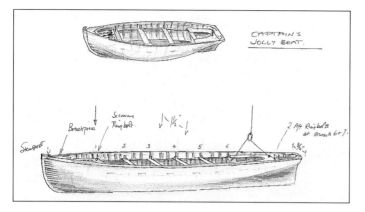

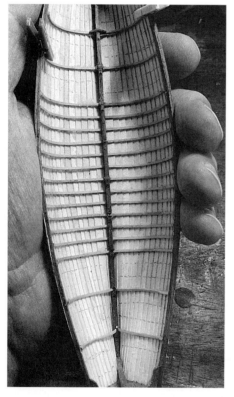

(Top)
Illustration of Captain's
jolly boat and gig.
(Author)

(Above)
Interior of 32ft cutter,
showing clincher build-
ing and steamed ribs,
held in the author's
hand.

paint on it. The handle on the end of an oar must not, in full scale, exceed 2in in diameter, or it could not be fully gripped. Small wonder then that when gazing down on the average offering of ship's boats many of them look a little bit lumpy. In fact, a micrometer would reveal on some of them that they would be impossible to manufacture if followed as builder's models.

Making a start

Given that there are physical limits as well as human ones, it is necessary, if building in the style of plank-on-frame, to start with rigidity in the form of a building board. You need to cut a straight slot which will accept the keel, not over-tightly: a sloppy fit, with masking tape stretched over it and carefully slit, should then give you a push fit, with the added advantage that this will prevent the keel being glued to the building board. Mark the right-angles of the frame positions from the plan. You do not really need to cut slots for these, their real use being for lining up the frames squarely to the keel.

The frames must be true and accurate, being the literal bones and rib structure of the boat. Leave plenty of over-length on the stem and stern, and depth to the keel. This all helps with clamping up, and generally providing points of grip in the initial stages. Likewise, the ribs need to have extra length, which can then be trimmed back at the assembly stage. In the pictures you will see planks of basswood (American lime) presawn to a nominal 3mm x 1mm (actual 0.126in x 0.042in). The keel is of mahogany $5/16$in x $3/32$in (actual 0.091in x 0.326in) and the top rail nominally 2mm square.

Wooden kebab sticks, with their special properties of flexibility and strength, can be ideal for making frames. Knowing what can be done with this cane-like material, I decided on my model to build the ribs from it, rather than solid frames. This

order to earn a living, auxiliary boats are an area where costs can be cut and to the customer the difference in the price is enormous. Amateurs who work for the love of the task are not so easily excused and some of the most excellent work, demanding great skill and patience, has been carried out by dedicated enthusiasts, and those who were not having to build to a deadline.

It is necessary to consider some of the facts about open boats before setting out on the task involved. Consider for a moment that, in full scale, the thickness of a plank or strake of a ship's boat is approximately $1/2$in thick, which at 1:48 scale is $10/1000$in (the thickness of modern veneer, in general terms). The frames or ribs of the ship's boat are approximately $3/4$in, equivalent to, let us say, $15/1000$in, marginally thicker than the planks. A stout keel of, say, 3in in full scale comes down to being approximately $1/16$in by the time it has a little

has several advantages, the most significant being that they can be steamed into the exact shape of the frame on the builder's plan, but still adjusted later when attached to the keel, before being attached to the top strake. This means that you can achieve a fair run with the planking, with judicious pushing and pulling of the ribs where required, and without distortion to the keel. With solid frames, one nearly always ends up having to use packing pieces and it is extremely difficult to deal with end grain accurately, as one must with any corrections to solid framing.

Miniature shooting board

At this point it is necessary to construct a special shooting board which can perform certain essential tasks. This is a simple device for gripping the planks of wood for accurate planing, and has the ability to open its adjustable jaws to accept two widths of planks at once, so making a matching pair possible, which is one of the secrets to achieving an even result on both sides of the hull. Because of the extension of the flat surface beyond the jaws it is possible to plane down the planks to a sharp end. The pictures and illustration will explain how it works, and the only details which call for any comment are that the jaw plates are made from $1/_{16}$in aluminium and the U-channel is simply a piece of drawer pull handle stock which slides over the plastic-coated board. The ability to hand-plane with this standard of accuracy has always presented difficulties in the past, but with this jig it makes it relatively simple to do.

So, it is with knuckle plane honed, the copper tube heated, and a bucket of water

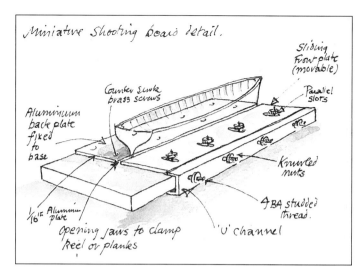

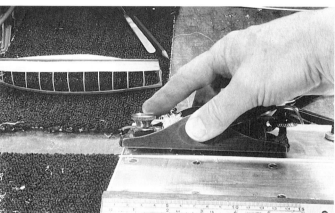

(Top)
Sketch of miniature shooting board.
(Author)

(Above)
Miniature shooting board.

(Left)
Matching pair of strakes, having been planed together on the shooting board. Mark the swell of the strake with a 'V' so that it is correctly applied when fitting to the hull.

to hand, that the journey of miniature planking begins. A reel of garden tying wire, of the thinnest variety and PVC-coated, is employed to trace out the curvature of the body plan frames and match the timber frame to its contour. The body plan shows only half the frame, but the

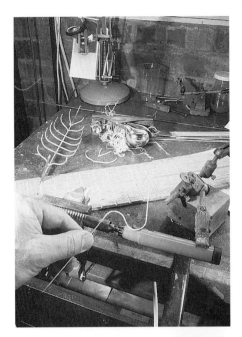

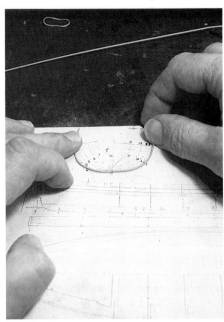

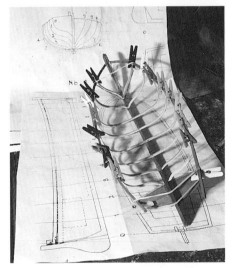

wire will replicate it for the opposite hand. Do not soak the timber for too long in the case of cane, or indeed the planks; a dip is sufficient at this thickness, and it is as well if the stick or plank is dried out in the action of drawing the timber over the copper tube. It prevents the planks from shrinking and aids the gluing-up process.

For the boat frames (ribs), kebab sticks are planed down into half-round section, which is not difficult to do. Then lie the flat surface down and plane the other half-round down to an overall thickness of $1/32$in; this leaves a miniature rounded edge on the strip, reminiscent of real ribs, and they are now ready for steaming.

Any way of getting the copper bending-tube touch-hot will suffice, but do watch the safety angle, particularly as wet material is involved. The little Portasol mini-blowlamp is ideal for this, or even an electric soldering iron, of the heavier variety (75 watt), up a copper tube will do the trick

Having got the ribs on station, the transom into the sternpost and the top strake positioned, some touch gluing provides the first sight of the boat in three dimensions. This is the moment when the sheer appears, always more marked on the vessel than on the sheer plan. The two horizontal bosom knees are added between transom and top strake, as is the breast hook at the stem, adding to the rigidity of the top sheer.

Natural lie of the planks

The secret to planking up a hull of any size is to determine the natural lie of the planks themselves. The less distortion that is put on a plank, the better the result, and for this reason builders of wooden boats have searched out hull forms to which the planks will lie most easily. Each plank needs to be tackled as a separate item. The maximum width of each plank is determined where the hull is at its fullest, and the minimum widths at both the stem and stern, where the planks go more tightly together. If you possess three pairs of dividers, and preset them to these given points, that is a quick and accurate solution to the task. The planks will do the rest.

In and out

Although it is wrong to talk of in and out strakes with carvel building, nevertheless there is an alternating trick which is useful to know about. You work two strakes at a time, the first strake being planed to half its width on *one side only* to both ends of the plank. In other words, throughout the process there is curvature to only *one* side of the plank, and this is laid with the rounded side towards the top sheer. The illusion of being tapered on both sides is caused by the bellying of the hull, and can easily be confused with double tapering. The first strake is spaced away the width of one plank at the fullest portion of the hull, and allowed to lie without strain against the ribs. The second plank is then used as a filler, or stealer, on the inside of the first plank. The stealer takes a lot more fitting than the plank taking the fair line of the hull, and you may well find that you have to splice the second plank and slide specially tapered pieces in to get a perfect fit at the extremities of the stem and stern.

By doing this in the fashion described, every alternate strake is being laid up against the flat side of the plank which is lying fair to the hull, and this is the secret to planking up carvel hulls without strain to the structure. It also keeps the strakes aligned when viewed at the stem and stern.

Inverted hull of the launch planked in carvel style.

When you come to the plank laid against the keel (the garboard strake), put a little relief angle on the side abutting the keel to relieve the stress caused by the plank having to go through 90 degrees in terms of the twist from the upright of the stem piece to the flat of the boat's bottom. You will also find it necessary to use some fantail stealers at the deadrise of the planking at the stern. Once again, the planks themselves will dictate the shape of these. A further tip is that you must plank both sides of the hull at once, or distortion will be introduced to the keel, making the matching process of the planks almost impossible.

The miniature clothes pegs and the alligator clips which you will need are fairly commonly available in shops. The latter need their teeth flattened: this is done by making them grip onto a piece of metal, and hitting them on the nose with a hammer. You then bend the ends in slightly, or turn into any useful shape you like.

Removal of the ribs

The initial frames are marginally out of scale and must be removed when the planking is complete. It must be appreciated that the final shape of the vessel is not dependent on the frames, but on the way

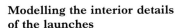

Ship's pinnace launch, showing interior details of athwartships windlass and trunks, 20pdr pivot gun, anchor davit, rudder, mast, bowsprit and oars.

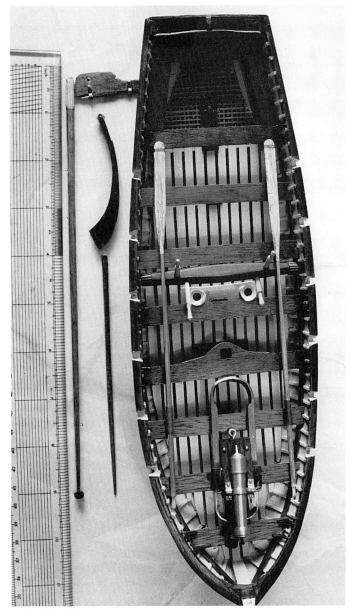

in which the planks have been cut. New ribs of boxwood replace the original frames which are removed at this point. These new ones are at proper scale and are applied to the interior of the launch once the planks are safely glued together. Ribs simply reinforce a hull structure: they are not strong enough to determine its initial shape. Once the hull is fully formed, seats (thwarts) and all the other details associated with a miniature scale model can be added.

Modelling the interior details of the launches

The model launch hull is now complete and the flooring placed, including the fiddley grating at the stern. It is tempting to start by inserting the risings, which is the correct term for the two internal strakes secured to the ribs which support the thwarts, but more properly the first items for insertion across the flooring of the boat ought to be the footwales: it is very surprising that this detail is so often omitted from models of boats built for rowing, because without this essential fulcrum point one simply cannot row a boat at all. Check at the outset that all the timbers are at the correct scale. For instance, the thwarts themselves, being in full scale no more than $1^1/_2$in thick, must reduce (at 1:48 scale) to approximately $^1/_{32}$in. It follows therefore that all the timbering in boats built for rowing and hoisting should be constructed as *lightly* as possible, relying for strength on knees, bracing pieces and skilled construction. Note that not all of the thwarts are permanently secured. Removable thwarts enabled large and unwieldy objects to be carried low in the boat for greater stability, thus in the launches not all the thwarts have hanging knees. Metal work has to include the iron hoops which secure the bowsprit, the anchoring of the pivot gun and slide, the trunks, the foot of the anchor davit and the pintles of the rudder. The tiller arms are also made of metal, simply because this is easier.

The oars

It is not easy to produce a convincing oar without giving it the consideration it deserves. The oar itself is divided very approximately into three equal parts: the blade accounts for one third, next the shaft and the inboard end (excluding the leather protection), and finally the loom and handle completing the full oar. In order to row successfully with an oar it must be well balanced when it is immersed in the water, so that the measurements for the oars of ship's boats are related to the length of the boat being rowed, being approximately one quarter of the total length of the vessel. Having said that, they are not all of the same size, and have to take into account the narrowing of the boat towards the stem where the thwarts are considerably reduced. For this reason oars were all marked for their positions and should, therefore, not all be modelled as identical. The sketch shows how the oars were modelled using barbecue sticks as the source material for the shaft and loom, and limewood for the paddle. A general observation about oars is that the stock diminishes from the loom until it disappears into the paddle, and that the paddle diminishes in thickness from its shoulder to the copper-banded tip. When one looks down a well-made oar, it fades to virtually nothing and thus presents very little resistance to the water at the point of entry and exit. There is not a great deal of point in making more than half the complement of oars, or the model will simply be overloaded, obscuring much of the other detail. Eight oars is quite sufficient to give the effect required.

Finally, do take a look at real oars; they are used and abused perhaps more than any other pieces of timber aboard ship, so do not make the mistake of making them look pretty. Paint the shafts as

though badly bruised around the leathered area, and do not varnish the handles, which should be left in the raw state. If you make them truly to scale, they are the final statement of scratch building, and they will be both seen and appreciated because everyone knows exactly how they should look.

Cutters

Although this section deals specifically with ship's boats as part of the complement for *Warrior*, these traditional craft and the method used for their construction can apply to any shape of hull using clinchered strakes. Just like a good piece

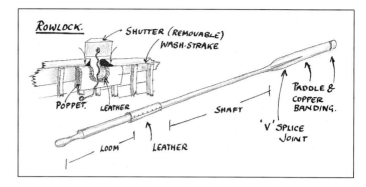

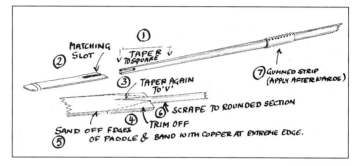

(Top)
Details of an oar.
(Author)

(Above)
How to construct an oar.
(Author)

Illustration of 32ft cutter.
(Author)

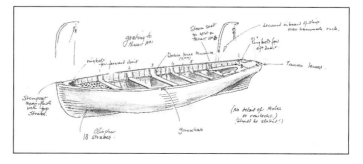

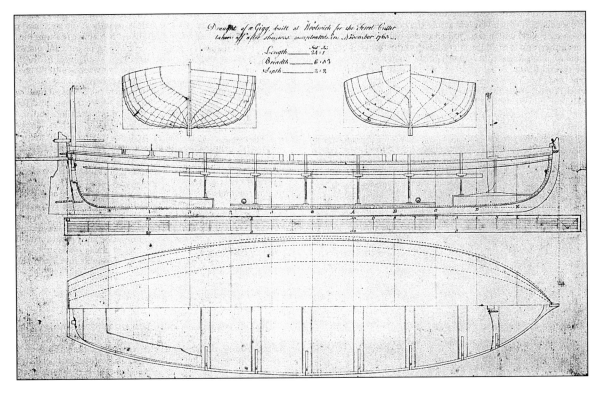

Detail of clincher-built gig.
(Science Museum)

of knitting or basketwork, clinchering must look as good on the reverse as it does on the face. It is harder to execute than carvel building, both in full scale and in miniature, because the strakes must be continuous throughout the length of the hull: in other words, no stealing, joggling or cheating. This is also the reason why the Royal Navy disliked clinchered boats, in that they were harder to repair than patching up a carvel hull. The advantage of the method was in its ratio of strength to lightness, given that a well-built clincher boat came out at approximately a quarter the weight of a carvel one of the same size.

Keel rebate

Cutting a rebate in the keel is the first essential, and this provides a surface on which the planks can land and be fixed. It also locates the rather difficult path which the garboard strake has to take, and gives the planks a proper fixing location at the

base of the transom, to which the planking can be pinned.

The stempost

The stempost should be steamed round to give the strength of a continuous piece of wood on the long grain. As a strengthener behind the upward curvature (technically known as the stemson and apron), a piece of timber was cut to shape with its leading edge sharpened to provide a rebate for the planks to shoulder into: a shape reminiscent of a penknife blade.

The sternpost

An open mortise and tenon joint cannot be avoided for the sternpost, which means the use of a slightly thicker piece of stock than the keel. Once jointed, it can be lightly sanded back on the trailing edge, but there is not much 'meat' on the mortise unless a thicker piece of stuff is used. Great care is needed with this vertical joint, to make

Clinchering on the 32ft cutters, from the keel.

Overhead of the clinchering process.

sure that it is perfectly aligned with the stempost, or the boat will be distorted from the outset. Such problems tend to worsen, so take extra trouble to assure yourself that all is fair and square. The two gussets, to be fitted between the keel and the sternpost, have the names of sternson and keelson, the whole area being referred to as the deadrise.

The gunwales

In general principle, it is easier to make matching pairs of any item if they are fab-ricated together. This is particularly true of something subtle like a boat's gunwale. Once again, wetted timbers, in this case mahogany, are drawn over the heated cop-per tube in tandem. Obviously, when these timbers are reversed they match exactly. This curvature will be perfectly stable, and can then be fitted between the transom and sternpost. Use superglue for this (which surprisingly likes the wood to be a little moist). Despite all the claims, it takes about twenty minutes for the glue to cure. This is a good moment to go and attend to something entirely different, and a hot tip is always to have a separate item in the workshop on the go all the time, which will stop you fiddling about with items which need to be left alone. Once the second strake is in place, the three-dimensional form of the hull produces the craft in embryo; she now only needs a ribcage and skin for completion.

Planking-up in clincher fashion

Final adjustments to the frames must now be made, checking out the fairness of the ribs in relation to one another. The eye is still the most useful piece of test equipment anyone has followed, in shipbuilding, by a set of dividers; and more useful than one set of dividers is three pairs of the same. Set the amidships pair to the widest setting (minus the overlap of course), and with the second pair calculate the width at the stem, and with the third, the width at the stern. This is old-fashioned mathematics, and it works better than fancy calculations on a computer. Think of it as homogeneous technology!

The plank shape

The plank has a flat bottom, and is planed in tandem with its opposite number at both ends to approximately half its width. The planks are in scale, measuring 4mm x 0.5mm (0.020in); the full-scale equivalent would be 1in. They are made from American lime (basswood). When measuring the plank's length, allow an overhang of an inch or so at either end, so that you can select the exact width required at the stempost. Very useful for planking-up purposes are a pair of endcutters from an electronic engineer's kit. These cutters can be used with great accuracy and save a huge amount of time: they are so sharp that they guillotine the ends without any sign of crushing to the timber.

Thumb, lick and forefinger

The planks are so thin that, to put curva-ture on them, all you need to do is moisten them and pass the timber between thumb and forefinger: they will curl naturally with the smallest amount of pressure, as would a piece of card or paper. Glue the edge of the plank along its length as neatly as possible using aliphatic glue, clamping it with the miniature clothes pegs, and cleaning up as quickly as possible afterwards. This adhesive sands very well and is well suited to the task, if a little lumpy. Every now and again, particularly on the transom, you need to use pins: lacemakers' pins (available from haberdashery shops) are the best. They are very fine, and it is possible to cover the piercing with the overlap of the next strake, like secret panel pinning.

It takes about fifteen minutes to pre-pare, fit and finish a plank at this scale. This is starting with a presawn plank 4mm x 0.5mm. This means seven hours' work simply on the planking, but do not try to do it all at once. It is very precise work for which you need good natural daylight if possible, together with that difficult combination of being at peace with yourself and the world, and an absence of interruptions. Finding this combination is perhaps the hardest task of all.

Natural beauty

Not everything translates well from big to small, but clinchering does, and when you have mastered the technique you will have a priceless understanding of the artistry involved. Do look at seascape paintings, and you will notice that few professional artists actually understand what is going on technically speaking, either in the way in which light falls on the planking, or how it is flat boards can be persuaded to adopt the rounded shape of a hull. No other method can imitate the sharpness of a planked hull, internally and externally, so by doing it properly, nothing is lost and much is to be gained. The final experiment ought to include a noise test to find out whether or not it is possible to reproduce that lapping sound which strakes produce against the waves of every harbour in the world where these traditional boats lie at anchor. Boats built according to the above instructions do float, and look particularly well alongside the mother ship.

The captain's gig

This vessel was deliberately different from the other nine working boats aboard ship. It represented the power and status of the captain, silently communicating his personal standing in society. Such things do not change from generation to generation; one has only to consider Royal Yachts through the ages to note that we expect the arrival and departure of royalty afloat to be carried out in some style. The first captain of *Warrior*, the Hon Arthur Auckland Leopold Pedro Cochrane, was himself not a commoner, neither was he a pompous man,[2] but from the beginning of his naval career as a midshipman he would have been taught what was expected of him in terms of taste in personal ownership. Within the constraints of life at sea, everything he owned would be of the highest quality available. Our generation gasps at the visible luxury of the captain's quarters, with its cut-glass decanters, French-polished furniture, silk cushions, the richly coloured wools of Turkey carpets and, in the very latest fashion, the black and white squares of linoleum floor (patented in 1860). This same luxury would also have extended to the 32ft galley (known as such after 1850, rather than

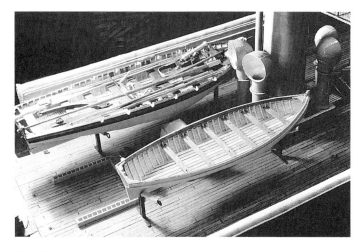

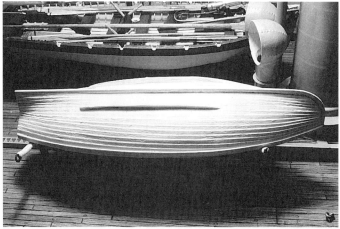

gig) which, according to custom, was the captain's own personal property. The change in terminology from the word gig, loosely translated as 'wanton woman', to

(Top)
The unfinished 32ft cutter, shown against the larger ship's launch in the boat crutches amidships.

(Above)
The magic of clinchering and the way in which low light levels fall on the strakes of a hull - even at midnight.

(Left)
The ship's launch alongside the grand entry port and ladderway.

2. Wells, Capt John, *The Immortal Warrior* (Emsworth, Hants: Kenneth Mason, 1987), p75.

Overhead of Captain's
gig.

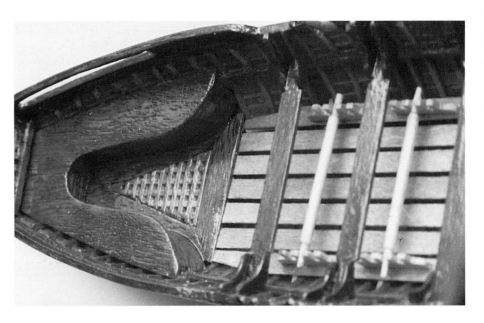

galley is interesting. There was a creeping respectability in referring to this vessel in terms other than that of being a 'fast woman' which is characteristically mid-Victorian in its aspirations towards gentility. A shame really, because the word gig well describes the difference in hull form of the boat's lean and hungry lines (emulating the wasp waists so beloved of the fashionable women of the times), as opposed to the full-bodied forms of the work boats. The Admiralty is said never to have officially recognised the new term, although it was an unpardonable offence in Crimean days for an officer of the watch, when the Captain of a ship of the line ordered his boat, to call away the 'first gig' instead of the 'galley'. This development, however, represents the finest excuse for indulging in red silk and gold leaf in the manufacture of this exotic waterborne carriage, being one of those rare opportunities for indulgence rather than restraint.

Mansonia

The exotic timber mansonia has a wonderful natural purple-brown shade, and a smooth hard surface. Sufficient strips of any similarly grained veneer should be sawn to plank up the clinchered hull, using the same technique as described for the earlier vessels, steaming the boxwood ribs from the body plan and fixing them on their stations to the keel. There is a temptation to leave the hull, both internally and externally, in its natural colour with a plain varnish, but this would have been bending historical truth too far. By the 1860s, all the auxiliary boats in the RN were painted white on the external side of the hull (no doubt for good practical reasons of being seen) but, for pure effect, the interior of the captain's gig was painted with a pink/red (Royal Purple), the distinguishing colour of consular rank, of which Captain Cochrane was, by both birth and office, a member.[3]

Luxury furnishings

The upper furnishings of this luxurious boat represent an amalgam of several ideas culled from Brian Lavery's book, plus a few thoughts of my own arising from other studies of regal craft. This includes heightened washstrakes on the bow quarters, a carved stempost, a canework backboard and banister in the stern sheets.

3. *Ibid.*

Jolly boat model under construction.

Added to this conjecture is the canvas-proofed cushioning on the stern seats and atop the painter locker, in a colour which matches the internal decoration. Another detail, which has more than a whiff of class distinction about it, is the absence of the sternmost thwart, giving those of officer class (including the odd gracious lady) a greater area of separation between themselves and the ordinary seamen pulling on the oars. In harbour service, this vessel would have been the equivalent of the courtesy vessel for esteemed persons, and to well-bred Victorians proximity to members of the working class was taken very seriously, and avoided wherever possible.

Connected to all this is the addition of a locker with a radiused edge to it. This was the result of study of a deluxe feature fitted to a large pinnace, and provides for the stowage of such niceties as a flask or two in transit from ship to shore. In this waterproof cabinet one would also expect to find racking for navigational instru-ments, such as compass and sextant, which could be locked away safely when the boat was moored to the quayside.

The second galley

This boat, despite sharing the same dimensions as her opposite number, had none of the decorative refinements of the first, neither did she have the bandbox finish, being simply an ordinary fast working sea boat. She nevertheless still required the extra tackle and fittings associated with the two masts and lugsails, and yet another set of oars.

The jolly boat

Captain Arthur Cochrane hated this little 18ft jolly boat, which was technically classed as a four-oared cutter. He claimed it was far too small to be of any use, not even big enough to bring aboard the fresh beef, which explains its nickname of the 'blood boat'. Despite complaints to the

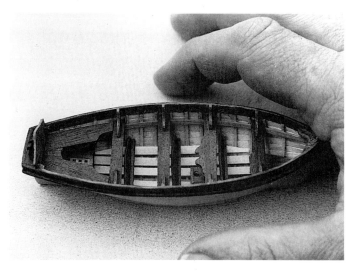

The blood boat before varnishing.

most difficult, simply on account of its size. There is a need to consider over and over again how lightly built everything must be, and the smaller you go so much the more must one concentrate on undersizing the scale. At the same time, the delicacy with which the approach must be made must not be allowed to interfere with the robustness of these working boats. They have to communicate their workaday purposefulness to the onlooker if they are to look truly authentic.

Admiralty, the despised vessel continued to be suspended from the stern davits, causing annoyance to all those who were obliged to use her. It is quite ironical that the name of Captain was attached to both the best and the worst boats of the ship's complement.

Delicacy *vs* robustness

With the construction of an item about the same size as a goose's egg, it is difficult to believe that the materials you use are going to be strong enough to withstand the stresses imposed on the structure in the process of building up from the keel. This is really born of a basic mistrust of timber itself, amounting to what is a disbelief that, at this kind of scale, wood will withstand the manipulation required of it to bend and twist through the shapes necessary to go from stem to stern. Given that you stick with the correct timber for the job, in the right scale, and you have a heat source to do the steam bending, then you will not fail in your efforts.

The challenge

I saved the challenge of the smallest boat until last, believing that clinchering a timber model of a mere $4^1/_2$in was going to require every last drop of concentration. Of all the ship's boats, the jolly boat is the

Illustration of draw plate.
(Author)

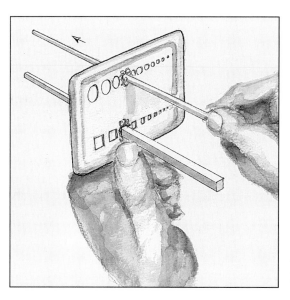

A round-up of timbers

Boxwood is absolutely essential for the ribs, and behaves beautifully under steam. The 0.5mm square is just about right at this scale. Limewood (basswood) with its smooth, creamy, knot-free grain, manufactures well into planks 2mm x 0.5mm, although you will probably not be able to believe that it is strong enough to plank anything. This again is available in presawn and sanded lengths. Mahogany does well for gunwales, transom, knees, thwarts, etc, and looks very boat-built. This is a subtle matter, and if you are fortunate enough to find some old mahogany with a tight grain, so much the better. Mahogany also darkens with exposure to the sunlight. This can be enhanced with the use of tinted varnish, but do not use the mahogany tint, always go for the darker ones which convey the effect of the grime associated with mud, sludge and so forth. Try dark oak on raw mahogany which produces a wonderful effect (furniture restorers call this vandyking).

With all the fitting out of auxiliary boats, if you are tempted to use timber which is thicker than that associated with veneer then you are probably overscaling. In a clincher boat, everything used in its construction is associated with lightness. For their size, clincher boats are very light indeed, and the finished model must look exactly that, robust and delicate, all at once.

Following the lines drawn up in Brian Lavery's book, I marked out the stations on a building board and worked in the old-fashioned style, matching the frames to the plan and setting up from the keel. Never having been taught this technique by anyone, the practice on the previous six boats provided me with the necessary confidence to tackle the jolly boat in the same style, going from relatively large to very small. One detail worth noting in the jolly boat is that the bottom boards follow the line of the bilge, whereas the other larger boats have flat bottom boards and stretchers for the feet of the oarsmen to press against. In this foreshortened vessel, all the depth of the boat is used amidships, with a raised platform to the painter locker at the stem, and grating in the stern sheets. This adds to its character, though it could probably do with a bit more sludge and a little less varnish: the mud and the blood together.

4. *Ibid*, p235.

Measurements for *Warrior*'s Boats[4]

Type	Length (ft)	Weight (tons)	Lifesaving	Oars	Sails	Armament
Launch (2)	42	8	140	18 DB	2 standing lug and staysails	20pdr
Pinnace (1)	32	$4^1/_2$	70	14 DB	2 standing lug and staysails	12pdr
Cutter gig (1)	20	-	19	4/6 SB	mainsail and staysail	-
Dinghy (1)	14	-	6	4 SB	foresail and mainsail	-
Cutter (2)	30	2	49	12 DB	dipping lug and mizzen	rocket launcher
Galley (1)	32	3/4	28	6 SB	2 lugsails	-
Gig (1)	30	3/4	26	6 SB	2 lugsails	-
Cutter (1) (jolly boat)	18	-	12	4 SB	foresail and mainsail	-

8
MASTS AND YARDS

*W*arrior has been an extremely fortunate ship not only to have survived physically, but to have so much documentation about her to help the modelmaker. John Scott Russell's engraved plans in his huge work entitled *Ships of War* are of prime interest to shipbuilders, whilst Midshipman Murray's internal drawings and sketches of the ship have been absolutely critical to the way in which the original restoration took place.[1] There are also paintings and photographs of *Warrior* extant which aid the process of historical research.

In 1862 there was published a second edition of a very important book, Nares' *Seamanship*, which had first been published under the title of *The Naval Cadet's Guide: or Seaman's Companion*. This book contains 308 illustrations detailing exactly the way in which the ships of the Royal Navy were rigged,[2] at a time when tradition was a respectable word, and was adhered to with an almost religious fanaticism. This book has the same kind of forceful implications as Scott Russell's plans; the manual is a piece of detailed primary evidence against which it is extreme-

Wooden bowsprit on the Science Museum model.

ly difficult to argue with any conviction whatsoever. Builders of vessels on the stocks would quite often deviate from ship's plans into a state which was referred to with the words 'as built', creating all those endless arguments of detail which have fuelled the pens of naval historians. But Nares' *Seamanship* shows exactly what the current established practices were in the early 1860s, accompanied by the question and answer style in which cadets were examined before promotion. Because it assumes no knowledge, apart from that which is taught and illustrated, it is as useful today to those who are trying to elucidate how rigging was set up, as it was to the ignorant cadet who had to learn it all by rote.

The bowsprit

The issues surrounding the bowsprit of *Warrior* in 1860 and the one adapted for the restoration have been complicated by the need to experiment. The 'as-launched' version, handsome as it was, was quickly changed – that is to say, shortened – in the 1862 refit in order to alleviate the undesirable weight at the bow. The one depicted in the Science Museum's model was this early version, and the exact style is corroborated in Nares' *Seamanship*. The restored vessel has also had two bowsprits; the first was fitted but, although fitted according to the plan, looked too thin and pole-like. This was emphasised by the fact that it was made of steel, and had none of the familiar diminishing chamfer and sturdiness of its wooden counterpart. So a new and bolder one was ordered, again in steel, but differing in design from the original, being much simpler in its form and detail on account of its inherent strength and welded construction.

Warrior was originally rigged at HM Naval Dockyard, Chatham. Although this novel ship had many entirely new features associated with her hull and machinery, the command given to Chatham Dockyard

over the matter of her rigging was simple and blunt: she was to be rigged as an 80-gun ship (despite her official classification as a frigate). The simplicity of this order is in total conflict with what our eyes witness in the complexity of both the standing and running rigging. Nevertheless, the standards and specifications were so well-understood that such fittings as were not available off the shelf would be quickly and easily manufactured.

The 1860s marked a period of great change for the Victorian Navy; as yet no Royal Naval Dockyard was able to produce an all-iron battleship, so it was not until the tow from the Thames Iron Works that she became by possession a naval vessel. It was reasonable to suppose that, had she been masted and rigged on the Thames, she would have been fitted with metal masts made from sections of wrought iron (as was the mainmast on the SS *Great Britain*), but once in the clutches of Chatham where there were ample supplies of timber, tradition was served and the masts were made from Baltic pine and banded with iron hoops. However, she and her sister were the only 'Black Battle-ships' to be fitted with wooden lower masts.[3]

The remarkable quality of the Science Museum builder's model of *Warrior* ensured that it was possible to compare the copper plate engravings of Nares' *Seamanship* manual with the evidence of the model, and follow the rigging and fittings, line for line. It is akin to having a clearly written set of instructions and illustrations, and points out that ships of this period were assembled and rigged on the principles of a factory production line.

Making the model bowsprit

Warrior's bowsprit has a handsome 20-degree steeve to it, a feature not enjoyed by her successors. Added to the proud upward rake is the extra attraction of the cruciform spritsail gaff booms (sometimes

1. Russell, John Scott, *Ships of War* (London: ?1866); Wells, Capt John, *The Immortal Warrior* (Emsworth, Hants: Kenneth Mason, 1987), Midshipman Murray's sketches, p112
2. Nares, Lieut George S, *Seamanship* (1862), first published in 1860 as *The Naval Cadet's Guide*: or *Seaman's Companion*), facsimile of second edition, introduced by David R Macgregor (Woking: Gresham Books, 1979).
3. Wells, *op cit*, p224.

wrongly referred to as whisker poles) which provide a spread of load for the whole spike, and also an area for the safety netting beneath the jibboom. The back-guys to the whole bowsprit contrast effectively with the whimsical forestays and running rigging. The dolphin striker completes the three-dimensional triangular effect and has an unusual forward rake to it. The whole spike bowsprit undeniably looks most impressive and viewed from dead ahead of the stem would have presented an intimidating sight to any potential aggressor.

The component parts are as follows. We will start with the heel of the bowsprit: this pierces the iron walls and breastpiece of the ship, and the heel locates into the knightheads forward of the main (gun) deck. The next item to note is the iron banding which clenches together the bowsprit timbers. The rubbing paunch runs along the topside of the bowsprit, providing a small flat walkway on an otherwise rounded mast pole. The bowsprit saddle supports the bowsprit outboard of the iron knee of the ship, just forward of the heads. The bowsprit spritsail gaff booms give lateral support to the bowsprit

and acts as the spreaders for the safety netting. The crans irons are the iron quarter bands to which the bobstay and back-guys attach just aft the bowsprit cap. The dolphin striker is in fact a jawed gaff boom. The bees are a platform on the bowsprit top, which support the sheaves of the lower topmast forestays. These stays pass through the jaws of the spritsail gaff booms and anchor to the iron forewall of the ship. Moving on to the jibboom (the middle pole), there is a saddle atop the bees and there ought to have been one at the heel, but this has been omitted on the Science Museum model. The bowsprit cap must be iron banded and mortised to the bowsprit, as well as being filed out to house the jibboom and the heel of the flying jibboom. The jibboom is held in place by the heel chain, which prevents the boom from being pushed inboard. This long chain passes round the heel of the jibboom, starting and finishing at the bowsprit cap, and has an adjustment with deadeyes and lanyard, thus keeping the chain tight into the niche carved into the jibboom's heel. The crupper chain lashes the jibboom to the bowsprit, passing over the heel chain, in the style of gammoning.

The model spike bowsprit.

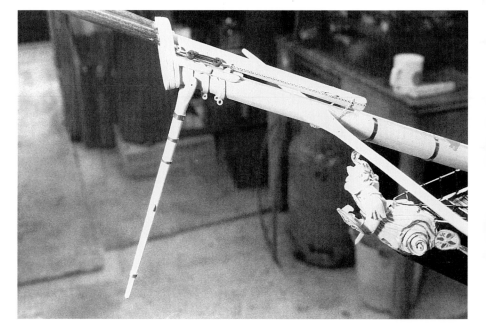

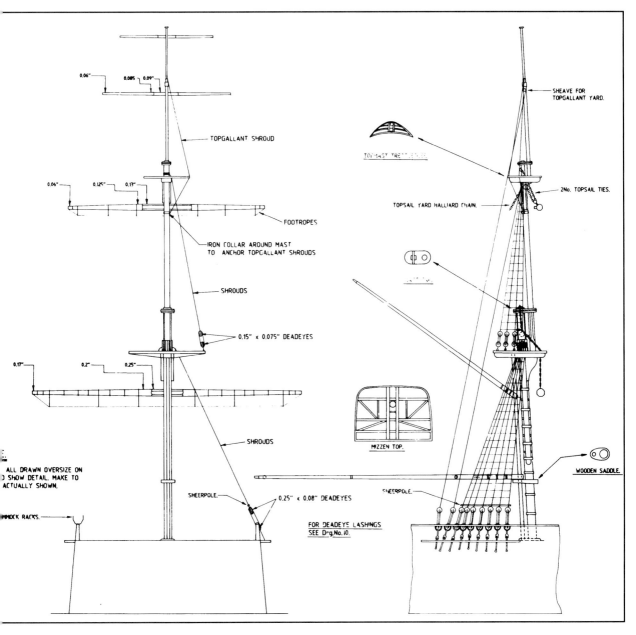

0.06"   0.085" 0.09"

TOPGALLANT SHROUD

0.06"   0.125"   0.13"

FOOTROPES

IRON COLLAR AROUND MAST
TO ANCHOR TOPGALLANT SHROUDS

SHROUDS

0.15" x 0.075" DEADEYES

0.17"   0.2"   0.25"

SHROUDS

SHEERPOLE.

0.25" x 0.08" DEADEYES

FOR DEADEYE LASHINGS
SEE Drg.No.10.

ALL DRAWN OVERSIZE ON
SHOW DETAIL. MAKE TO
ACTUALLY SHOWN.

HAMMOCK RACKS.

SHEAVE FOR
TOPGALLANT YARD.

TOPMAST TRESTLETREES.

2No. TOPSAIL TIES.

TOPSAIL YARD HALLIARD CHAIN.

MIZZEN TOP.

WOODEN SADDLE.

SHEERPOLE.

Mizzen mast.
(Author & J D Metcalf)

It does this at an angle, and is held in place by a stop-cleat on the underside of the bowsprit and in an angled slot, at the heel of the jibboom. There is a horizontal sheave cut into the base of the jibboom for inhauling and outhauling. On the aft side of the bowsprit cap is fitted the jackstaff holder, used when in port. The flying jib-boom is lashed with hemp at the heel, and belly-lashed by use of a quarter boom iron, also known as a clip. This double iron band produces the effect of 'crossing the finger', the two booms being not exactly parallel one another, but intention-ally offset. All three booms are pierced for vertical sheaves in order to reeve the rele-vant rigging through them.

Manufacture of the spike bowsprit

Because of the complexity of carving some of the components, hardwood is prefer-able, whilst the rest of the poles can be made from mature Scots' pine. All three booms are best constructed from sapele, as are the gaffs, with the exception of the dolphin striker and bowsprit cap which can be made from teak. It will be neces-sary to construct a V-groove shooting board for reducing masts from square to round. This continues to be a very useful item, even when the masts have been made, for marking up the horizontals and verticals in preparation for cutting sheave slots and placing other fittings accurately. It is not necessary to use a lathe for mak-ing masts: it is not the way they are made in full scale, and a freshly sharpened knuckle plane does the job with ease and a lot less fuss.

Start always with square stock for the initial reduction and taper. Keep the tim-ber square until you start to come within the specified measurements. Then start to plane off into octagonal shape until the final moments of reduction when it can be rounded off. Always cut an extra few inch-es for the left hand to grip and roll when the mast has to come out of the V-groove

for final finishing. It is useful to keep a set of three O/S callipers handy, preset to the prescribed widths of heel, middle and top. The golden rule is to ensure that you do not overscale, and that you have the courage to believe that it is the rigging which provides the strength to masts, rather than the thickness of the timbers.

The bowsprit cap

A properly set up bowsprit cap has its top edge running parallel with the jibboom and its underside squared off to the reeved angle. In geometrical terms, whenever there are differing angles to tyre around with iron banding, this will make a demand for smithing, or heating and ham-mering. The tenon joints must be cut at the reeving angle of 20 degrees, and the mortises to match. The best way to do this is to start with an oversized piece of squared timber, and cut the mortises first, and then trim back to the rounded shape of the cap. (This procedure will be dis-cussed in more depth in the section deal-ing with the fabrication of the lower mast caps.) Even on a model, the banding of the cap is essential, in that a great many stresses meet at this point, and it needs inherent built-in strength.

As the gaff jaws are banded, including those of the dolphin striker, they are wrapped round with softened copper shim (0.005in) and soft-soldered. As with the anchor stock banding, they are then knocked up to ensure a really tight fit. The shim is very thin; a pair of O/S callipers can be used for holding the bands in place when soldering them up. When the bands are painted they hardly show at all but, as in full-sized practice, they do strengthen and enhance the final effect.

Lower masts

Victorian wooden masts were made from resinous Baltic fir, banded together with iron hoops on the exterior face, and

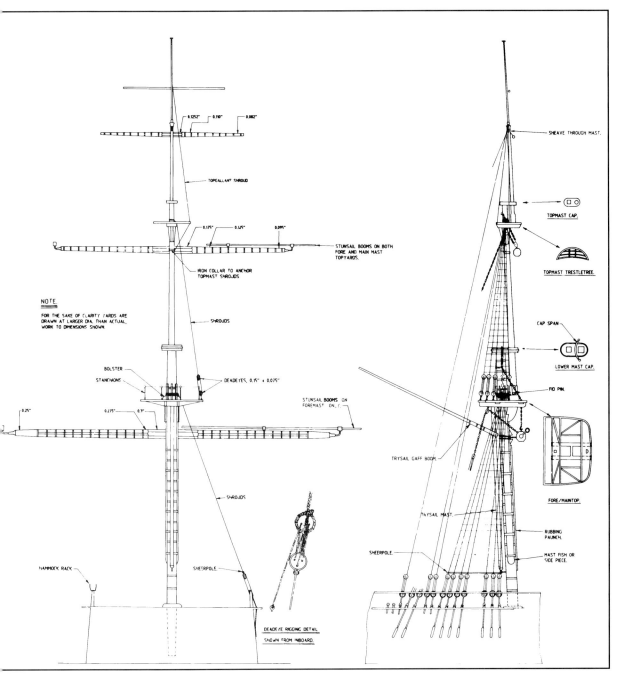

0.1252" 0.110" 0.082"

TOPGALLANT SHROUD

SHEAVE THROUGH MAST.

TOPMAST CAP.

TOPMAST TRESTLETREE.

0.175" 0.125" 0.095"

STUNSAIL BOOMS ON BOTH
FORE AND MAIN MAST
TOPYARDS.

IRON COLLAR TO ANCHOR
TOPMAST SHROUDS

CAP SPAN

LOWER MAST CAP.

NOTE.

FOR THE SAKE OF CLARITY YARDS ARE
DRAWN AT LARGER DIA. THAN ACTUAL,
WORK TO DIMENSIONS SHOWN.

FID PIN.

SHROUDS

BOLSTER

STANCHIONS

DEADEYES, 0.15" × 0.075"

TRYSAIL GAFF BOOM

FORE/MAINTOP.

STUNSAIL BOOMS ON
FOREMAST ONLY.

0.25"

0.275" 0.3"

RUBBING
PAUNCH.

TRYSAIL MAST.

MAST FISH OR
SIDE PIECE.

SHROUDS

SHEERPOLE

HAMMOCK RACK

SHEERPOLE.

DEADEYE RIGGING DETAIL
SHOWN FROM INBOARD.

Main and foremasts.
(Author & J D Metcalf)

4. Bramwell, Martyn, *The International Book of Wood* (London: Mitchell Beazley, 1979), p184; Underhill, H, *Masting and Rigging the Clipper Ship and Ocean Carrier* (Glasgow: Brown Son & Ferguson, 1988), p55.
5. Longridge, C Nepean, *The Anatomy of Nelson's Ships*, revised by E Bowness (Watford: MAP/Argus, 1977), Ch XI.

coaked internally with long mortise and tenon joints, which locked together the scarfed faces of the timbers.[4] The iron hoops were shrunk straight from the forge onto the timber, using the long-standing technology acquired in fitting metal tyres to carriages and carts. Mastmaking was a specialist job in the shipyard, separate from ordinary shipwrighting and, because of the need for the shipwright to be master of both timber and metal, it was regarded as a highly specialised craft.

The central cores of all three lower masts stepped into *Warrior* were made up from composites of timbers and fished, that is to say, reinforced with cheeks, at their second and third quarters. Lower masts were divided from head to heel in the following fashion. The head was at the topmost end of the mast and led down to the stop of hounds. These provided the platform for the fighting top. Below this

Mainmast in the V-groove.

were the third, second and first quarters of the mast, which led to the point of fullest diameter, before passing through the deck, supported by the partners. The mast also passed through all the lower decks, diminishing in size to the point of the heel, which had a square step cut into it to locate it to the keelson, and to prevent it from revolving.[5]

Manufacture of the lower masts

As with the making of the bowsprit, the tools for making masts are very simple: a shooting board with a V-groove cut in it, a set of preset callipers, and a finely-honed knuckle plane. Start by marking out the top and the bottom of the timber stock with a series of concentric circles, horizontals and verticals. These will indicate any unevenness as you reduce the stock from square to round section. An engineer's centre-finder is an extremely useful tool, but most of its tricks can be replicated by placing the mast in the V-groove, and using an engineer's square for marking up the end grain. If you want to mark off other points of reference on the timber face, use a very fine drill in a drill press. (This technique will be discussed more fully when the yards are constructed.)

If you can find some pitch pine out of which to make masts, then that is an excellent solution. Less satisfactory are the more obvious choices: ramin, which is so closely associated with dowel, is not a good idea, and unseasoned softwood must be avoided at all costs. Old furniture is the best source of matured timber for model shipwrighting and, of course, a jointed mast, even in miniature, is less likely to warp and twist than a single pole. It is also stronger. As the taper starts to diminish, the stock disappears at an increasing rate, so a helpful hint is to use the callipers constantly at the finishing stage.

When you are reaching the closing stages with rounding off, you can use the callipers on a scratch basis, that is to say, the scratch marks which they make on the surface of the soft wood as they are coming close to the required preset diameter can be planed smooth until the timber stock slips through the callipers uninjured. Leave sufficient extra length to grab hold of when planing from square to round, typically 4-5in.

A fished mast must have a flat planed on either cheek of the mast, unless you are planning to go through the difficult process of making a concave groove; this could be done with a gouge, but the suggested method is to plane a flat onto the sides of the lower mast. Ripsaw from a piece of round stock, planing an edge onto the halved strip, in order that the wedges under the iron hoops can be knocked in.

With the flats planed off the sides of the mast, and the grooves for the iron hoops made on the underside of the halved dowelling, the process of iron banding can begin, watching carefully that the adhesive does not block up the grooves cut for the bands. If you can find some copper strip with adhesive backing, as used by the stained glass fraternity, so much the better. It protects the mast from being badly scorched by dissipating the heat; it also solders itself nicely to the underside of the brass banding.

All the brass strips should be prepared, and then given heat treatment to soften them up. Getting the bands on tightly needs a little knowhow, and the following may well help. Measure the circumference of the hoop with the brass band $\frac{1}{2}$in or so back down the taper. Cut to length, allowing a small overlap, and taper file the ends so that they will fit together without too much bulk. Gently hammer to shape at the back of the mast to take out the softness of the metal band, and clamp in the vice. Now hammer the front and the joint, and then squeeze some soft-solder with pliers, and slip it between the ends. Add the killed salts flux (Baker's fluid).

Before you solder it is important to

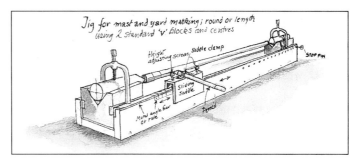

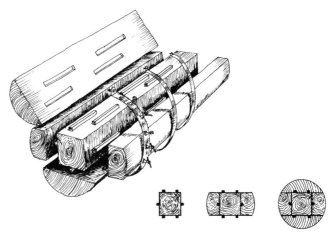

(Top)
Illustration of jig for mastmaking and measuring.
(Author)

(Above)
Illustration of built-up masts.
(Josh Mowll)

(Left)
Mainmast with fishes taped to it. The fishes have been previously grooved on their inside faces to allow for the alternating 'iron' bands.

have ready a sharp pointed instrument (I use a needle file), which is used to bring together the two brass ends when the solder is still in a fluid state. Hold the wooden-handled needle file between your teeth, as

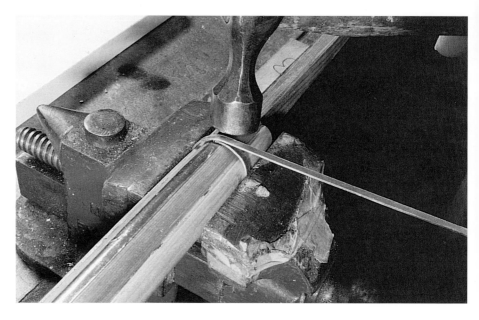

there is no time at all to pick it up. This is certainly both dangerous and unhealthy, but there it is, it is what has to be done until a better system is developed. Solder it with the iron, as quickly as possible. Now knock it up the taper and, with some luck, it will be so tight that the band starts to plane the timber with little curls on the leading edge. You would think at this point it could not go any tighter, but it can and it must. Once again, you must hammer the back of the mast band then squeeze it in the vice jaws, and resolder the original joint (file in teeth again!). The point of this last exercise is that the timber is eventually going to shrink and, if the band is not literally clenching the outer fish in a marked groove, it will come loose. The alternate bands which only go round the pole of the mast are captive, and cannot be knocked up but, by the same token, they cannot work loose either.

When all this is done, the rubbing paunch on the fore side of the mast is fixed over the soldered joints, hiding up all the joins, the good, the bad and the ugly. Do not oversize the paunch: it is less than half the width of the fish, and is only there as a rubbing strake, not really as a strengthening feature. The last job is to slip in all of the wedges, which really brings the work alive, giving it all the authenticity of a truly built-up mast, and is well worth the extra trouble.

The construction of the yards

As with the lower masts, the lower yards on fore, main and mizzen were built-up. They were also iron banded and battened at the centre of the bunt, as it was called, giving the appearance of a solid octagonal mass of timber around which the truss chain was attached. They were also strengthened against the lateral forces which the wind exerted on them, by baulks of timber stretching out as far as the yardarms, on the fore and aft side. The most obvious part played by the yards was as a horizontal pole to which the sail was bent: attached by the head rope of the sail to jackstay stanchions approximately 1ft apart. These lower yards were not only at the centre of the powering system of a sailing ship, but were also equally important was their role as the ultimate hoisting davit. Ship's launches, the barrels of guns, and the upper masts and yards were all lifted using these monster composite poles with block and tackle attached.[6] The yards

6. Nares, *op cit*.

are further complicated by their use as the messenger system for routing all the sheeting lines of the sails, so that they fairly bristle with detail needing careful research before they are set up on the model. Further accommodation on the fore and main yards has to include provision for stunsail booms, set in their irons at 45 degrees forward of the yard. These booms were used to catch the wind in light airs, or when the ship was being driven hard, and are part of the features of a complete masting system.

Square to round

My lower yards started off in the form of square stock, of timber which was felled at approximately the time that *Warrior* was launched in the 1860s. It is pitch pine, sweet-smelling and, although it was a cheap timber years ago, it is now extremely precious; it is also still full of resin, even after 130 years, and is a perfect delight to work. In the form of square stock, it is easy to mark up, with essential stations drilled out as guidelines. The most difficult part of yardmaking is knowing where you are as the yard is being planed down. By drilling out a series of very small holes, top and bottom as well fore and aft, you can tell exactly where you are at any given moment.

The dimensions of *Warrior*'s masts and yards are carefully documented both in length and diameter, and are given in the table overleaf. These dimensions differ slightly from those on the restoration, which follow those of a steel-masted clipper ship, rather than a timber-masted ship.

Manufacture of the yards

With the precious stock carefully marked up, and the O/S callipers close to hand, the first job in making the lower yard is to remove the timber next to the centre bunt. (The bunt of the yard is the central octag-

onal portion, which is battened both to strengthen it and to prevent it slipping in the chainstrop.) On the model this has to be done in order to get sufficient access for the spokeshave between the shoulder created by the bunt, and the portion of the yard which has to be planed down. The yard is too long for the lathe bed and, at this stage, too fat to pass through the headstock barrel, so the lathe is of no use - a comfort, no doubt, to those who do not possess one anyway. If you have a lathe, the easier method by far is to make the bunt of the yard separately, and bore it out at either end to receive the yard, a piece of information which should also be exercised later when it comes to the manufacture of the topmasts and topgallant masts. Despite the fact that I did this the awk-

Marking up positions for the iron banding on the main yard from scaled-up drawing.

Dimensions of Masts and Yards on *Warrior*[7]

Masts

Lower masts, deck to cap

Foremast	79ft 3in	diam 40in
Mainmasts	86ft 3in	diam 40in
Mizzen	67ft 6in	diam 26in

Topmasts

Fore and main	65ft 0in	diam 22 in
Mizzen	50ft 6in	diam 16in

Topgallant masts

Fore and main	52ft 6in	diam $12^1/_2$in
Mizzen	39ft 6in	diam 9in

Yards

Fore and mainmasts

Lower yards	105ft 0in	diam 25in
Topsail yards	74ft 0in	diam 16in
Topgallant yards	46ft 0in	diam 11in
Royal yards	32ft 6in	diam $6^1/_2$in

Mizzen

Crossjack	71ft 0in	diam 17in
Topsail yards	51ft 6in	diam $11^1/_2$in
Topgallant yards	33ft 6in	diam 8in
Royal yards	24ft 6in	diam 5in

Gaffs

Foremast	41ft 0in	diam 11in
Mainmast	49ft 0in	diam 11in
Spanker	49ft 0in	diam 11in

Bowsprit

Length outboard	40ft 2in	diam 35in
Length including housing	63ft 0in	
Jibbooms	44ft 6in	diam $15^1/_2$in
Flying jibbooms	44ft 9in	diam $8^1/_2$in

7. Ballard, Admiral G A, *The Black Battlefleet* (London: Society for Nautical Research, 1980), p250.

ward way, it was not that difficult to do, and it is always a pleasure to hand-plane masts, a pleasure enhanced by the pungent smell of spruce and resin.

The V-groove

Experienced modellers will know that it is handy to start off the reduction of the yard by using a V-groove shooting board, which helps keep the diminishing process

equal. It is normal to work with eight planed faces, until the final strokes are required to put it into the round, at which point the yard is fetched out of the V-groove and finished off on the flat surface of the bench, rolling it and planing it at the same time. For the octagonal section of the bunt, place the yard back into the jig and plane off the portion representing the battens at the centre of the bunt. A touch of sandpaper leaves nothing more to be done, but the manufacture of an identical twin.

The iron banding

This feature of both masts and yards is very distinctive and important, more so perhaps because the livery in which this ship is painted is not black, but buff, and this detail is therefore highly visual, with the shadows it casts being conspicuous even in a low light. When leathering the oars of the auxiliary boats, the use of old-fashioned brown gummed paper strip was put to good use, and this prompted my thought processes regarding possible further applications. The animal glue with which the paper is coated is moistened with water which temporarily expands the paper. When it dries out, it shrinks – which is ideal for the purpose of banding, because it shrinks so tightly in on itself that it squeezes out its own moisture and clings limpet-like to the timber. Experiments with strips of paper have shown that six turns around the yard perfectly mimic iron banding when painted.

The stunsail boom irons

These are the metal ferrules on the extreme ends of the yards which carry the stunsail booms. Their manufacture requires a little reflection in that if you make them and fit them in the original fashion, they must be soft-soldered *in situ*. An easier way is to take a piece of brass tubing which will slide over the end of the

Rolling and planing at the same time; sweet smelling pitch pine.

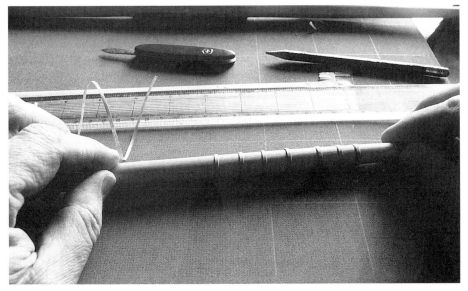

Banding made easy with the previously drilled holes marking locations for the gummed strip.

yardarm tip and cut the tubing so that it can be folded over its own end, filed down and silver-soldered. This will allow the ferrule to be centre-drilled (the object now looking like a spent cartridge case), and a piece of brass rod to be introduced, which will carry the arm and the iron hoop. On this second soldering, it will be possible to get a nicely-rounded blob, a feature of the metal ferrule. This is one of the advantages of hard-soldering, in that one can have more than one go at it, and in each case the flow of solder is controllable, quite unlike soft-solder.

Fighting tops

The Masting and Rigging of English Ships of War, by James Lees,[8] contains plans of fighting tops which exactly match those of the builder's model. From 1833 onwards, fighting tops of warships stopped using

8. Lees, J, *The Masting and Rigging of English Ships of War 1625-1860* (London: Conway Maritime Press, 1984 edn).

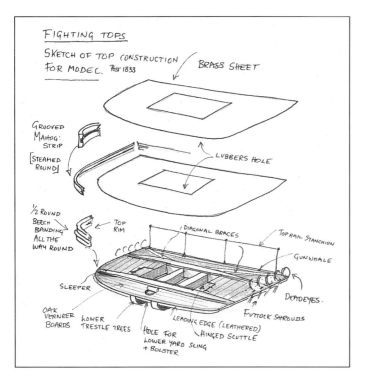

the fan-tailed strutting, and were flush-decked, except for the rim, the upper crosstrees, sometimes called sleepers, and the diagonal riders. The construction of fighting tops can be done by starting with a metal platform made from brass sheet individually boarded over in oak veneer. The outer rim should first be grooved in mahogany strip, and then steamed into shape, so that the top itself is enclosed mechanically all the way round its outer edge. A beech strip in half-round form can then be steamed and glued on the outer edge of the mahogany strip. This means that the fighting top is greatly strengthened, whilst still retaining scaled dimensions. As it is a meeting place for all kinds of roping to the topgallant masts, as well as futtocks to the lower masts, it needs this kind of inbuilt strength to resist the pull and tension of the ropes permanently attached to it. One may see the results of

(Above)
Illustration of fighting tops.
(Author)

(Right)
Underside of the main fighting top: below the outer rim, note the trestletrees, crosstrees, bibs, hounds, cheeks, necklace fittings for futtock shrouds, iron bands, iron hoops around the fish with chocking pieces, and the trysail mast abaft the mainmast; the fore section of the lower mainmast is protected by the rubbing paunch.

(Far right)
Fighting top viewed from the topside. Note the diagonal bracing, the bolsters and the mast battens. The top rope upper sheave can also be seen in the 'eighth squaring' of the top mast heeling. The sheave is set diagonally across the mast heel.

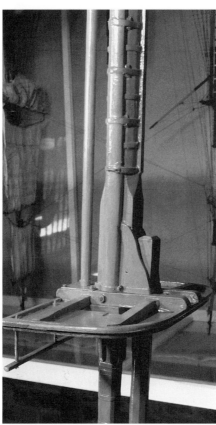

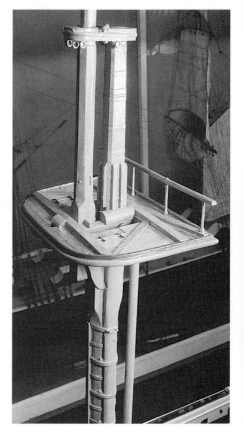

timber-built tops on old models, where they have assumed the shape of a broad-brimmed hat on their leading edge. Metal will not allow this to happen.

Trestletrees and crosstrees

Thoughts about metal platforms further up the masts continue with the subject of what to do about the topgallant trestle and crosstrees. Experience of working models dictates that they be made of metal; they have, of necessity, to appear to be lightly made, and yet be strong. The crosstrees perform three tasks: the provision of a platform, the housing of the topgallant mast, and the spreading of the topgallant backstays. The restoration crosstrees show small sections of fiddley grating, following the draft design of William Symonds, Surveyor of the Navy.[9] The model ones have metal bar grating for reasons of strength and, let it be truthfully said, because of the difficulty of fitting fiddley grating to a curved edge of metal. The ellipses involved with shaping this object present no problem to annealed brass. It can be effected with a pair of smooth-jawed pliers; were it to be made from timber, quite thick section would have to be steamed round and fitted to the outer rim, involving some difficult joints on the leading edge. The other plus factor for using metal is that the squared holes used for the mast heels and housing can be adjusted to shape, allowing for the rake of the royal masts. It is yet another example of using metal instead of wood wherever intrinsic strength is required.

Mast caps

The construction of these important items requires care. Decent hardwood stock is required: it must then be halved, then dowelled, and finally glued together,

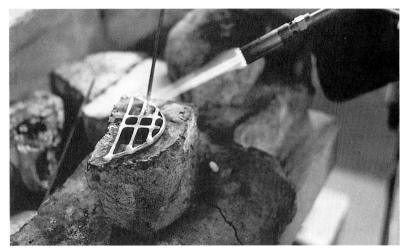

preferably contra-graining the joint. The reason for this is that, even where excellent timber is used, the mortise joint will have a tendency to split the cap in half, putting unacceptable strain on the grain of the timber where the mortise joints come close to the edge. The cross dowels prevent this happening, and the edge banding (steamed beech meat skewer planed to half-round section) takes care to bind the whole cap into compression. In full scale these caps were dovetailed together on the long grain, and that would be a perfectly acceptable way to construct them in miniature as well. This business of splitting mast caps is not just an issue with model shipwrights. All fighting vessels

(Top)
Trestletrees and crosstrees being silver-soldered.

(Above)
Bar grating on the crosstrees; brass rod soft-soldered.

9. *Ibid,* section 1, illustration 20.

Illustration of mast cop
construction.
(Author)

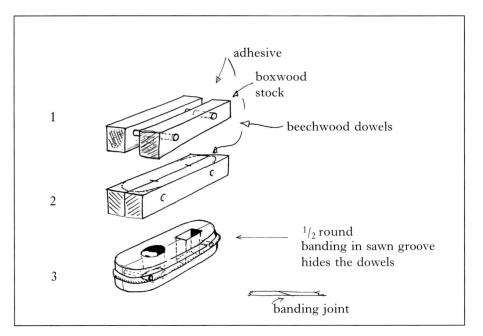

adhesive

boxwood

stock

beechwood dowels

1

2

$^1/_2$ round
banding in sawn groove
hides the dowels

3

banding joint

The masts and yards in
place.

carried spare caps, as a failure of one of
these could easily cause chaos aloft, and in
extreme cases immobilise a vessel.

The last consideration with the cap is
that the angle of the two centre mortises
must allow for the rake of the individual
mast and match the waterline of the ship,
and also be in parallel with the doublings of
the mast. Put more simply, where the heel of
the upper mast meets the top of the lower
mast, these two must be in parallel with one
another, and this is dependent on the gap
between the centres of the cap. There is no
room for error here, and allowance must be
made for the fact that both masts are in
tapered section. Expect to put in quite a few
hours into making these fittings, and expect
to make a few for the scrap box.

9
RIGGING AND THE ROPEWALK

It is possible to rig a model ship using a single thickness of miniature thread, but in order to capture the essence of both standing and running rigging in scale there is no escaping the need to spin your own ropes, in the different ways demanded by a full-size vessel. Thus arises the need to build your own ropewalk.

The ropewalk

My machine has been developing in stages for twenty years. Refinements have taken place during that time which mean that it is now almost totally automated, able to produce scale rope, hawser-, cable- and shroud-laid rope, in any required circumference. The same machine can be used for worming and parcelling the rope as well as serving it. This last technique, which is really just a final wrapping round the rope with fine thread, is particularly important as *Warrior* was wire-rigged in places, and serving the wire effectively is therefore an essential function. All the strops are made with a central core of copper wire wrapped with thread.

A trip to Chatham Dockyard to see the full-sized ropewalk in action convinced me to return home and cut the original machine in half. The fact that their ropehouse is a third of a mile long underlined the necessity of lengthening the distance between the headstock and tailstock, so that it is possible to increase greatly the manufactured length of the miniature rope, and save a great deal of precious time.

How rope is made

There are basically two functions to rope-making: first it must be spun from the headstock, and second, it must be hardened ('given back-twist' is the correct expression). Only when these two functions have been performed will it hold together without coming untwisted. The mechanical problem is that when rope is spun and hardened it shortens, so that any ropemaking machine must have some kind of slide built into its tailstock. Rope shortens by approximately 20 per cent during the process of manufacture, so that over a 10ft length for instance, it effectively shrinks by 2ft, thus giving a guide as to the ratio of travel needed at the tailstock end.

Essential parts and functions of the ropewalk machine

The headstock consists of a baseboard on which is mounted an electric drill in a stand. This drill has a reverse facility and variable speed. The ideal speed for rope spinning is approximately 150rpm: many

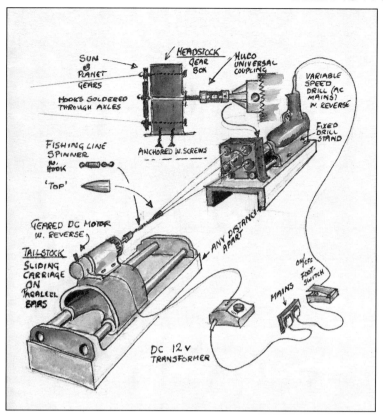

SUN & PLANET GEARS

HEADSTOCK GEAR BOX

HUCO UNIVERSAL COUPLING

VARIABLE SPEED DRILL (AC MAINS) W. REVERSE

HOOKS SOLDERED THROUGH AXLES

FIXED DRILL STAND

FISHING LINE SPINNER W. HOOK

ANCHORED W. SCREWS

'TOP'

GEARED DC MOTOR W. REVERSE

ANY DISTANCE APART

ON/OFF FOOT-SWITCH

TAILSTOCK SLIDING CARRIAGE ON PARALLEL BARS

MAINS

DC 12V TRANSFORMER

Sketch of ropewalk.
(Author)

whirls as they are properly called, are formed by drilling through the axles and inserting some $1/16$in wire hooks. The solid block of hardwood is anchored to the baseboard very securely. A good deal of strain is exerted on this item, so it needs to be sturdily built. The sun and planet cogwheel set-up allows the four outer hooks to travel at the same speed and in the same direction. The centre axle and hook of course revolve in the opposite direction.

Universal coupling

Unless your engineering is exceptional, it is a good idea to use a Huco universal coupling between the electric drill and the gearbox to take out any misalignment. These couplings are remarkably tough, even though they may not look it. Try to centre the height of the electric drill in the stand to the centre of the gearbox, as this will remove all strain and vibration as far as the drive is concerned. Apart from the electric drill having a cut-out foot switch, which is useful when emergency snarl-ups happen, that concludes the headstock, and it may be placed as far apart from the tailstock as the slide travel will allow. It will be kept in place by its own weight, and a piece of carpet underneath it will considerably muffle its noise.

The tailstock

In a basic machine, there are only two requirements of the tailstock. The first one is that the cradle can be dragged along effortlessly against the pull of the shortening rope as it is formed; it should be noted that some of the ropes are very fine indeed, so that there must be almost no resistance against being drawn along the parallel bars. One refinement is to tip the end of the bars up slightly, to facilitate the sliding motion with a touch of gravity.

of the cordless screwdrivers now available revolve at 120rpm, which is perfectly acceptable; they also have a reverse function, so that left- or right-hand rope can be laid with them, but you will need to adapt the switch.

Gearbox at the headstock

The set-up has five gearwheels, four of them planet wheels to a large central cogwheel, with the advantage of higher gearing for the rope spinning, and a lower gear for the centre driver when used in serving mode. (Although the gear wheels I use are old Fischer-Technik products, similar things are available from Lego and other companies such as Proops Bros.) Each gear wheel has an axle through it, which ends on the foreside of the gearbox with an open hook, and on the aft side with a collar to keep it captive; the box is a block of hardwood fitted with metal tube bushes in which the axles run. The hooks, or

Second, a spinner must be introduced between the tailstock motor and the single hook fitted in the chuck. The spinner spins as the rope is being twisted and closed, and it is immaterial as far as the spinner is concerned which way the rope is being laid up. These spinners are available from fishing tackle shops, and are ball-raced against the strain of a really heavy catch.

Other possibilities

The same effect on the tailstock can be had by using weights and pulleys according to the strengths required by the different sizes of threads and cottons being used. Many of the hand-cranked versions of ropewalks use this idea. A sliding bar tailstock does have the advantage over the weights and pulleys idea in that it will stay wherever it is placed, and this is useful when going from the process of spinning to the process of hardening, as will be described below. It also makes tying up the ends and tensioning easier, and allows operations to take place without any need for a gravity drop at the end of the bench.

Power in the tailstock

It is not necessary to have power at both ends of the ropewalk, but it is a feature which saves time. The very precise rheostat fitted to the type of transformer used for model railways gives real precision to serving rope, and the reverse function is useful when the thread misbehaves and one needs to unwind the wrongly-applied turns with the flick of a switch. The DC motor itself is geared, and this adds to its versatility in the different roles required of it.

Yarn

Linen threads and best quality mercerised cotton are two favourite standbys of mine; traditional cobblers and leatherworkers use a thread which is waxy in appearance and made in shades of dark brown and black in a glacé finish, sometimes described as mercerised thread.[1] The 50g spools are in the region of 500m long: they are expensive, but of wonderful quality, and as strong as the proverbial old boot. The thread is 0.018in thick, and this is ideal for the yarns of shrouds and forestays, etc, at 1:48 scale. A trip to the upholsterer's is the next port of call: they use a linen thread straight off the hank, and you get very good value for money this way. They do different shades in the darker colours which nicely ape the real thing, in that not all ropes either in the standing rigging, or the running rigging, are of the same age and colour. Tar-pitch, when it is ageing, goes back to a nut-brown colour, which many of these threads are produced in. The only trouble is that you have to spool these hanks, and that means an extra pair of willing hands. This material is slightly thicker than the Barbour thread at an average of 0.021in (an exact inch diameter, in scale of 1:48). The last of the favourites is mercerised cotton made by Sylko. This is a cotton thread, available in deep brown (code 217), which does not go fluffy when spun into ropes. The mercerised cotton is just 0.005in thick, so it can be used for the very finest running rigging, as well as in multiple yarns for all other sizes.

Right- and left-hand laid

All of these threads and cottons are manufactured in right-hand lay. When you come to lay up ropes, right-hand lay becomes left-handed rope. This is a nuisance, because it means that the first action of spinning the rope on the machine has to unravel the natural lay of the thread or cotton before it can be laid up right-handed. As the majority of ship's rope is right-handed, there is a great deal of rope-spinning to do: thus arises the need for variable speed on the headstock end, if possible. As the yarn untwists from

1. Available from Barbour (see list of suppliers).

its natural lay, first of all it slackens and the tailstock needs adjusting to keep the yarns tight, the operator pushing it away from the headstock. As the yarns tighten up again, so the tailstock cradle will be dragged towards the headstock once more. The slack in this operation is only an inch or so, and not as marked as when the yarns are being spun into rope.

Hawser, cable and shroud

Hawser-laid rope is the most commonly used and is constructed from three strands of rope, laid right-handed. Cable-laid rope is thick and strong, and used for the heaviest work, as the name suggests. It is laid up left-handed from three ordinary ropes twisted together, nine strands in all. If it were not laid left-handed, the strands would become untwisted and the rope would fall apart. Gun tackle is also laid up left-handed, but the yarns and strands are both right-handed, which makes the rope much softer and easier to handle. Few are aware of this, and all sorts of odd explanations are offered in a half-understood way. The disadvantage to rope laid in this way is that it is more liable to soak up water, and, of course, gun decks were made artificially wet by use of the hoses under general quarters in order to prevent fire.

Using the ropemaking machine

Having selected the thread or cotton according to what sort of rope is required, it is a question of tying up individually from the hooks at the headstock, feeding them through the spinner/looper in the tailstock, and tying them off together in equal tension using a single knot: a pair of miniature pliers with offset tips is an indispensable tool for knot-tying.

The top

There is one important free-standing item which has not yet been mentioned. This is the top, a cone shaped from hardwood, with either three or four grooves in it. It should really be the shape of a bullet, with a piece of robust wire let into the aft end of it. Two of them are required for either three- or four-stranded rope. They should be made from hardwood, polished and waxed, so that they slip down the rope being formed easily. The top controls the lay of the rope and, to some extent, the hardness of the finished rope. What happens is that when the headstock whirls start turning, the top will be squeezed along the rope as it closes in on itself. In hand operation only, by pressing the top against the tension, one can alter the angle of lay; the narrower the angle, the tighter the rope. In the automated version of the machine, this top can travel suspended from an overhead wire, and this saves much walking up and down. The skill is in knowing how much pressure to use, and the penalty for trying to make it too hard is that one can snap the strands. So speed, feel and practice are essential ingredients.

Rope hardening: applying back-twist

Once the ropes are closed together, the rope is only half made. The next operation is to harden the rope. In full-sized practice this means cutting off the strands from the hooks on the headstock, tying them together, and tightening the whole rope, so that the strands bite together. This process is done between a fixed hook, on the tailstock motor in place of the spinner, and the centre driving hook on the headstock. It is driven from the tailstock end. Because it is possible to drive from the tailstock, you leave the strands on the headstock hook in place, remove the spinner and knot the rope over the fixed hook in the tailstock motor chuck, and spin the rope into the hardened state. The process of hardening does not use up so much energy as the process of spinning the yarns, but it does visibly shorten the rope, giving it that special property of stretch which is so useful when it comes to rigging the vessel.

Shortened operating instructions

Tie the threads individually to the headstock hooks.

Roughly trim to length at tailstock.

Leave sufficient length for tying the knot.

Run hand through the threads to ensure no tangles.

Make sure the tension is even.

Tie off all the strands to spinner at tailstock, in one knot.

Insert the appropriate top.

Drive from the headstock. Top will be forced from tail to head.

Disconnect rope from spinner (but see comments below).

Tie the rope to the fixed hook at the tailstock end.

Spin the rope until fibres are tightly formed.

The rope is now formed and ready, and will not unravel.

In my machine I have a fine hook fitted into the pin chuck to which the spinner ring on the front end can be attached, obviating the need to remove the spinner and knot the rope. One simply hooks the front of the spinner directly to the hook in the pin chuck, making it into direct drive.

Serving process on the ropewalk

Serving is the outer wrapping of a rope or wire, and is what you see on the standing rigging many of the old restored ships. What goes on in the inner part of the rope is, from a modeller's point of view, somewhat academic, provided the finished scale of the rope is correct, and the served wrapping of suitable size and strength. This means that what goes on in the inside in the centre core can be of any material you wish, and silvered copper wire can be used as the central core for all the yard

Close-up of the fisherman's spinner and the hardwood 'top' (three-grooved). The spinner allows the rope to be spun from the headstock end, until the strands automatically squeeze the top along the length of the rope.

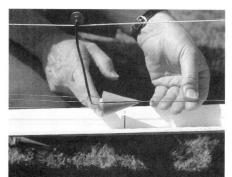

Controlling the top as the rope is spun; by pressing the top against the rope, it is possible to control the tightness of the lay.

strops, as this makes it very much easier to attach them tightly to such locations as yardarms, where they can be spot-soldered in an almost invisible way. The silvered copper wire is served on the ropewalk with an outer wrapping of thread, using aliphatic resin wood glue to hold it all together. When and where the two ends of the strops need to be soldered, the wrapping can be pulled off exposing the copper wire for the process. This makes a strong and neat joint, and saves many traditional hours of stropmaking.

Serving

The difficulty with serving (or wrapping) rope or wire is that one must adapt the machine to produce long lengths of very evenly-wound miniature rope. The introduction of a slope in the form of a long V-groove, which runs from the tailstock end of the ropewalk towards the headstock, means that the spool can be made to feed automatically using gravity, without demanding the skill required to push it gently by hand. Experiment has shown that a 5-degree slope is ideal for letting gravity do its job. But there is also a secondary problem, concerned only with the thread spool that, just occasionally, where the thread has been too tightly wound by the manufacturers onto the spool, it leaves the bars, and is hauled up to the central core causing chaos. Thread, by its nature, is variable in thickness, so wherever it is used this problem is going to be present. It particularly applies when coming towards the end of the spool where it compacts together. It never happens with mercerised cotton, which is perfectly even. The problem of the lifting spool can be cured by inserting a short length of brass bar into the spool centre to weigh it down, with miniature pegs to keep it captive.

The outrigger

When you unwind a spool, as seen from top dead centre, the unwinding comes from the side of the spool, which is its most direct feeding point. Therefore, it behaves best when the V-groove is offset to half the width of the spool from the point where it is being driven. Now, one could rejig the whole machine to allow for this, but in practice it is not necessary. An outrigger, initially in the form of a clothes peg, will be sufficient to overcome the problem. With this simple attachment, lining up the feed to the spool, it works faultlessly.

Finish

The wrapping needs to be treated with varnish, both for its appearance and to hold it all together. (I have found that Ronseal Mattshine does the job well, as does Rustin's Button Polish.) The easiest way to apply varnish to rope is to leave it under tension on the ropewalk and use a piece of angle bar, with some varnish in the V-groove, which can be moved along the backside of the thread, whilst at the same time brushing it with varnish on the front. In this way it all gets a good soaking. The angle bar needs to be approximately 6in long and fitted with a small handle. Matt shine varnish enhances the dark brown colour and gives it a dull sheen, reminiscent of that slightly glazed appearance of tar and without the weighty look of

The top nearing the end of the run.

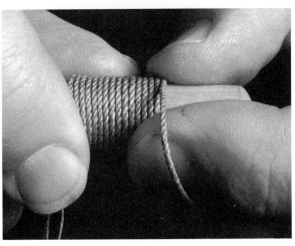

Miniature rope does not look or behave like string. The righthand-lay (hawser) clearly shows when coiled.

paint. The larger diameters show the serving very clearly, whilst the smaller diameters can be felt more than seen, but very close observation will show that this process has been correctly done, if by somewhat devious means.

The extended V-groove, down which the reel of thread descends using gravity as it wraps itself around the central core of miniature rope. The rope is driven at approximately 150rpm from the small DC motor at the tailstock end.

Blocks

Sir Marc Brunel, father of Isambard Kingdom Brunel, invented a blockmaking machine which to all intents and purposes automated the production of blockmaking for the Royal Navy. It saved the Admiralty £24,000 per annum, and greatly improved the product, which is food for thought for those intent on buying in the item rather than tooling up to make it mechanically. Even in miniature, there are literally hundreds of these blocks to be made, in their various versions, and it is therefore necessary to consider automating the process wherever possible.

These blocks are small, so if they can be made in a strip, as far as the machining is concerned this considerably reduces the 'fiddle factor'. If they are going to work, they must also be accurately and uniformly made. Insistence on the very finest hardwoods is essential because of the forces exerted upon them during the manufacturing process. In my travels I have discovered some prepacked hardwood ends, cut to the right sort of dimensions (5in x $1/2$in), used by those who turn fancy lace bobbins for lacemakers. The woods include such exotica as black ebony, wenge, tigerwood, satinwood, greenheart, rosewood, etc, as well as kingwood and cherry.

Following the legend of the sketched drawings, you do not have to possess a miniature circular saw or a lathe to produce these blocks, as every process can be done with hand tools.

Use aliphatic glue and a short length of copper wire twisted up in the presawn groove to compress the joint tightly. The copper wire is dispensed with when the joint is dry. It is much easier to file off the corners with a scrap of timber passing through the block. Do not file away too much, as you must leave some thickness of timber between the slot and the edge.

For the sheave, anything which will revolve on an axle will do. Only very close inspection reveals whether or not a sheave

Details of thimbles.
(Author)

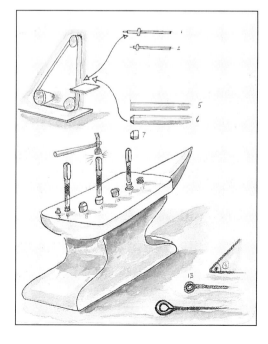

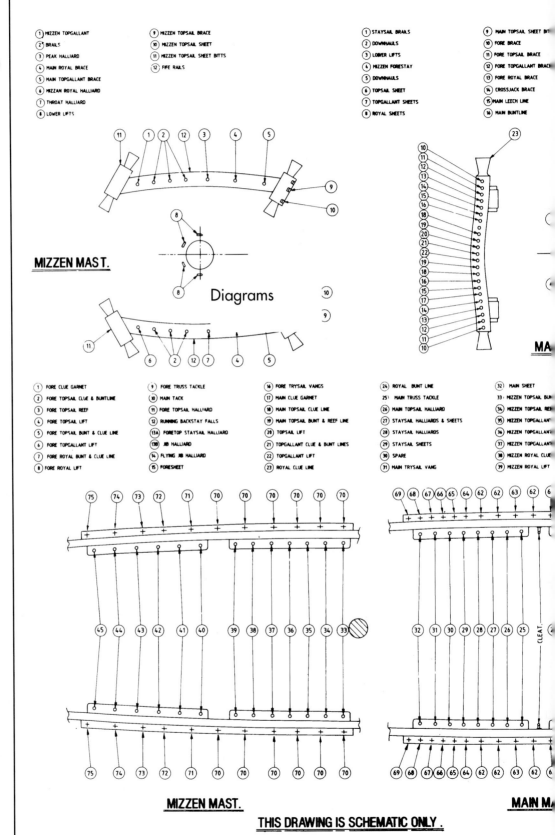

1 MIZZEN TOPGALLANT
2 BRAILS
3 PEAK HALLIARD
4 MAIN ROYAL BRACE
5 MAIN TOPGALLANT BRACE
6 MIZZEN ROYAL HALLIARD
7 THROAT HALLIARD
8 LOWER LIFTS

9 MIZZEN TOPSAIL BRACE
10 MIZZEN TOPSAIL SHEET
11 MIZZEN TOPSAIL SHEET BITTS
12 FIFE RAILS

1 STAYSAIL BRAILS
2 DOWNHAULS
3 LOWER LIFTS
4 MIZZEN FORESTAY
5 DOWNHAULS
6 TOPSAIL SHEET
7 TOPGALLANT SHEETS
8 ROYAL SHEETS

9 MAIN TOPSAIL SHEET BITT
10 FORE BRACE
11 FORE TOPSAIL BRACE
12 FORE TOPGALLANT BRACE
13 FORE ROYAL BRACE
14 CROSSJACK BRACE
15 MAIN LEECH LINE
16 MAIN BUNTLINE

MIZZEN MAST.

Diagrams

1 FORE CLUE GARNET
2 FORE TOPSAIL CLUE & BUNTLINE
3 FORE TOPSAIL REEF
4 FORE TOPSAIL LIFT
5 FORE TOPSAIL BUNT & CLUE LINE
6 FORE TOPGALLANT LIFT
7 FORE ROYAL BUNT & CLUE LINE
8 FORE ROYAL LIFT

9 FORE TRUSS TACKLE
10 MAIN TACK
11 FORE TOPSAIL HALLIARD
12 RUNNING BACKSTAY FALLS
13A FORETOP STAYSAIL HALLIARD
13B JIB HALLIARD
14 FLYING JIB HALLIARD
15 FORESHEET

16 FORE TRYSAIL VANGS
17 MAIN CLUE GARNET
18 MAIN TOPSAIL CLUE LINE
19 MAIN TOPSAIL BUNT & REEF LINE
20 TOPSAIL LIFT
21 TOPGALLANT CLUE & BUNT LINES
22 TOPGALLANT LIFT
23 ROYAL CLUE LINE

24 ROYAL BUNT LINE
25 MAIN TRUSS TACKLE
26 MAIN TOPSAIL HALLIARD
27 STAYSAIL HALLIARDS & SHEETS
28 STAYSAIL HALLIARDS
29 STAYSAIL SHEETS
30 SPARE
31 MAIN TRYSAIL VANG

32 MAIN SHEET
33 MIZZEN TOPSAIL BUN
34 MIZZEN TOPSAIL REE
35 MIZZEN TOPGALLANT
36 MIZZEN TOPGALLANT
37 MIZZEN TOPGALLANT
38 MIZZEN ROYAL CLUE
39 MIZZEN ROYAL LIFT

MIZZEN MAST.   **MAIN M**

THIS DRAWING IS SCHEMATIC ONLY.

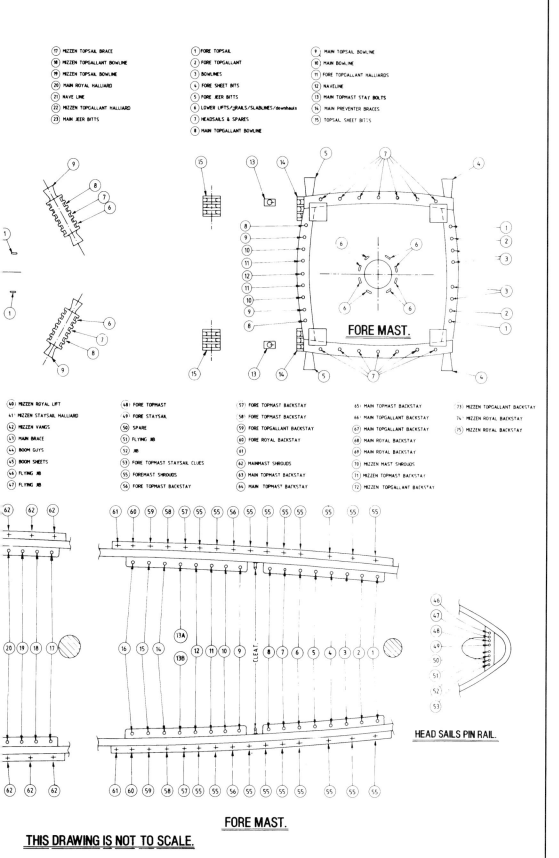

17 MIZZEN TOPSAIL BRACE
18 MIZZEN TOPGALLANT BOWLINE
19 MIZZEN TOPSAIL BOWLINE
20 MAIN ROYAL HALLIARD
21 NAVE LINE
22 MIZZEN TOPGALLANT HALLIARD
23 MAIN JEER BITTS

1 FORE TOPSAIL
2 FORE TOPGALLANT
3 BOWLINES
4 FORE SHEET BITS
5 FORE JEER BITS
6 LOWER LIFTS/RAILS/SLABLINES/downhauls
7 HEADSAILS & SPARES
8 MAIN TOPGALLANT BOWLINE

9 MAIN TOPSAIL BOWLINE
10 MAIN BOWLINE
11 FORE TOPGALLANT HALLIARDS
12 NAVELINE
13 MAIN TOPMAST STAY BOLTS
14 MAIN PREVENTER BRACES
15 TOPSAL SHEET BITTS

FORE MAST.

40 MIZZEN ROYAL LIFT
41 MIZZEN STAYSAIL HALLIARD
42 MIZZEN VANGS
43 MAIN BRACE
44 BOOM GUYS
45 BOOM SHEETS
46 FLYING JIB
47 FLYING JIB

48 FORE TOPMAST
49 FORE STAYSAIL
50 SPARE
51 FLYING JIB
52 JIB
53 FORE TOPMAST STAYSAIL CLUES
55 FOREMAST SHROUDS
56 FORE TOPMAST BACKSTAY

57 FORE TOPMAST BACKSTAY
58 FORE TOPMAST BACKSTAY
59 FORE TOPGALLANT BACKSTAY
60 FORE ROYAL BACKSTAY
61
62 MAINMAST SHROUDS
63 MAIN TOPMAST BACKSTAY
64 MAIN TOPMAST BACKSTAY

65 MAIN TOPMAST BACKSTAY
66 MAIN TOPGALLANT BACKSTAY
67 MAIN TOPGALLANT BACKSTAY
68 MAIN ROYAL BACKSTAY
69 MAIN ROYAL BACKSTAY
70 MIZZEN MAST SHROUDS
71 MIZZEN TOPMAST BACKSTAY
72 MIZZEN TOPGALLANT BACKSTAY

73 MIZZEN TOPGALLANT BACKSTAY
74 MIZZEN ROYAL BACKSTAY
75 MIZZEN ROYAL BACKSTAY

HEAD SAILS PIN RAIL.

FORE MAST.

THIS DRAWING IS NOT TO SCALE.

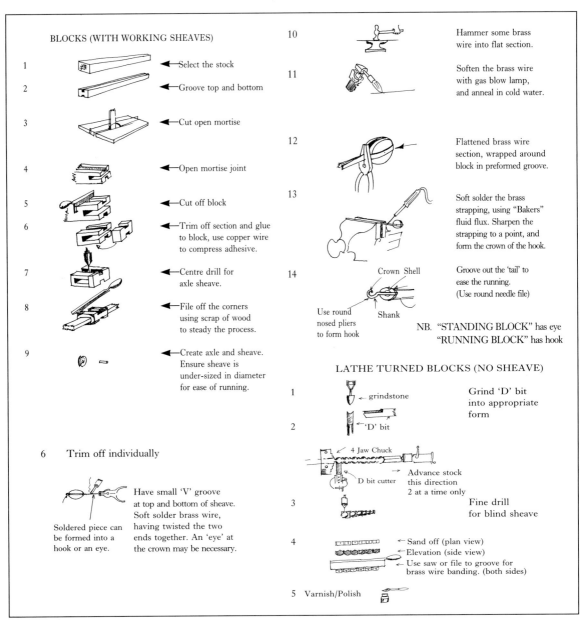

BLOCKS (WITH WORKING SHEAVES)

1 — Select the stock

2 — Groove top and bottom

3 — Cut open mortise

4 — Open mortise joint

5 — Cut off block

6 — Trim off section and glue to block, use copper wire to compress adhesive.

7 — Centre drill for axle sheave.

8 — File off the corners using scrap of wood to steady the process.

9 — Create axle and sheave. Ensure sheave is under-sized in diameter for ease of running.

10 — Hammer some brass wire into flat section.

11 — Soften the brass wire with gas blow lamp, and anneal in cold water.

12 — Flattened brass wire section, wrapped around block in preformed groove.

13 — Soft solder the brass strapping, using "Bakers" fluid flux. Sharpen the strapping to a point, and form the crown of the hook.

14 — Groove out the 'tail' to ease the running. (Use round needle file)

Crown   Shell

Use round nosed pliers to form hook

Shank

NB. "STANDING BLOCK" has eye "RUNNING BLOCK" has hook

LATHE TURNED BLOCKS (NO SHEAVE)

1 — grindstone — Grind 'D' bit into appropriate form

2 — 'D' bit

— 4 Jaw Chuck — Advance stock this direction 2 at a time only

D bit cutter

3 — Fine drill for blind sheave

4 — Sand off (plan view) — Elevation (side view) — Use saw or file to groove for brass wire banding. (both sides)

5 Varnish/Polish

6   Trim off individually

Soldered piece can be formed into a hook or an eye.

Have small 'V' groove at top and bottom of sheave. Soft solder brass wire, having twisted the two ends together. An 'eye' at the crown may be necessary.

Illustrations of blockmaking in miniature. (Author)

is present, and some modelmakers find the axle itself is quite sufficient.

Use 0.032in brass wire, which hammers out to approximately $\frac{1}{16}$in. The trouble is that the hammering process hardens it, so that it will not follow the contours of the block unless you soften it with heat to red hot. After that it behaves well and will hug the contour of the block prior to soft-soldering in the vice. After soldering, sharpen the joined brass strip to a point half an inch or so from the shell of the block and use a pair of miniature round-nosed pliers to form the hook of the eye. Grooving out the tail adds that little bit of professionalism and allows the sheet/rope to lie within the parallel of the shell. One often sees models where the ropes bulge out of the sheaves, looking unrealistic and awkward.

Although these blocks look like coffee beans, they do have a great deal of grace and charm about them. A well-made block has the smoothness of a bar of soap about it, and it should have a smile on its face as well. If they do not smile at you, then the slot is not going far enough to the extremity of the shell, or you are not using a sufficiently wide strip of timber. When they are right, they smile on both cheeks!

The sheaveless blocks

Even on a working model, not all the blocks will need to be sheaved, and a hole or holes will be quite adequate for the vast majority of the single-stropped blocks. A very simple lathe is required for this method. It could be done with an electric drill, and it is within the capacity of DC equipment as well. You will need a grindstone to make the shape of the tool bit cutter, which is basically oval in nature. The tool bit will need to work close to the jaws of the chuck for the best result, and the idea is to produce a string of wooden beads, out of a piece of square timber.

Next sand or grind away the sides of the beads, still in a strip, having first drilled the hole or holes through the block. Note that when making a sheaveless block, the hole should not be drilled through at top dead centre; you must make allowance for the fact that the sheave brings the rope out near the end of the slot, so that there is a right way up. Next make a light saw cut for the groove, which will house the strap

or strop. After a coat of varnish, saw the blocks off, and make a V-groove top and bottom with a saw or file. With these tiny blocks it is acceptable simply to use annealed brass or copper wire, and twist the ends into either a hook or an eye and soft-solder them accordingly. Use a round needle file across the hole on the tail end to complete the process.

All shapes and sizes

There are a great many types and shapes and sizes of these blocks, and different ways of stropping them as well; sister blocks, jeer blocks, hanging blocks, jewel blocks, etc, and a personal favourite, the fiddle block which, as the name suggests, looks like a violin hanging upside down. But they can all be made on one or other of the two principles outlined above, and what a difference it makes to see them fabricated from the different dark-coloured hardwoods now available.

Rigging the bowsprit: the cat's whiskers

The javelin shape of the the bowsprit, pointing the way forward for the whole ship to follow in fair weather and in foul,

Production of blind sheaved blocks in satinwood. Note the crescent shape of the tool cutter D-bit.

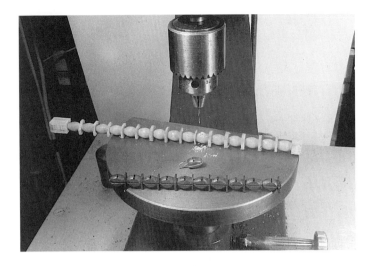

This particular bowsprit, being timbered, has very little to do with that as fitted to the restoration, which is made from steel. The original style of bowsprit is as depicted on the builder's model and in the very early photographs of the ship. The main visual difference is in the girth, and

(Above)
Piercing through the blocks. This operation needs to be done from both sides for greater accuracy. They ought *not* to be drilled at top dead centre. The square section from which these blocks are turned presents the timber conveniently for drilling, and makes easier the saw cut on the (planed) side of the blocks, which takes the stropping. This is shown on the front row of blocks on the drilling machine table.

(Centre right)
Setting up the initial rigging lines. The different sizes of the handmade rope and the sag of the chains look well together.

(Right)
Block with working sheave made from rosewood, stropped with brass banding ending in a hook.

epitomises the fast sailing ship. The appeal of this spiked projection has to do with both the setting and the rake of the three sections of timber (bowsprit, jibboom and flying jibboom) which in the case of *Warrior* together make a protrusion of 40ft 2in. Crossing this handsome feature are the spritsail gaffs, which are somewhat of an anachronistic feature in that there was never any intention of bending a sail to them, but they do provide some spread and back tension to both the dolphin striker and the tip of the flying jibboom.

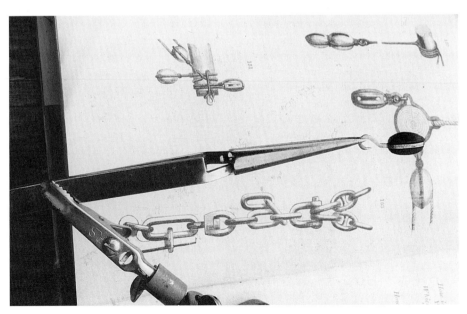

the presence of the spritsail gaffs which are sited well aft of the bowsprit cap in the traditional place for such items. The restoration ones are no more than whisker poles, and belong to the period of the 1870s rather than the 1860s. It is interesting that all of the paintings so far done of this ship following the restoration have this detail copied from the restored ship, rather than the original: this underlines how thorough one needs to be in one's research before attempting a truly accurate pictorial representation. In 1878 there were plans for re-rigging *Warrior* with steel poles, but they were never carried out. When it came to the 1980s restoration programme, steel was chosen for a number of quite logical reasons, with the most important considerations being cost and maintenance. The thought of restoring timbered masting was totally out of the question.

Vulnerability

The mere thought of attempting to rig this mighty projection must cause considerable feelings of excitement, given that there is an immense visual appeal in the dramatic contrast engendered by the juxtaposition of all that weight with the will-o'-the-wisp nature of the rigging lines themselves. Because this part of the ship's rigging lies almost horizontally, one can not only see, but also appreciate it more fully than the rest, containing as it does all the different sizes of roping and chain. There is also an accompanying look of vulnerability, which forcibly reminds the onlooker how skilfully these ships had to be handled in order to avoid the indignity of collision and entanglement, especially when in harbour.

The demand of what is really a three-pointed anchorage of support for the spars accounts for the attractive look of rigging in the way that it quickly builds into a series of triangles, a geometry which is echoed in the fore and aft sails, and the staysails throughout the ship. Why these

shapes should appear so attractive is beyond my remit to investigate, but it is certainly true that there is a deep appeal to the emotions in the combination of shapes encompassed in the display of rigging and canvas presented by sailing ships.

Chained down

You must move cautiously when rigging a ship model, and it is a process which must be preceded by thorough research. You must read as much of the classical literature on the subject as possible, and look at as many good-quality models, particularly contemporary ones, which are now housed in museums and collections. Much can be learned by looking at the major full-scale restoration projects, and perhaps most important of all, by schematic sketching. No-one these days has first-hand experience of sailing Victorian ships. This means that we have to learn from books, of which there are plenty, just how the sailing ship developed, both in the commercial world, and in the Royal Navy, at the end of this glorious period of shipping.

There are five books which ought to be consulted by anyone wanting to rig a warship of the period 1860-80, and without the expertise which they contain one simply could not make any accurate headway at all. The first is Nares' *Seamanship* , a facsimile book of a work first published as *The Naval Cadet's Guide:* or *a Seaman's Companion*.[2] This is particularly good in terms of the high technical quality of the contemporary drawings and illustrations which it contains, and the instructions of how a ship of this period was

Bowsprit on restoration, built from steel. Note the position of the spritsail gaff booms and iron-banded cap, plus single chain bobstay.

2. Nares, Lieut George S, *Seamanship* (1862), first published in 1860 as *The Naval Cadet's Guide: Seaman's Companion*), facsimile of second edition, introduced by David R Macgregor (Woking: Gresham Books, 1979).

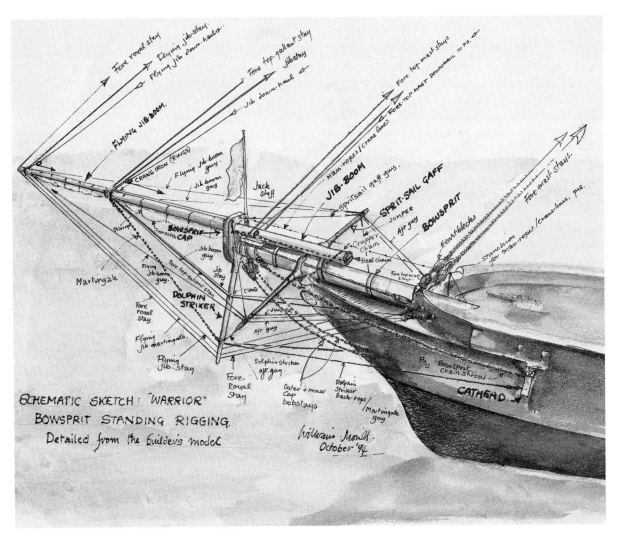

Within the illustration (schematic sketch labels):

Fore royal stay. Flying jibstay. Flying jib down-haul. Fore top-gallant stay. Jib down-haul. Fore top-mast stays. FORE-TOP MAST DOWNHAUL TO P.S. Man-ropes/crane lines. Fore top mast stays to P.S. Fore-mast stays. FLYING JIB BOOM. CRANE IRON (RINGS). Flying jib boom guy. Jib boom guy. Jack staff. JIB-BOOM. Spritsail gaff guy. SPRIT-SAIL GAFF. Jumper. Aft guy. BOWSPRIT. Heart blocks. Stanchion for man-ropes/crane-line. P.S. Stirrups. BOWSPRIT CAP. FOOT ROPE. Jib boom guy. Crupper Chain. Heel chain. Fore top-mast stays. Martingale. Jib boom guy. Flying jib boom guy. Fore top-gallant stay. Jib stay. Cleats. Jumper. Fore royal stay. DOLPHIN STRIKER. Flying jib martingale. Aft guy. Fore-Royal Stay. Flying Jib-stay. Dolphin striker aft guy. Outer + inner Cap bobstays. Dolphin Striker Back-rope/Martingale guy. P.S. Bowsprit Chain Shroud. CATHEAD.

SCHEMATIC SKETCH: "WARRIOR" BOWSPRIT STANDING RIGGING. Detailed from the Builder's model.

William Mowll. October '94.

Schematic on bowsprit standing rigging. (Author)

rigged and worked. *The Masting and Rigging of English Ships of War 1625-1860*,[3] written by J Lees, is useful in the logical way in which it is put together, and also for the illustrations (many of which are taken from Nares' *Seamanship*). It also describes chronologically the development of masts, rigging and sails throughout the 235 years which it covers. H Underhill's *Masting and Rigging the Clipper Ship and Ocean Carrier*[4] is an aid to understanding what the restorers have done to *Warrior* in the way of wire rigging and steel masts. It is also profusely illustrated, but one must bear in mind the original *Warrior* was wooden masted and sparred, although rigged on the lower masts with iron wire. John Wells' excellent book, *Immortal Warrior*,[5] is indispensable for its wealth of

technical and historical detail, as well as carrying some very detailed and accurate illustrations by the Technical Illustration Department of the Bournemouth and Poole College of Art, who have developed a highly-regarded expertise in this particular field. Finally, *The Black Battlefleet*[6] by Admiral G A Ballard is the contemporary *vade-mecum* of the capital ship in transition.

Wood and iron

In the 1860s the art of shipbuilding and of ship rigging were both poised on the cusp between the use of wood and of iron. *Warrior* was equipped with wooden lower masts with iron wire rigging, as had been the SS *Great Britain* seventeen years before. Wood and armour-plating, in the form of a sandwich, were also used for her protection, and the masts and spars of this ship were covered with wrought iron hoops and bands at all the points where strength was required. Wrought iron chain was used wherever strains occurred over and above what hemp could stand, and this included trussing the masts, as well as the bobstays and backguys, to say nothing of the forged iron anchors and other mast lashings; the ship fairly bristled with chain.

A first glance at the issue of rigging a bowsprit of the 1860s is a bit daunting, but so long as panic does not set in, it is all very logical and practical. Nares' *Seamanship* manual makes several bold statements about rigging which reduce the terror factor by appealing to simple logic: 'Every spar must be supported by ropes led in three different directions. A rope supporting any mast from forward is called a stay; and the side supports are called either shrouds, backstays or guys'.[7] The function of the bowsprit was to provide a rigid, near-horizontal projection to the rest of the vertical rigging. It was all about restraining the masting system and rooting it to the vessel, which accounts for the chains of the bobstay and martingale, which prevent the tendency of the stays to pull the rigging upwards and outwards. The second effect of this forward projection was to provide a point of leverage at the extreme of the vessel, which improved the steering of what was known to be a very stiff ship, so that the jib and flying jibsails were, operationally speaking, two of the most important sails aboard.

On the underside of the bowsprit, the outer and inner cap bobstays were anchored to the ship's iron knee, continuing the curve of the cutwater in a very eye-catching way. Side pull to the bowsprit was checked by the chain shrouds, port and starboard, anchored to the cathead knee. The same function was provided for the jibboom by the martingale, and the flying jibboom was restrained in upward pull by the flying jib martingale, which is the middle rope of the extreme headstays, reeving through the dolphin striker.

Wire rigging

Such is the integrity of the Science Museum model that wherever iron wire rigging was used on the original, so the modelmakers have faithfully reproduced the work using braided brass wire. The use of brass braided wire for a working model is fraught with difficulties, and when you look closely at the builder's model, the reasons are very obvious. One small injury to brass wire kinks it in an irreparable way, added to which the tensions of brass wire have to be nearly perfect at every fixing, because there is virtually no stretch in the material. The Science Museum model has only had one move in its life, but that does not include surviving two World Wars, during which times the model must have been put into storage. At some stage in its existence it has been badly handled, with the result that the bowsprit rigging has been damaged and somewhat spoiled.

Waxed linen thread

For the working model, it seems foolish to use anything apart from spun linen thread throughout the ship. The handmade rope has as one of its most delightful features a good deal of elasticity, which is imparted to the rope in the hardening stage of manufacture.

Metal stropping

Metal wire (copper) has been introduced into the stropping of the heart blocks to make both the seizing and the thimble through which the length of rope is threaded. This is the most practical way of rigging a working model, where all injuries and snagging to the lines can easi-

3. Lees, J, *The Masting and Rigging of English Ships of War 1625-1860* (London: Conway Maritime Prss, 1984 edn).
4. Underhill, H, *Masting and Rigging the Clipper Ship and Ocean Carrier* (Glasgow: Brown & Son, 1988).
5. Wells, Capt John, *The Immortal Warrior* (Emsworth, Hants: Kenneth Mason, 1987).
6. Ballard, Admiral G A, *The Black Battlefleet* (London: Society for Nautical Research, 1980).
7. Nares, *op cit*, p5.

ly be repaired by snipping off the rigging line at the thimble, and reeving through a replacement length which can be quickly lashed with cyano glue.

Heart blocks

All the bowsprit blocks are closed heart blocks with lanyards riven through them for the adjustment of the stays, guys and back ropes. Heart blocks do the same job as deadeyes but, because they are passing through two large holes rather than six small ones, the adjustment is easier. The bobstay chains also use the same method, being tightly lashed. It is worth mentioning that, in full size, the heavy chain acts as a downward tension on the outer end of the bowsprit, and the bowsprit would ride to the chain, as a ship rides on the weight of the anchor chain rather than the anchor itself. The mechanical effect of this is the same as a large expansion spring. The manufacture of heart blocks is not all that easy. This hole (which is the exact shape of a modern lavatory seat) must be hand-filed, and the groove to take the strop is difficult to do because of the smallness of the item. If mechanical production is in your mind, the jig might well include an upturned hacksaw blade with an adjustable fence, but the advice would be to drill the hole first, and jamb a suitable piece of dowel in the centre, so that the block is at least captive before you work on it. The bowsprit cap heart blocks should be cast in low-melt metal in a silicone mould, using the technique described for the auxiliary guns. The smaller ones are hand-made from black ebony.

Setting up the bowsprit

This is begun by positioning the outer and inner cap bobstays and the chain shrouds, port and starboard, followed by the spritsail gaff aft guys, which are anchored to the front wall of the ship, and the first tri-

angle completed by the addition of the flying jibboom guy. It is a good idea to work from the inner ropes first. The headstays will have to wait until some of the engineering has been completed, but it is satisfying to make a preliminary start on what will be a long and complicated journey. The bowsprit provides a good practice run in anticipation of all that is to come.

Rigging to the lower masts: dead man's eyes

In the sailor's world, populated with sea monsters and water-spouts, accompanied by the ever-present threat of a watery end in Davy Jones' Locker, it is no wonder that the naked deadeye acquired the sinister aura of the human skull, a object which, before it is riven through with its lanyard, it resembles quite markedly. The word deadeye also quite vividly conveys the fact that there are no moving parts set within these adjusting blocks: thus it ought to be a simple enough task to produce these round blocks, each with three small holes and a groove around the edge. However, the phenomenal number of these blocks sold over the counter in model ship shops indicates that it is not quite so easy to make them as it might first appear. In fact, my advice to anyone who is not a completely dedicated ship-modeller is to buy them in, and be grateful that someone produces them at so moderate a price, and to so high a standard! But there are plenty of lathes and lathe conversions about these days, and many scale shipmodellers have invested in these machines, with the thought that they would like to make their own fittings, masts and deadeyes being at the forefront of their minds.

Ebony

Ebony is a dense hardwood, more often than not jet-black in colour. Over three thousand years ago, it was regarded as a highly prized timber by the Egyptians, who traded actively with Ethiopia in order to obtain this wood for their craftsmen. It has only ever been available in small sizes, and was often used in the ancient world as a veneer. It turns well on a lathe, providing its own polish and shine before any additions of wax or other compounds. It is so dense that the end grain will polish up as well as the long grain, and with no more effort. One must be cautious of tearing the grain out when planing, but in general terms it is more like working in metal than in wood. The texture and the feel of ebony is one of the ultimate tactile sensations, and fortunately it is available in small quantities as turning blanks for lace bobbins and pens. Scratch-built deadeyes were a must for the model of *Warrior*, but information as to how to manufacture them is a bit thin on the ground. Two of the books that I consulted mentioned different procedures, but neither were concerned with how to produce the swelling meniscus which gives deadeyes their distinctive character.

Jigs and tool bits

The great advantage of having a metal turning lathe is that you can make the tools and jigs to do the job. Many people rightly observe that in model shipwrighting there are not that many round fittings to be made (deadeyes being one of the notable exceptions). Lathe owners will quickly counter this by saying that the primary function of a lathe is the ability to perform between the final object and the raw material in the manufacture of accurate jigs. But before any of this can take place, every lathe owner must learn how to grind the tools used in the lathe not only to sharpness, but also to shape.

The usefulness of the D-bit is well known to turners, but less appreciated elsewhere. It is basically a piece of high speed steel, ground off to half width at its tip, and backed off for clearance on the underside. It is not easy to make a forked end to it, because miniature grinding stones are ineffective for anything other than dressing: a way to do this is to offer up the HSS bit to the revolving strap of the (Dremel) linisher, on the edge of the abrasive band. In passing, the linisher is, without a shadow of doubt, the single most useful machine tool for sharpening and finishing small parts.

The ebony stock arrives in square form: in order to plane it into round section, you must eighth square it before offering it up to the chuck, just to clean off the edges. The stock can then be reduced to the required diameter in the lathe, after which it can be polished up with emery cloth, and finally flower paper and microcrystalline wax, of which more in a moment. The joy of a ground form toolcutter for the lathe is that it will always reproduce the same shape, and you can make small objects in a 'stick'. Once the cutter bit is correctly contoured, manufacture is assured, although you must learn to cope with the whip, which is worsened by the many little grooves made in the stock which you are machining. A hand-held V-groove used as a travelling steady, backing the machined object, is the kind of thing that can be helpful, but these are matters of personal preference. Set the tool height slightly above centre, so that it can be pressed down by the hand held steady where the whip is at its greatest in the middle of the stock.

With the stick still in the chuck, make the groove on what will be the outer edge. Use the parting-off tool for this, coming from the back of the lathe's cross slide. Do not make this groove too deep, or you will either be drilling holes through it, or it will break off during the next procedure. In order to part the stick off in the lathe, it must be fed from deep within the chuck. (An extremely important feature of any lathe is the fact that the stock can be fed through the body of the chuck and the mandrel.) To cut the deadeyes off cleanly,

Ebony deadeyes in production on the lathe with specially ground D-bit

and pierced with a smaller drill to be in scale with the lanyard.

Wooden dolly

A wooden dolly is then set up in a vice, the deadeye placed between the dolly and the blind end of the brass bar which acts as the drill guide. With moderate downward pressure and a sensitive touch on the drill press, the first few I made came out well until the fine drill broke. There was no doubt in my mind that this had to do with the density of the ebony, heating up the fine drill, expanding it and then breaking it. Further breakages followed until, in near despair, micro-crystalline wax was used to lubricate the process.[8] This wax is a wonderful product, of which it is difficult to speak too highly, for putting a restoration shine on wood or metal. It is not, however, advertised as a lubricant for machining hardwood, which it certainly should be because it makes a world of difference. As cutting fluid is to machining metal, so this specially formulated wax is to machining hardwood. All that is left to do is some polishing, which can be done on a scrap of leather impregnated with the aforementioned wax, and finally comes the gouging out of the deadeye holes with a gouge or needle file, to relieve the angle of the lanyard and facilitate the adjustment as in full size. You may not get thanked for this final effort, but do it if you must. This might all seem pretty crazy, but if a model is to be truly 'all your own work' and judged as such, any adjudicator can tell the difference between the Italian jobs and your own work, and anyone who knows their timber knows the difference between dark brown stain and *bona fide* hardwood with a hand-polished finish to it.

The restoration deadeyes must be some of the largest and most handsome examples of the art of blockmaking. Notice how the iron wire shrouds are turned in cutter stay fashion, as it is called, and not lashed as one would normally

and not damage the grooves, it will be necessary to wrap a single length of masking tape around the stock, to protect the timber from damage which would be caused by the chuck jaws, and to feed no more than two deadeyes at a time for parting off. Any greedier ambitions result in breaking the stick, and having to saw off the rest by hand. The tape does work, and anyone worried about concentricity in the lathe can relax as it will be barely noticeable.

Brass drilling jig

The jig is a piece of brass bar, marked out on the top end with a triangle of dots. (Note that the triangle of dots should be sited with the base line just below the diameter.) The brass bar is bored out to a sliding fit on the stock, and parted off leaving a blind end of approximately $1/4$in. It is then carefully marked out on the top with a centre drill in the three positions,

8. Available from Picreator Enterprises (see list of suppliers for further details).

expect to see if used with hemp rope. This is relatively rare, and its technical name is a racking seizing. The builder's model in the Science Museum is faithful to this important historical detail.

Seized by the throat

As can be seen from the close-up photography, the shrouds have been served on the ropewalk machine with an outer wrapping or winding around the central core of the rope. This is to imitate the prototype wire rigging which has been similarly treated in full scale. This makes the shroud more inflexible than ordinary spun rope, and means that when it has to be seized at both the masthead, and around the deadeye, it needs to be seized by the throat with wire. There are three possibilities for this: good old annealed brass wire which is difficult to obtain; copper wire, which has a slight tendency to break when twisted tightly; and soft wire of the type used by florists for wiring up flower arrangements (this is normally gal-

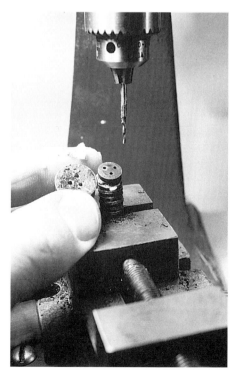

vanised). Any or all of these can be made to disappear into the rigging, given that real standing rigging is covered in tar, and the model reflects this by having touches of black paint in the appropriate places. (Try Hammerite black for a very interesting effect.) The use of a small pin chuck means that you can work singlehandedly in drawing the two lengths of wire together, by closing the chuck jaws together until they grab the ends of the wire, and then twisting until tightened.

Rigging the shrouds

Different people do this in different ways but, before anything can happen, the pendants of tackles, called Burton pendants, must be placed on the mizzenmast. Historically these were used for lifting heavy tackles aloft, and are placed at the very bottom of the masthead rigging on all three lower masts. They were cut-spliced over the mast and round-thimbled on their ends, with the forward one rigged approximately 2ft above the aft one. Thereafter, the order for the rigging to go around the masthead is one and two (all one shroud, seized in the bight) to port; one and two to starboard; three and four to port; three and four to starboard, and so forth to the ninth shroud which, being an odd one out, is once again rigged with a cut splice.

(Left)
Brass bar, pierced with the triangle of holes which act as a guide for the drill bit. After heavy use, the holes are silver-soldered and rebored for continued accuracy.

(Below)
The magnificent full-scale restoration deadeyes on the shrouds of the mainmast. Note the sheer pole and fancy ropework giving protection to the lanyards.

Once the masthead end has been dealt with, whether or not racking seizing is involved, it is necessary to measure and mark the point at which the deadeye is rigged to the shroud. Do this with typist's white correction fluid. The line of deadeyes has to follow the top of the bulwarks, but small variations in height are quite acceptable, in that deadeyes are themselves adjusters, although this was less the case with iron wire rigging than with hemp rigging, which needed constant attention. Before they are set up, it is a good idea to let these rigging lines stretch with the weight of clamps or reverse action tweezers, or even clothes pegs, which will do the job just as well.

Lanyards

By the 1860s, the lanyards were rigged slightly differently, in that the standing end was fixed to the channel (chainwale), riven through the lanyard from the aft end to the forward end, and tied off above the bight of the racking seizing. On my model, because the backstay rigging, particularly on the mainmast, will seriously interfere with the ability to get at the engine room, it will be rigged with fewer shrouds and backstays, although all the lower deadeyes are in place. A number of modellers reject certain prototypes as working models because they fear that the rigging will interfere with the operational aspects.

Seized by the throat! Tourniquet applied around the shrouds with the pin chuck.

This is a pity because, with a bit of planning, it is only necessary in such circumstances to give an indication of rigging for people to feel that the model 'looks right'.

In my workshop there lives an energetic female spider. She has been rigging the model to her own plan ever since the masts were stepped into their housings. The webs she spins are exquisite, and a solemn reminder that the very essence of rigging a model ship, even a large one like this, is to keep the work as fine as nature will allow.

The logic of working sail

The weight of all this research and knowledge can seem somewhat intimidating and quite daunting in prospect, but it all turns out in the end to follow its own simple logic. The stays and shrouds are about not allowing masts to move, and all the rest is about hoisting and shifting sails to catch the wind. As far as the sails are concerned, items of running rigging likewise give the sailors aloft the ability to have control over the canvas sails: sometimes requiring an increased spread, and then, under other conditions, needing a shortening of sail by reefing, brailing and clueing up.

With the upper masting, every single item aloft must be removable, including the topmasts, topgallants and royals. All the items above the fighting tops must be of a size and weight which could be manhandled into position. That is why the upper masts and yards are so much lighter than the lower masts (and yards), which were stepped into their positions from specially adapted sheer hulks moored in the Royal Naval dockyards. *Warrior* was first masted and rigged at Chatham, where exactly this system was used.

Rigging to the upper masts: going aloft

Rigging the upper masts on a model of this size will need a decent pair of step-

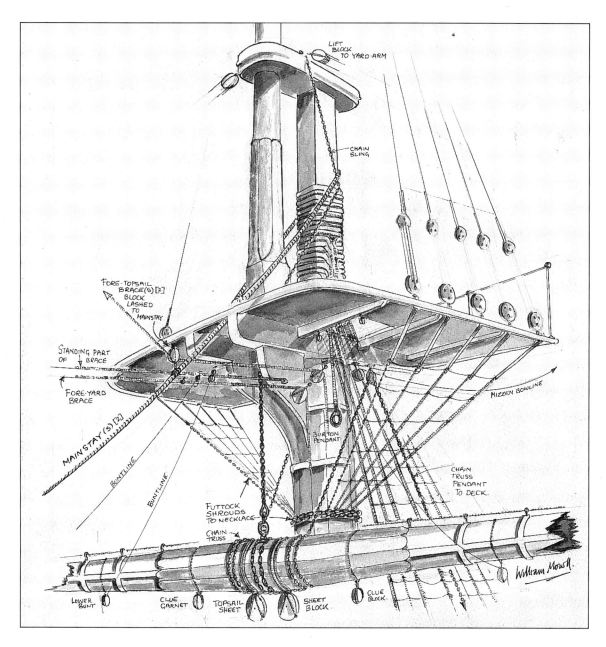

Illustration of underside of mainmast detail. (Author)

ladders to reach to the top of the fore and main topgallants and royals, which are almost at the level of the rafters of my workshop. Check that your ladder has wide treads, and be aware that you will spend many hours standing aloft. When one is concentrating on an item of rigging, it is very easy to flatten the whole project by missing your footing. In an ideal world, one would buy two ladders,

because in rigging one is forever having to work from both sides.

Return of the ropewalk

In correct scale-model practice, each rope is made for its individual purpose, in the same way as all the other items are made and fitted in a scratch-built model. Setting up the ropewalk can be a bit of a nuisance,

Sketch of standing rigging to fighting top.
(Author)

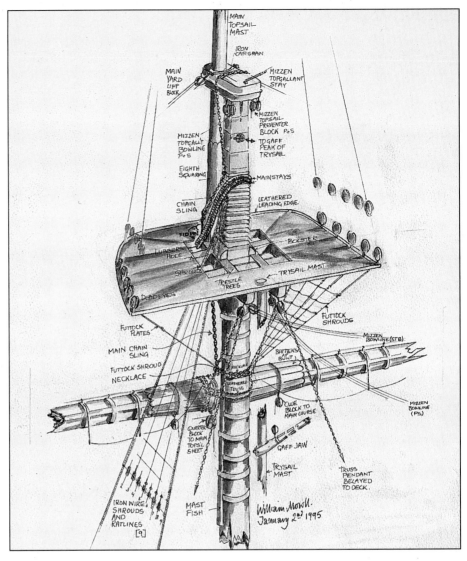

as one really needs a minimum length of 8ft between headstock and tailstock to produce the longer lengths required. This is particularly true of the pendant falls and backstays of the upper masts. It is also necessary to produce this kind of length when using purchases between double blocks. Finding an 8ft length of space in any workshop is difficult, and my ropewalk is seriously interfered with by the pillar drill which shares the same bench. Besides the laying of the rope, whether left- or right-hand laid, there will be considerations of the thickness and hardness of the rope, as well as the finished colour. There will also be a decision as to whether the rope will be served, which is the wrap-

ping of the rope with an outer layer of protection, where the rope perhaps goes round a masthead, or in the case of a stay, may be chafed by other ropes rubbing against it. It is a good idea to experiment with different raw materials, cottons and linens in particular, as they lay up more easily than man-made fibres. Then stretch the resulting lengths of miniature rope over a piece of white card, from the thickest hawser-laid forestay to the thinnest ensign halyard, and make a note on the card of how it was done and with what materials, etc. This will prevent you from making the basic error of finding that you are manufacturing rope which is too weighty for the upper works, and is also

that when natural linen thread is dyed it does not have a single standard colour. Barbour threads all have varying hues, so that some can be used for lanyards, others for braces and so forth, and this gives the hint of individuality which silently makes the point that it did not all come from one ball of string. Thread supplied in any other colours than dark brown or black should be viewed with the utmost caution. Sometimes kit manufacturers show models with bright white rigging on the box, in order to enhance the visual appeal of the product, but it has nothing to do with the way real ships appear, and could lead to disappointment if offered for competition. The trick with model shipwrighting is always to understate, rather than overstate, the full scale. So one degree softer in all colours throughout the model (including the paintwork) is what is required, and this is the reason why

Full-sized spider's web.

out of scale with the blocks through which the rope has to be riven.

Keeping it all in scale

The blocks on the upper yards are surprisingly small, particularly with an item such as a clue block: no more than $^3/_{16}$in at the scale of 1:48. At this scale, if they are larger than a ladybird they are certainly too big. As the work progresses, you begin to get a feel for what looks right. In the selection of the threads for roping, choose the dark brown and deep ashen grey colours characteristic of manilla roping after it has lost its golden glow and been exposed to salt sea air.

Small and dark

Distinguish between the different kinds of cordage for different usages. It so happens

Rigging the topmast shrouds on the model. Note that they are turned in cutter stay fashion as with the lower mast shrouds.

9. If you cannot find these, look in a CeKa catalogue (available from good tool shops) under the electronic tweezers.

Underside of restored fighting top, with a mass of detail, for both standing and running rigging.

Group of clamps.
(Josh Mowll)

dark brown rigging actually looks better than harsh black, a colour which ought to be reserved only for the heaviest forestays.

Tools and gadgets used in rigging

It is much easier to tie a knot with a pair of pliers or tweezers if they have cranked ends - bent is the official description. You will also need a pair which are self-gripping (sometimes known as cross-pattern, or reverse-action, tweezers).[9] You will also need what are technically known as weaver's scissors, which have two sharp points for getting into very inaccessible places. A good range of clothes pegs is also

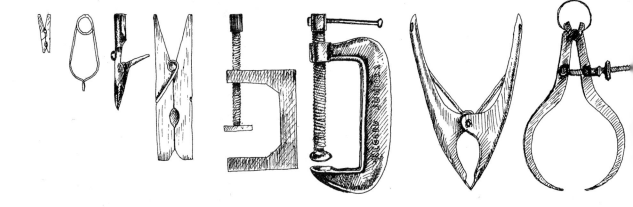

very useful, going from the large wooden blanket pegs, right down to the miniature plastic ones as supplied by stationers. I have also found that fishing tackle shops, where there are supplies for fly-fisherman to tie their own fly hooks, are also a useful hunting ground. And finally, some electronic alligator clips, which you can file

Detail of rigging to the topmast.
(Author)

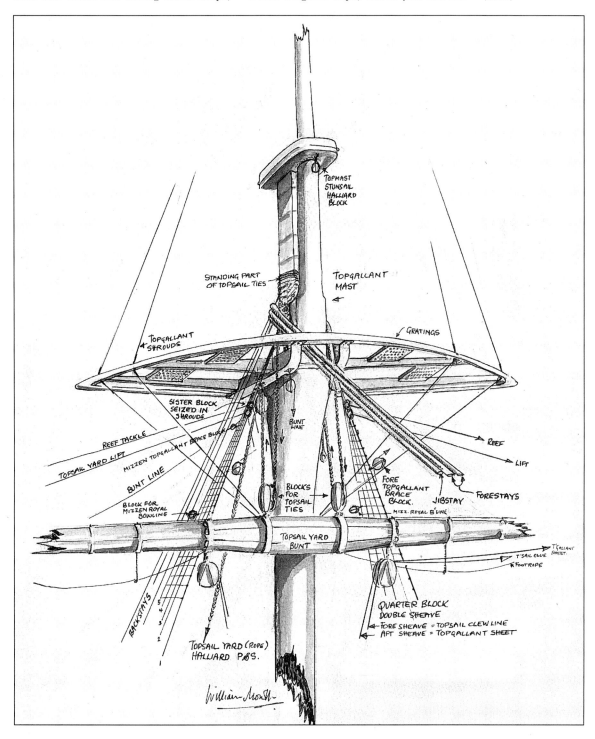

and bend into whatever shape you find useful.

Cyano

The use of Cyano superglue has changed the face of rigging model ships forever, and virtually done away with the need for needles and splicing ropes. The glue will also act as an agent which creates a rigid end to miniature rope, which can then easily be fed through sheaved blocks like a bodkin. It has taken me a long while to realise that you should never use this glue without also having some kitchen paper

(Below)
Setting up the ratlines on the mizzenmast, using spun copper wire righthand-laid.

(Bottom)
The copper wire thread is lashed with .004 copper filament, which disappears in the knot.

handy to wipe the nozzle every time you replace the cap. This way you will prevent the inevitable build-up of surplus adhesive which ends up blocking the spout with excess glue in the cap. A further tip for the use of this adhesive is to clean out the cap at the end of the day with a cotton bud. Also keep some cocktail sticks ready nearby, because they will provide a more efficient way of gluing an inaccessible strand than just squeezing the tube and hoping for the best. The glue will happily run down the cocktail stick, and you can be very precise in its application. If you overglue an item, just put a piece of the kitchen roll paper against it, and draw the excess off by capillary action.

If you wish to imitate a spliced rope end, for instance say the standing end of a rope attaching itself to a sheaved block, twist left-hand laid rope anticlockwise on itself and apply the Cyano glue into the strands; then twist it even more tightly on itself until the glue hardens, which will be within thirty seconds or so. This gives a very convincing imitation of a spliced rope, and an excellent tough join with whatever item it is secured to.

One more rigging tip is the making of a loop to imitate the becket, or thimble, at the crown of a sheaved block. Assuming that you are using either copper or brass wire to strop the block, and that you are dealing with two strands of wire twisted into one at the top of the block, the trick is to pierce the two strands of twisted metal, just above the block, with a metal spike; use an engineer's scriber. Do this on a soft piece of wood, or it could easily be you that lands up with the piercing rather than the strands of metal! What happens is that the spike will make a round loop, stretching the twisted metal strand without breaking it. The piece can then be soldered just beyond the loop before snipping it off, making a very strong but light fixture through which the attendant rope may be secured. This is also a neat way of attaching a turnbuckle to a stropped block where there is a hook needed at one end and a loop at the other.

Sister blocks

The yardarms on the topsail yard and topgallant yards are supported by the lifts which reeve through sister blocks seized between the first and second shrouds, which is a very awkward location to deal with. Because the sister blocks are so fine, I made the decision to manufacture them out of metal. The way to do this is to solder two small round pieces of brass tubing together into what is virtually a figure of eight. They should then be grooved with a hacksaw blade to suit the size of the shroud rigging. Then place them into the apex of the leading rigging and seize with a copper wire tourniquet. It took me all day to do these nine fittings, but they do represent correct practice for this period of shipping. In common with full-sized practice, the ratlines on the model ought not to be tackled until all the standing rigging is complete. This is because the inbuilt tensions in the rigging need to even themselves out before this final exercise in knotting takes place.

Rattling down the rigging

It is a guess that the original ratlines fitted to *Warrior* in 1860 were made of iron wire, and crossed the shrouds by being lashed to them, either with roped knots, or, more likely, with lengths of softened single-stranded wire. My caution about this statement has to do with the awareness that sailors in this period went barefoot, and iron wire rusts up very easily, so

(Above)
Tarring the ropework and trimming up. The rigging trucks are lashed to the shrouds and running rigging lines will run through them to the belaying pins below.

(Left)
Underside of foremast on the model.

wire strands would cause unnecessary injuries to the feet of sailors, but certainly from contemporary pictures it looks as though it was either iron bar, or inhospitable iron wire, which was used. The restoration ratlines are fitted in the con-

(Opposite)
Detail of rigging to the
topgallant mast.
(Author)

ventional manner, with rope and jamming clove hitches, ignoring the fact that they are crossing steel shrouds.

Nearly all models of ships which involve ratlines get into difficulties with the natural sag of the ratline rope when it is made in the traditional way with a clove hitch. There simply is not enough weight in the cotton or thread to impart that well-used look, and worse still, the rope tread is inclined to reverse, something which never happens in full scale. The way round this is to use copper wire, which is sewn through the shrouds, and the treads imparted by pulling the copper wire into a crescent shape (watching out that it does not distort the lie and line of the shrouds) and, when satisfied, touching the wire with Cyano instant glue. The second advantage to this system is avoiding the trap of oversized knots, so often the downfall of otherwise beautifully-rigged models. Unfortunately, with my *Warrior* model, the shrouds had all been served for their full length (as on the prototype), which meant there was no chance whatsoever of getting a needle through the tight binding. The only option for me was to go back to the 1860 practice of lashing each point of contact, rather as you would do for a solid bar, or as seen at the bottom of the rigging, with the sheer pole.

On the model the lashing points can be marked out by using a short length of timber, correctly scaled in width for a 16in ladder rung, with double-sided tape attached to it. This tape is sufficiently tacky to adhere to the aft side of the shrouds, and keeps the spaces level and even. The positions should be marked off with typist's correction fluid. For the lashing, use copper wire which is very fine (0.004in): this disappears into the paint work without trace. Reverse action tweezers are the tool for the job of twisting the fine copper wire until it breaks of its own accord.

Experiments with producing the ratlines in copper ended up by spinning long lengths of three-stranded copper wire into

right-hand lay (which means anti-clockwise if you are using a hand brace to do the spinning). Measure with dividers the diminishing distance between the shrouds, which of course narrows with each rung, and prick out the fixing points on a piece of squared paper. This is followed by making the sag in the rope like a series of small scallops, to match the fixed points exactly. The ratline is then offered up to the shroud, and clamped at either end with clips. This means that you can now lash from the centre and then work towards the outer shrouds. From the inboard view, which one sees athwart the ship, the ratlines do appear to be knotted, and not just applied. In the final few inches towards the masthead, where the shrouds go very close together, use a row of pins marked out on the squared paper, against which the scallops can be made by just indenting the wire between the upright pins with a pencil point.

None of this represents a quick solution to the painstaking work involved with detailing the ratlines. It takes longer to do than conventional knotting, but it is very sure and certain when it is done. Having said that, ratlines ought not to be self-conscious affairs. If they are made in too strident a fashion, it can easily spoil an otherwise well-rigged model. Once done, they ought to melt unremarkably into the background and will only really be picked out when they have canvas against which they contrast.

Technically speaking, the ratline ought to be thimbled at either end, so that it can be seized to the fore- and aftmost shroud, but I am afraid that, in the interests of personal sanity, that detail will not be shown on my model.

Control systems of square sails on a man o' war c1860

The standing rigging, by which is meant the forestays and backstays, as well as the shrouds, give firm support to the masts. To cross a yard to a mast, there must be some way of hauling the yard up to the

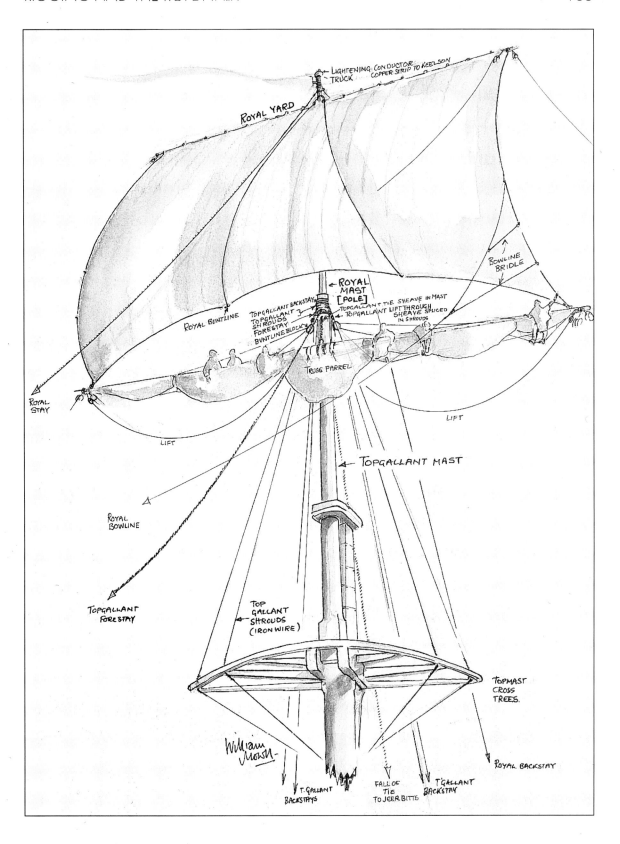

LIGHTENING CONDUCTOR
TRUCK — COPPER STRIP TO KEELSON

ROYAL YARD

BOWLINE
BRIDLE

ROYAL
MAST
[POLE]

TOPGALLANT TIE SHEAVE IN MAST
TOPGALLANT LIFT THROUGH
SHEAVE SPLICED
IN SHROUDS

ROYAL BUNTLINE

TOPGALLANT BACKSTAYS
TOPGALLANT
SHROUDS 3
FORESTAY
BUNTLINE BLOCK

TRUSS PARREL

LIFT

ROYAL
STAY

LIFT

TOPGALLANT MAST

ROYAL
BOWLINE

TOPGALLANT
FORESTAY

TOP
GALLANT
SHROUDS
(IRON WIRE)

TOPMAST
CROSS
TREES.

William Mowll

T. GALLANT
BACKSTAYS

FALL OF
TIE
TO JEER BITTS

T. GALLANT
BACKSTAY

ROYAL BACKSTAY

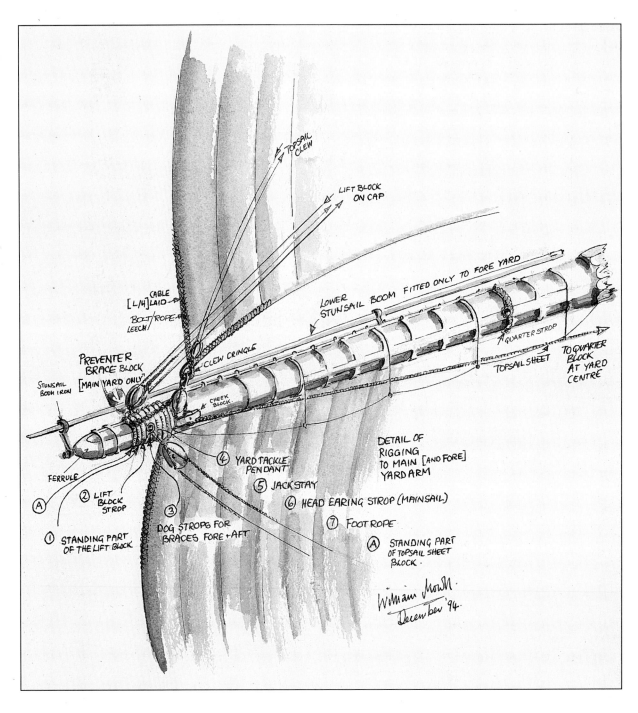

TOPSAIL
CLEW

LIFT BLOCK
ON CAP

LOWER
STUNSAIL BOOM FITTED ONLY TO FORE YARD

QUARTER STROP

[L/4] CABLE
LAID

BOLT/ROPE
LEECH

CLEW CRINGLE

TOPSAIL SHEET

TO QUARTER
BLOCK
AT YARD
CENTRE

PREVENTER
BRACE BLOCK
[MAIN YARD ONLY]

STUNSAIL
BOOM IRON

CHEEK
BLOCK

DETAIL OF
RIGGING
TO MAIN [AND FORE]
YARD ARM

FERRULE

④ YARD TACKLE
PENDANT

② LIFT
BLOCK
STROP

⑤ JACKSTAY

Ⓐ

③

⑥ HEAD EARING STROP (MAINSAIL)

DOG STROPS FOR
BRACES FORE+AFT

⑦ FOOT ROPE

① STANDING PART
OF THE LIFT BLOCK

Ⓐ STANDING PART
OF TOPSAIL SHEET
BLOCK

William Mowll
December '94.

Illustration of rigging to
the main and fore
yardarm.
(Author)

sailing position. On the lower masts, these very heavy yards were hauled into place using jeer blocks, and kept in place by use of a chain sling which went round the aft side of the masthead, above the standing part of the shrouds and backstays. By 1860, these jeer blocks were removed once the lower yard was in place, and safely attached to the chain sling hook. Lift blocks, attached to the cap span of the masthead cap, supported the tips of the lower yardarms only. In order to tie the yard into the mast, a collar needed to be fitted at the centre, or bunt, of the yard. This was called a parrel, or truss, and allowed the yard to swing within a fairly limited axis on the lower mast. By the 1860s the truss, like the sling, was made of chain. The lower yards were infrequently raised and lowered, and could be considered to be permanently fixed.

If we now move up to the topsail yard, a slightly different system was used for hauling the yards up and down. The jeer blocks on a topsail yard were permanently fixed with iron bands around the bunt of the yard. Tye blocks were fitted to the underside of the trestletrees on the crosstrees at the topsail masthead. The halyard was riven through these with the standing part above the shrouds and backstays, and the hauling part taken down to the upper deck. When in harbour, the yardarms were supported by the topsail yard lifts, the point of purchase of which was through the lower sheave of a sister block spliced between the leading two shrouds. Shrouds were often used as convenient fixing points for brace blocks and bowlines, as well as providing trucks for the falls of the running rigging attached to the inner side of the shrouds. The truck was like a little grommet seized to the shroud just above the deadeyes.

The topgallant masthead provided yet another hoisting system, which this time used a simple sheave through the mast itself. This single rope was known as a tie (or tye) hitched around the yard. As with the lower masts, a parrel (or truss) tied the yard into the mast; the lift blocks were seized between the shrouds rather like a captive thimble. The royal yard used a sheave for the tie, and a simple truss, as with the topgallant.

Catching the wind

With the yards raised into position, controlling the sails was the next consideration. Brace blocks sited on the yardarms

Main course clued up to the yard.

provided for this. Brace blocks lead aft, whilst preventer blocks lead forwards. When sailing close to the wind, the windward edge of the sail (known as the leech) can flap when the wind is escaping at a tangent. To stop this happening, bridles were fitted to bowlines on the leading edge of the sail, and belayed forwards. Other conditions called for a reduction in the spread of canvas, which was achieved in several different ways, but comes generally under the heading of reefing.

By the 1860s, topsail reefing was by use of jacklines, which can be most easily described as the system used in the operation of Venetian window blinds. These single topsails were huge spreads of canvas: the driving force of the whole ship, and therefore much tended. On steamships the main courses were not so

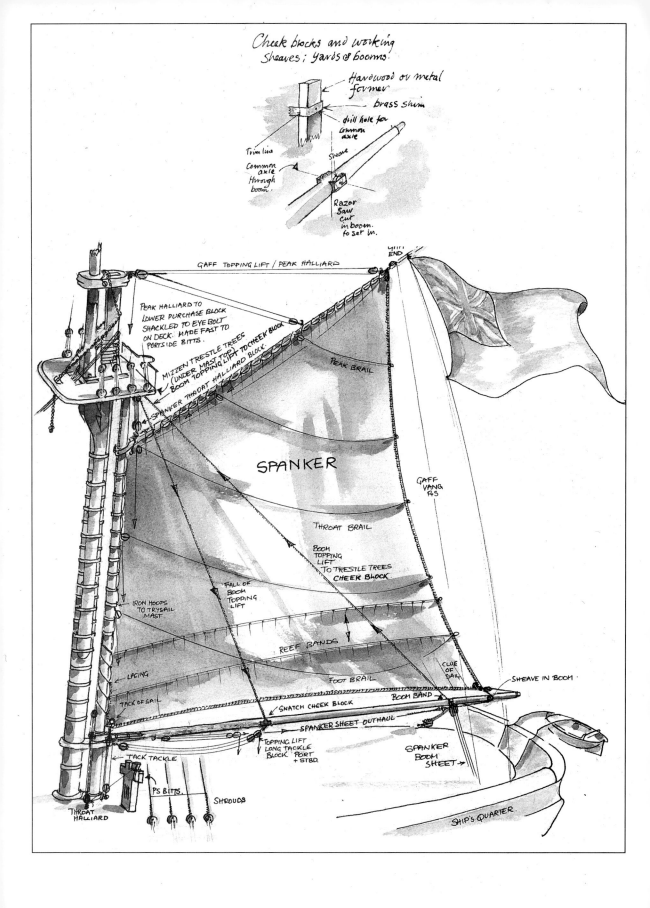

Cheek blocks and working
Sheaves; yards & booms.

Hardwood or metal
former

brass shim

drill hole for
common axle

Trim line

Sheave

Common
axle
through
boom.

Razor
Saw
cut
in boom.
to set in.

GAFF TOPPING LIFT / PEAK HALLIARD

GAFF
END

PEAK HALLIARD TO
LOWER PURCHASE BLOCK
SHACKLED TO EYE BOLT
ON DECK. MADE FAST TO
PORTSIDE BITTS.

MIZZEN TRESTLE TREES
(UNDER MAST TOP)
BOOM TOPPING LIFT BLOCK
SPANKER THROAT HALLIARD BLOCK.

SPANKER THROAT TO CHEEK BLOCK

PEAK BRAIL

SPANKER

GAFF
VANG
R4S

THROAT BRAIL

BOOM
TOPPING
LIFT
TO TRESTLE TREES
CHEEK BLOCK.

FALL OF
BOOM
TOPPING
LIFT

IRON HOOPS
TO TRYSAIL
MAST

REEF BANDS

LACING

CLUE OF
SAIL

FOOT BRAIL

SHEAVE IN BOOM

TACK OF SAIL

SNATCH CHEEK BLOCK

BOOM BAND

SPANKER SHEET OUTHAUL

TACK TACKLE

TOPPING LIFT
LONG TACKLE
BLOCK PORT
& STBD.

SPANKER
BOOM
SHEET

PS BITTS.

SHROUDS

THROAT
HALLIARD

SHIP'S QUARTER.

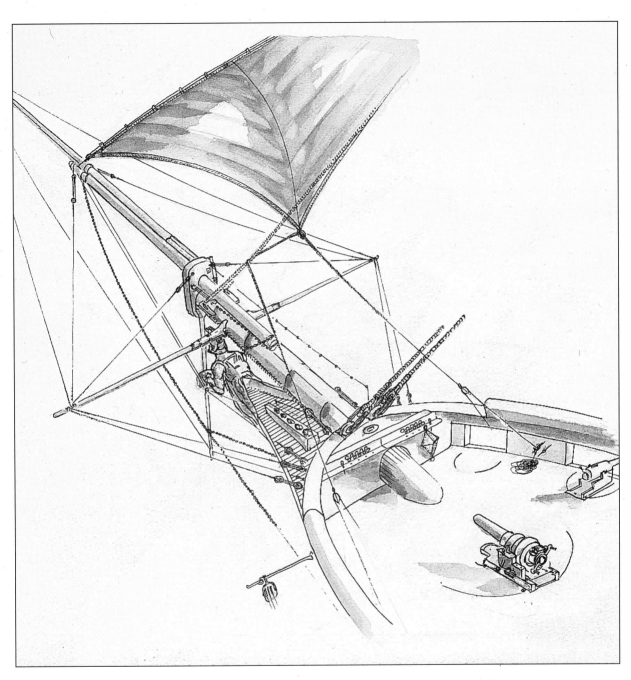

often used as the topsails, interfering as they did with the deck hamper, funnels and other furnishings. Standard reefing was used on the spanker sail at the stern of the ship, with brails fitted to the leech. These brails on a fore and aft sail are the equivalent of the cluelines on a square sail, which, when the sail is being furled, gath-er the bottom corner of the sail, and lift it to the bunt or centre of the yard. The cluelines operate from the aft side of the sail. On the fore side, another set of ropes (buntlines) gather the foot of the sail, and haul it up to the yard in the familiar three loose folds so often depicted by artists. Gaskets were provided for the final tight

(Opposite)
Spanker sail illustration.
(Author)

(Above)
Illustration of jibsail.
(Author)

Spanker sail. Note the curved foot of the sail, the Red Squadron flag is worn from the gaff peak.

block attached to the clue cringle. This allowed the sail to billow out in light airs.

On the fore and main courses, the sheets were lead through fair-leaders in the ship's side and belayed to cleats. It is easy to make the mistake of thinking that the sheave slots cut into the yardarms of the upper yards are for the sail sheets to reeve through. They are in fact for hauling up the reefing gear attached just below the reefing lines on the leech of the sail.

Apart from the gear associated with stunsails, and various oddities like nave lines and tricing lines, that covers the basics of how square sails work, and the reason why there is so much rigging associated with their operation. The 1860s is at the tail end of the development of sailing warships, and all the little refinements are there which had evolved over hundreds of years of square-rigged sailing ships. Although nearly all drawings and paintings of sailing warships show a curved foot to the sail, the truth is that warships had no roaching and paid the price for this in terms of wear to the foot of the sail on the mast stays. In the Royal Navy, this was thought to be less important than speed, whereas merchantmen saw the issue the other way round: for them more wear and tear equalled less profit.

furling of the sail, and steamers then had canvas steaming covers fitted to prevent the sails from becoming saturated with soot.

The foot of the sails had all to be adjustable. To achieve this, sheets were provided for the bottom corners of the sails, and these ropes were led up to the sails through quarter blocks at the bunt of the yard below. The sheet was then riven through a cheek block fitted to the aft side of the yard, and through a single sheave

Electronic sail and rigging

The running rigging on the model must be effected in a slightly different way from the original, because the braces must be rigged on a 'closed loop' system to an electronically-controlled winch at the stern of the vessel. This miniature winch must have an adjustable length of travel, something which not all of these possess; it also needs strength enough to pull the whole suit of sails onto the opposite tack and keep them braced against the wind. The model I have used is the Marathon which has a pull of 30lb and has a remote adjuster, giving a sheet range of 8-15in. It also plugs straight into the existing R/C, using the nicads of the receiver.

Installation

This was not an easy task on my model: it was necessary to cut through the underside of the gun deck, with no overhead access, a job only made possible by the use of a miniature circular saw held freestyle at arms' length in the dark, with a silent expression of gratitude that the gun deck had been individually planked. This meant that it was only necessary to cross-cut the deck beams to get a reasonably neat result, being able to break the planking away. However, it is inevitable that where one has to design working parts on what is a prototype model that these sorts of adjustments must be made.

Once the winch is in place, it must have an extension piece fitted to go through the upper deck, forming what in fact can be matched to original practice, that is a link between the main and upper capstans together through two decks for greater purchase. The base of this winch/capstan must be machined on the lathe and very carefully fitted in a precision-cut hole in the upper deck, the hole acting as a top bearing.

The closed loop system

Once fitted and secured with bolts, it is possible to see whether or not the winch works. A loop system requires one length to be wound left-handed and the other right-handed, and you need to wind the rope around the capstan/winch for the amount of turns that it will have to travel. This unit is completely waterproof – not the fastest of its kind but just right for the purpose. It does exactly what is asked of it, in a business-like manner, with the length of travel set in a neat device with assistance of a small screwdriver.

The simplest solution

As is common with miniature working square sail rig, the main yardarm is linked up with the winch, and the loop continues to the fore topsail yard. This is virtually in a straight line and can include the fore yard in the loop. Once the model ship is rigged with sails, this system alone will bring all the yards round, particularly if downhauls are rigged to all the yardarms. It is, even to scale, quite a sight to see the whole rigging on the move, and the slower this happens, the more majestic the sight. There would be no reason at all not to apply a winch to the foresails and spanker, but in practice this side of things is best kept as simple as possible, especially as it is more than likely that when the model is under sail it will be under steam power as well. This way the fore and aft sails can be positioned to the most advantageous quarter of the wind by use of propeller and rudder.

The stern chaser

The winch can be used to perform just one more task, and that is to make the Armstrong breech-loader stern chaser gun come round on its racer arcs, port and starboard. On the model, the naval gun carriage should be attached by gun tackle to the rudder yoke, so that when the vessel moves to starboard the gun moves to port. This is also a check that the rudder mechanisms are working.

10
SAILS AND FLAGS

nd now to the worsted stuff.
Sailcloth and bunting can both be
described technically as soft
materials, although canvas made from
hemp must have felt anything but soft
when being manhandled on the yards of
ships, or being repaired by the sailmaker
after storm damage.

Sailmaking

The decision whether or not to include
sails on a model ship is not lightly taken.

First sign of sail. Note
that the ratlines are not
yet set up.

For several good and practical reasons, it
may be better not to get involved with
them at all. Nepean Longridge set his face
against flying any canvas with his famous
model of *Victory*, claiming that sails not
only greatly complicate the rigging, but
also obscure much of the deck detail.
Certainly, sails radically alter the way a
ship model looks, and not always for the
better in terms of a glass case model: some
very well-made model boats have been
totally spoiled by the quality of the sailmaking. It is only when wind and tide
become involved in the equation that
things alter. Bare poles on the water simply looks wrong. In reality, even a square-
rigger in tow would still fly a topsail or jib,
so that a working model cannot really justify its title unless working sails are on display. However, if you are after the particular magic and mystery of working sailing
ships, you must face up to the myriad of
difficulties which lie behind that first
moment when the canvas fills with wind
and billows out in full orchestra and cho-
rus. All the work and preparation which
precedes that magical moment must be
planned and executed to perfection if the
effect is to be truly convincing.

When the restorers were first considering how best to display the masts and
yards, they did not initially intend to do
anything other than mock up the furled
sails. They discovered soon enough, as

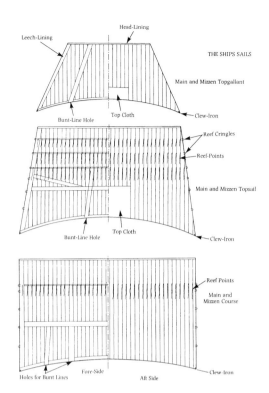

THE SHIPS SAILS

Leech-Lining
Head-Lining
Main and Mizzen Topgallant
Bunt-Line Hole
Top Cloth
Clew-Iron

Reef Cringles
Reef-Points
Main and Mizzen Topsail
Bunt-Line Hole
Top Cloth
Clew-Iron

Reef Points
Main and Mizzen Course
Holes for Bunt Lines
Fore-Side
Aft Side
Clew-Iron

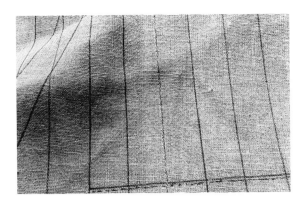

increasing mechanisation of mid-Victorian life, sails were all hand-stitched, and repairs at sea were laboriously carried out with patience and determination.

This section, as an introduction to making scaled-down versions of sails, ought to be accompanied by a warning that model sailmaking requires exactly these two qualities of patience and determination, as well as the finesse of a court dressmaker. The material gains of modern life have also been accompanied by losses, and in our disposable society there are fewer and fewer people left who have the ability to repair, stitch and mend. My sailmaker, Phyllis Checkley, belongs to an age when small girls were made to sit and sew, embroider and patch, and such training made her the obvious choice for the long and laborious work of making a full miniature wardrobe of sails with the delicacy of touch that is required to emulate the original suits of canvas.

The first sight of miniature sail

Muslin cloth is my choice for sailmaking: although it is very light, it also has a roughish texture not dissimilar to sailcloth. There are lots of arguments about what one ought to use for the most realistic material, and most of them hinge on the fact that man-made fibres simply look

(Left)
Sails, after the late Harold A Underhill. (*SS Great Britain: The Model Ship*, Author)

(Above)
The right choice of cloth is important: muslin is soft but grainy. Note the stiched line in the centre and how the cotton blends in with the drawn line (Edding 141 felt tip pen).

modelmakers discover in their turn, that unless you do make the items in full, they never look right, even when they are furled or merely clued up. Sailing steamships are a particular case; more often than not they relied on their topsails, jibs and spanker, rather than their fore or main courses, for propulsion when in steam. This was to avoid the difficulties of huge areas of canvas fore and aft of the funnels being endangered by sparks and being covered in soot. Under these circumstances, one can see and understand why these ships were, out of preference, sailed rather than steamed for the greater part of any voyage; it was also cheaper.

The sailmaker

Traditionally, the sailmaker was held in high regard. His strong fingers were the only thing which stood between success and disaster in the aftermath of a storm at sea, and his skills in ropework and repair were absolutely vital. Even with the

The author marking out the stitching lines for the sails.

(Right)
Using the sewing machine to simulate the sewn line down the sail cloth of a topgallant. It has been previously marked with a brown waterproof fine point pen.

needle is adequate, although some machines might be happier using a finer needle when stitching a fabric as fine as muslin. Use dark brown thread for over-stitching and the bunt line cloths; the machine-stitched lines are in a lighter colour to match the hue of the dyed muslin used as canvas. (We used Molnlycke 9796 and 9720, but any easily available brand of mercerised cotton or polyester thread is suitable.) It is most effective to machine over the drawn brown lines of the canvas cloths, effectively lessening the impact of the brown-coloured ink with which they have been marked up. If the machine stitch line is not absolutely accurate, the drawn line still dominates, giving the effect of stitched cloth with its shadows along the seams.

The cloth can be guided through manually, or a quilting guide (an accessory

and feel wrong, so that one needs to seek out natural fibres like cotton or linen. (It is interesting that nautical slang for canvas was 'muslin', and that sailors also referred to their girls and women as 'a bit of muslin'.)

Six yards of muslin should suffice and, before getting the material on the drawing board, soak in a bowl full of black instant coffee at the strength you would make it for yourself to drink. Leave for around half an hour and then rinse out with plain water. It is now the right shade for canvas, and to mark it up the cloth can be laid over scaled up drawings as if it were tracing paper. It is easy to see through, which is one of the material's attractions, and the drawing can be done with a fine-point, waterproof felt-tip pen. (I used an Edding 141 EF.)

Needles and pins

Muslin cloth is easy to work because it has a fine weave to it, which means that it stitches and hems well; this is important because the edges must be turned in to stop fraying. For the hand-sewing, use a crewel, or embroidery, needle (1$\frac{1}{2}$in), and for the machining a size 14 (medium)

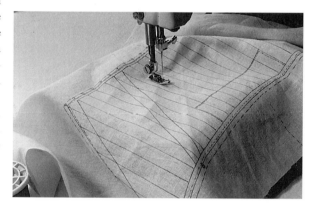

which comes with many modern sewing machines) can be used when guiding the cloth through the machine, to ensure that the stitch lines are straight. It is also important to ensure that the stitching lies flat to the muslin without any puckering of the material. Lightweight fabrics such as muslin generally need a stitch length which is on the short side, but you will need to experiment with tension and stitch length to find out which combination your machine is most happy with.

The cloth bands, which are the pieces which protect the sails from fraying, are

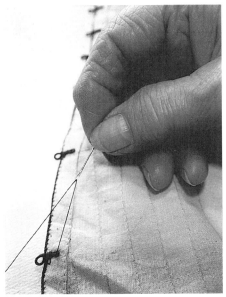

the sail by overstitching by hand. The reef bands are one third of the size of the cloth bands. To achieve this width, use a steam iron to make a new fold in the bias binding. The reef band also has a thick piece of thread which has to be led through like a shoelace. The only way to do this is to thread it through every inch or so as it is being machined, as there is no way in which it can be threaded through afterwards; it must also be ironed throughout the process as well. Quite frankly, reef bands are bad news for the machinist.

The little loops at the heads of the sails and the earing cringles must all be stitched on by hand; use an embroidery gimlet/pricker to ensure uniformity of loop size, something which is most important. The clue cringles are all sewn from the back of the sails.

In summary, the order of tasks is as follows. First, machine stitch the lines of cloths in light-coloured thread, then stitch the bias binding, inserting the thread where necessary. Next stitch the top cloth, but not through the bias binding, and machine stitch the edges in light-coloured thread. Oversew the bolt rope (using dark waxed linen macramé thread) by hand, making the cringles where necessary in the dark brown sewing thread. Make a separate line of loops at the head of the sail. Make the bunt line holes, using buttonhole stitch, and finally finish off the top cloth with hand sewing.

(Upper left)
Machine-stitching the reef tackle patches made from bias binding.

(Left)
Reef cringles, hand-sewn to the bolt rope.

(Above)
Basic requirements for sailmaking: macramé waxed linen thread in dark brown (for the bolt rope); Molnlycke (light and dark brown) with Barbour thread in background; thimble, scissors and sewing machine needles.

made from $1/2$in wide bias binding, easily available from haberdashers. Use this width for the middle bands, although the reef tackle patches go down first, so that the middle bands can be sewn over the top. Like the sails, the bands should be dipped in a stout mixture of instant coffee. They look even better if they are a little streaky where the stain gets into the turn of the bias binding. Attach the bolt rope to

Flags and pendants

There are a number of areas where model-shipwrighting can lead into realms well beyond the safety of mere modelmaking. With the flags it is necessary to proceed with caution, because in 1861 the old system of squadron flags being either red, white or blue was itself under review in the Royal Navy, and an Order in Council was proceeding through Parliament during the first commission of *Warrior*, and finally passed in 1864, confirming the use of the White Ensign only for Her Majesty's ships of the Royal Navy. Thus the builder's model, completed in 1859, shows the White Squadron flag, accurate for the pre-launch period, but all other sources, that is to say, the ship as painted, photographed and restored, show the Red Squadron, or senior, flag, later adopted for the Merchant Navy Service as the Red Ensign: *Warrior*, in fact, flew both.[1]

The Red Squadron flag for *Warrior* was a gigantic piece of bunting cloth, some 30ft x 15ft, flying from the mizzen gaff, and visible and recognisable as far as the eye could see. At the time, warships' ensigns were the only feature recognisable from afar and capable of identifying friend from foe: this is the reason for their immense size. Note that the ensign was flown from the staff when in harbour, and from the gaff when at sea. Likewise, the jack was only flown in harbour and virtually never at sea; this was logical in that its position at the bowsprit cap was an already overcrowded site in terms of sails and running gear and further interference was uncalled for.

Thermofixable dyes

The most pressing concern has to do with dyeing the fabric in the manufacture of the flags. Dyes, and their uses on fabric, have come a long way in the past few years, responding to the apparent need for everyone to have something written on their chest. This has led to a new generation of thermofixable dyes, which are basically dependent on a heat source to convert them into the fixed state. Fixing is something which can be done domestically with an iron with the fabric between two sheets of paper.

The key to being able to use fabrics such as silk in much the same way as you would treat paper is an agent called gutta,

a water-based sealant used by silk painters, which stops the inks and dyes from bleeding across the weft and warp of the material. When the design is complete, the water-based, transparent gutta can be rinsed away, allowing the cloth to return to the floppy state which is important in miniature flagmaking. If cotton voile is used then gutta is not necessary. If the dyes are being used in an undiluted state, one can paint directly onto the surface without the colours either running into one another or bleeding into the material itself. It is possible to allow the dye to run by thinning it down, but that is not really applicable to flagmaking, although one can achieve some very interesting fading effects by experiment with the paints, and the red colour of the ensign can be deliberately salt-stained. A good tip is to keep a hairdryer handy for where the lines go tightly together, drying off the colours in blocks as you proceed. This way there is no chance that the colours can interfere with one another. I used Setacolor fabric paints by Pebeo of France: in the fixed state these dyes are totally water-resistant, and thus have a very much longer life expectancy than pen dyes.

Instructions for flag and pendant making

Chose your material carefully: use a very light, but quite grainy, cotton voile, a material much like muslin cloth. One ought to be able to see through it very easily, important with flags, big and small: their appearance is quite different against the light compared to when the light is shining on them. As they trail in the wind, flags can appear translucent in places, or as blocks of colour, according to the way that the light falls on the cloth bunting. This is why they are so difficult to interpret and need subtle techniques in order to model them effectively and accurately.

It is essential to soak your material in tea or coffee, to stain down the white

1. Kemp, Peter, (ed), *The Oxford Companion to Ships and the Sea* (Oxford: Oxford University Press, 1976), p827.

colour of the cloth: this gives the flag an appearance of age and use, important because most flags are pretty dirty, especially those which have been flown in the wake of two smoking funnels. When the material is dry from its soaking to stain, you can proceed straight away with the dyes, unless you are using silk, which is notorious for colour bleeding. With silk you will need to insulate the drawn pattern with gutta, as described above, to seal the lines wherever they coincide. As mentioned, a hairdryer is a very useful piece of tackle in preventing bleeding, and experiments with it are well worthwhile.

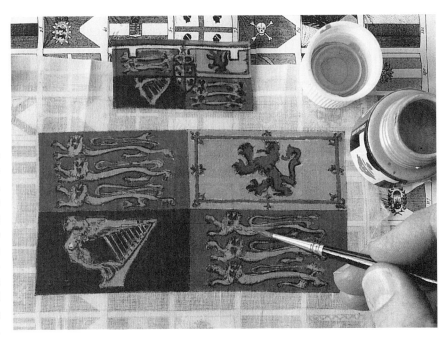

The material should be stretched out evenly on a board with some absorbent paper (blotting paper, kitchen towel, even lavatory paper will do) behind it to soak up the excess dye. The pattern should then be marked out with a waterproof fine tip pen and the dyes painted on with an ordinary watercolour brush. A good tip here is always to remember to use the *tip* of the brush when lining, and never its blind side. By rotating the board you will always have a top edge to paint, and the accuracy of your freehand painting will be improved.

If the borders of your flags are to be turned in with edge stitching, you must allow for mirror imaging along the edges, or they will not come together as a completed pattern when the flag is finally stitched together. Frankly, this is hardly worth the effort, and it is better to treat the edges with a matt varnish, which will prevent fraying and allow the flag to hang more naturally.

After painting the front side of the flag, reverse it, delineate the pen markings again, and block in the remaining colour. Try not to overdo the colouring or the pigment will spoil the translucency.

As a bit of indulgence, and because it was cold outside, I experimented with the production of the Royal Standard, as introduced in 1837, which flag has remained unchanged since then. It is not technically a flag at all, but perhaps one of the most complicated banners in heraldry, with lions passant and the Scottish lion rampant, as well as a harp of gold on a blue field representing Ireland. It is an impressive design and the dyes do it justice. The Admiralty flag, known as the Anchor flag, is another handsome flier, originally the flag of the Lord High Admiral, and always flown in conjunction with the Royal Standard at the launch of a ship. This flag is flown by the Sovereign on the foremast of the Royal Yacht, with the Royal Standard on the mainmast, and is most certainly part of the wardrobe of a major warship for use on royal occasions and reviews of the fleet; Queen Victoria's birthday was taken very seriously by her Senior Service.

The Royal banner, using Pebeo thermofixable dyes.

11

ENGINE AND BOILER

The Stuart Score engine used in my model arrived unassembled in a kit of parts which had been machined by Stuart Turner's factory. The engine is a horizontal form of the popular vertical Double Ten with a few alterations to the bedplate. The horizontal units do not normally have Stephenson's link reversing gear fitted, although the vertical ones do. The necessary modifications for going astern include lengthening the valve rods and a bit of judicious filing away at some other points which protrude on the cast iron bedplate. These projections would otherwise interfere with the motion of the link gear.

Illustration of Stuart Turner Score engine. (Author)

Engine assembly

The engine should be assembled according to the instructions. Expect to spend some time on this; it is a machined set of castings only, and not a proprietary ready-to-run unit. Common to full-sized practice, the crankshaft bearings should not be overtight when the engine is being run in, particularly the centre bearing. The cylinder head covers can also be difficult to access but, overall, the engine does look like a period piece of Victorian engineering, and is visually very pleasing.

Setting the valves

One snag encountered with the adaptation of this engine to reversing is setting the inside set of valve guide rods on the eccentrics of the crankshaft. This is not easy because there is no way of pinning the inside eccentrics to the crankshaft whilst this process is being set up. You might think that there would be a collar on the eccentric sheave to do this, but there is not. A way to overcome this is to use a product, made by Loctite, which is a non-permanent screw lock fluid for preventing screw threads from working loose.[1] This

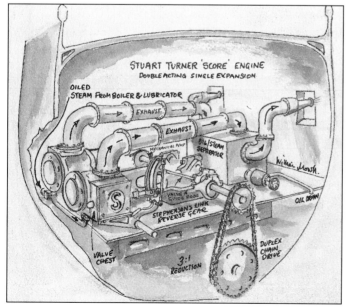

sets the eccentrics tightly in place so that the valves can be set up with the correct amount of lead and lap to allow for expansive steaming to work properly. With the Loctite product, it is just possible to move the eccentrics round the crankshaft. To set the valves by eye is nearly impossible; by far the best way of doing this is to connect the engine to a source of compressed air, and to disconnect the piston rods from the connecting rods. With the valves still connected to the crankshaft via the eccentrics, the engine can be rotated by hand, when the pistons will shoot backwards and forwards as the valves open. With suitable marks on the flywheel, the points at which this happens can be ascertained, and adjustments made to the position of the eccentrics until the valve timing is perfected. This is a ticklish job because, as always, there will be a compromise to be made on the ideal points at each end of each cylinder. It can, and nearly did drive my colleague to distraction, and as a *bona fide* engineer, he actually knows what he is doing.

Once the inside valves are correctly set, with much judicious oiling the engine turns over well enough. As with any new engine, there is a bedding-in process, where all the parts have minuscule high spots which need to be polished off by friction. The colour of the oil will tell you exactly how much of this is going on in the initial stages, and this is one of the further difficulties of valve-setting with an engine that has not yet been run in.

Setting the outside valves on their eccentrics is much easier, because these have collars and grub screws which attach directly to the crankshaft. Once their positions have been determined, and the engine run up in both directions, the two eccentric sheaves will have to be pinned together, but as the amount of shared

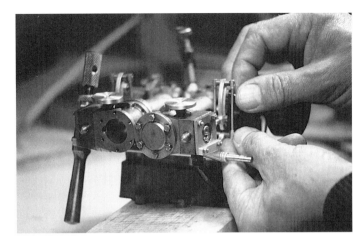

land on which to do this is so limited, some of the outer eccentric sheave's collar will have to be cut away to enable this to be carried out. This does not matter in terms of strength or engineering, but it would be kinder to novices if such things were mentioned in the instructions accompanying the kit of parts. For a complete tyro (which is where we all begin after all), the instructions badly need rewriting.

(Top)
Adjusting the reversing gear valve.

(Above)
Running in the newly assembled engine on compressed air, applying liberal amounts of oil to the crank bearings, and everywhere else.

(Left)
Preliminary siting of the model engine (Stuart Turner Score) with overhead condenser pipes.

1. This, along with the bulk of my education in boilermaking, I have learned from Geoff Sheppard, who is my longstanding mentor in this field.

That having been said, there is, in this engine's defence, nothing else on the market which so very definitely gives off the correct impression of a late-Victorian steam engine in miniature. Possibly because Stuart Turner's engines are simply miniatures of their larger full-scale units, the babies look just like their parents, and there is an uncanny resemblance in this engine to John Penn's trunk engine, of 'one thousand, two hundred and fifty horses' power' (as it is described on the Victorian plans), designed and made for *Warrior*.

Working pressure

There is a big difference, however, in terms of motion. The original engines of *Warrior* were slow-turning, low-pressure steam units operating from rectangular boilers producing 20psi at the top end of their output. The maximum revolutions of *Warrior*'s propeller was 53rpm, which in practical terms would mean that normal steaming would have averaged 30rpm, particularly as not all the boilers were used at once, and the top figures were always quoted from steaming trials. Stuart Turner engines are designed for high-pressure steam, for pistons which are quite happy running at 500rpm, provided there is a good supply of steam. This immediately suggests that for the purposes of this model it would be wise to gear the engine down, gaining extra power and realism. In passing, it is worth mentioning that at top scale speed, this model ought not to move at more than 2.25mph, which would represent approximately 15 knots.

Scale speed

There is a useful method for working out scale speed: if the vessel is known to have a top speed, for example of 14.02 knots, and a scale of 1:48, take the square root of the scale, $\sqrt{48}$, which in this case equals

6.928, then divide the known speed by this square root (14.02 ÷ 6.928), which gives a scale speed of 2.02 knots.

Chain drive

Chain was much used by Victorian engineers, and there seems no good reason to employ any other means of transmission when this option is so readily available.

With the *Great Britain*, Brunel faced exactly the same problem in reverse: that of gearing up a slow paddle-steamer engine to a suitable speed for a propeller. He used a double duplex chain drive wheel, with teeth made from *lignum vitae* timber for quiet running. No model made by my generation is really complete without some items of Meccano in it, and it so happens that this company still produce a 3:1 ratio toothed gear with chain to match, and in order to provide both belt and braces, two pairs of these have been fitted to give it that air of Victorian confidence.

'Tween decks

Gearing down the engine means raising the engine bed and putting lifting blocks under the unit. This has the advantage of bringing the engine closer to the underside of the main deck, and therefore making it easier to access and operate. Under the chequer plate is a lower bedplate, which is a kind of reinforced and heavily braced tray that will catch the drippings of the sump, and is bolted to the coverplate of the bilges and ballast compartment. The chequerplate pattern came from the railway fraternity and is made from etched steel. This 9in x 4in plate was used as a pattern for the overlay of sheet pewter, which is soft enough to be persuaded to replicate the diamond pattern. It is very laborious, but each little diamond shape has to be pressed home with a pencil; the overlaid sheet can then be contact glued to a flat piece of aluminium or any other flat surface, it is then sprayed with matt black and when dry cut back with wire wool to reveal the diamond pattern.[2] Finally, spray it over with matt shine varnish.

Pipes and condenser

The most prominent features of the original Penn trunk engine were the huge steam pipes which fed the monstrous cylinders and the exhaust pipes which carried the used steam from the cylinders to the condenser. It is these exhaust pipes (or what the Victorian engineers called eduction pipes) with their bolted flanges going across the engine that steal the limelight every time. All trunk engines have this as their birthright, because the condenser (a heavy object in full scale) balances up the weight of the cylinder heads opposite, and means that the whole engine is kept relatively compact, with a low centre of gravity. The prototypes were very popular, and John Penn's company could have engined more for the Black Battlefleet had he had the capacity to produce them more quickly. Incredibly, one of these engines made in 1857 is still in use, powering the paddle steamer *Diesbar* on the River Elbe - and is in perfect running order. The other large object to appear in the model's engine room is the boiler feed pump which, like the propeller shaft, is chain-driven rather than using skew gears off the crank. This largely covers the area of chequerplate but, as with many details, it is the glimpse of such things which adds to the final feeling that one is looking at an object that has been carefully observed. Unlike the boiler room, the engine room is approximately on a scale of 1:48, but it is interesting that steam plants in general can readily mix scales without the eye being at all offended. Something which works will transcend the squabbles about the sizes of hexagon nuts and so forth, simply because it has the ability to perform the full-scale function, and therein lies the granting of final respect.

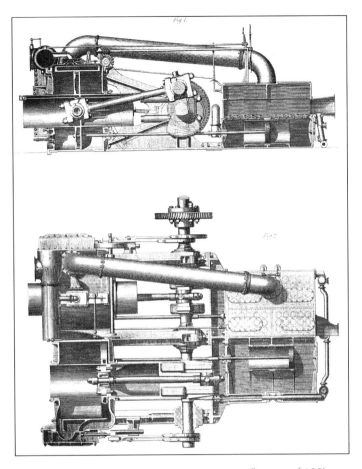

Illustration of 600hp John Penn trunk engine from Macquorn-Rankine's *Shipbuilding Theoretical and Practical*.

Boilers

The boilers which were installed in *Warrior* were of a type which was developed in the middle years of progress in the raising of marine steam. As with her contemporary, the *Great Eastern*, ten boilers were fitted on the latest pattern of Boulton, Watt & Co, but were centrally stoked from the gangway running the full length of the fore and aft stokehold. The stoking of the boilers was aided by the coal arriving in trucks on railway lines running from the bunkers to the furnace doors, with facilities provided for ash and clinker removal by using a system of buckets suspended from overhead rails. These buckets were hauled up to the weather deck, and the ash deposited down the ash chutes on either side of the sideheads. The ten

2. The sheet pewter comes from Fred Aldous Ltd; they also supply soft sheet copper which is extremely useful.

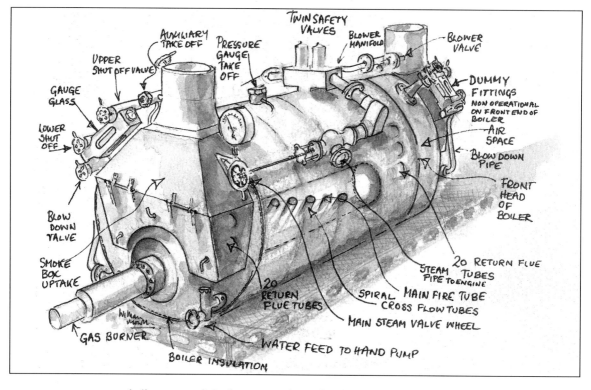

Illustration of model boilers. (Author)

Labels on illustration:
- TWIN SAFETY VALVES
- BLOWER MANIFOLD
- BLOWER VALVE
- AUXILIARY TAKE OFF
- PRESSURE GAUGE TAKE OFF
- UPPER SHUT OFF VALVE
- DUMMY FITTINGS NON OPERATIONAL ON FRONT END OF BOILER
- GAUGE GLASS
- AIR SPACE
- LOWER SHUT OFF
- BLOW DOWN PIPE
- FRONT HEAD OF BOILER
- BLOW DOWN VALVE
- SMOKE BOX UPTAKE
- 20 RETURN FLUE TUBES
- STEAM PIPE TO ENGINE
- 20 RETURN FLUE TUBES
- SPIRAL CROSS FLOW TUBES
- MAIN FIRE TUBE
- MAIN STEAM VALVE WHEEL
- GAS BURNER
- WATER FEED TO HAND PUMP
- BOILER INSULATION

boilers were of the box-type – iron-plated and riveted – and fitted with multi-tube flues which were ducted in such a way that they could exhaust up either one of the two funnels. Such boilers were not considered to be in the forefront of design at the time and were not even fitted with superheaters to dry out the steam between leaving the boilers and entering the steam chest of the engine, in spite of the fact that the practice was well understood by 1860.[3] The boilers were very susceptible to corrosion and were only just capable of producing the required working pressure of 22psi. However, this design was adopted because it had a proven record of reliability, and that was deemed to be more important than efficiency ratings. All marine boilers suffered from salt encrustation inside their shells, which had the undesirable consequence of insulating the boiler casings against the manful attempts of the stokers to bring them up to their working pressures. Only six in the aft stokehold would normally be in steam, whilst the others were held in reserve for such occasions as manoeuvring in harbour or when called to action stations.

No real improvement came about in boiler design until the use of steel rather than iron, and this development would not take place until almost thirty years after the launch of *Warrior*. In the later water tube boiler the internal workings were reversed, with the furnace heating the outside of the tubes containing the water enabling a steam pressure of (typically) 250psi to be achieved.

Box boilers acquired their name from their external features. Aboard *Warrior* they were 14ft 7in wide by 12ft 7in long by 12ft in height, with 440 brass tubes giving 20,755 sq ft of heating surface. The unladen weight was 3.35 tons, with four furnace grates per boiler, each 7ft 3in in length by 3ft in width.[4] Sadly, none of this has much relevance to miniature practice, because of the need for high pressure steam to feed the Stuart Turner horizontal engine.

Miniature boilermaking

The manufacture and production of a good, sound pressure vessel, is a highly skilled art, as well as a precise science.

3. Main, Thomas J, and Thomas Brown, *The Marine Steam Engine* (London: Longmans, 1860), p38.
4. Wells, Capt John, *The Immortal Warrior* (Emsworth, Hants: Kenneth Mason, 1987), p220.

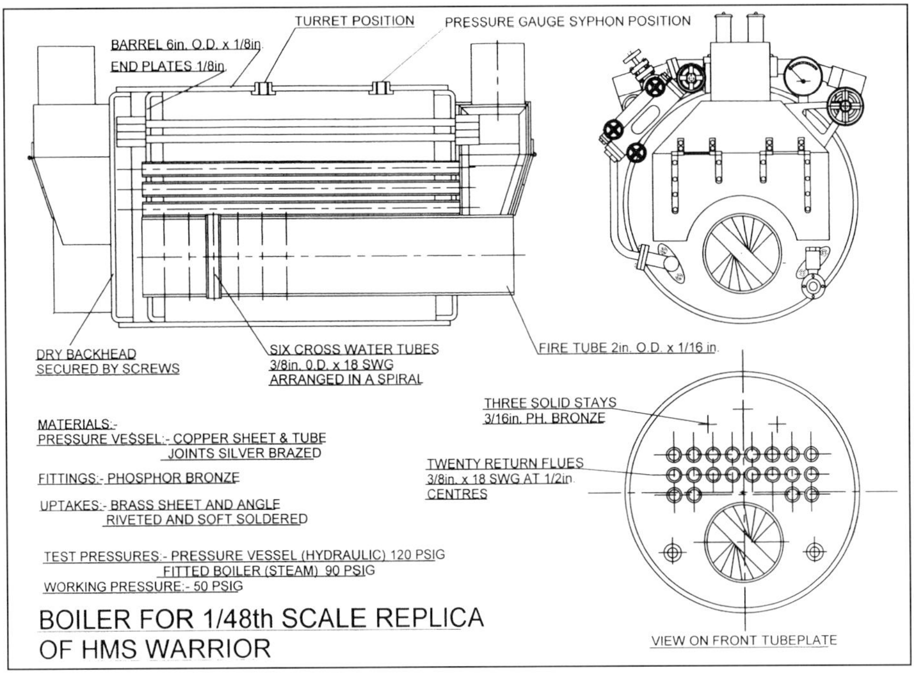

(Left)
Scale drawing of return flue boiler.
(Geoff Sheppard)

The silver-soldered seams must be perfect. The front and back plates as well as the fire tubes and boiler stays, which themselves must all be silver-brazed in such a way as to be able to withstand twice the normal working pressure of the boiler under test conditions, have to resist buckling and internal collapse. (Note that the term silver-brazing is correct for this process, although it is commonly referred to as silver-soldering.) These processes are reached by several separate heating stages involving drawn copper tube and copper plate, a metal notorious for its expansion and contraction. As with all soldering processes, if you can get it right first time, it is extremely satisfying. If your first attempt fails, it becomes progressively more difficult to repair. This means that much depends on good preparatory work in the initial design of the boiler and very careful fitting and machining in its construction.

Boiler pressures

The specific requirements for a miniature working boiler for the model of *Warrior* are very different from those demanded by the prototype. The initial working pressure for a model boiler like this needs to be approximately 60psi for the type of engine being used, although this pressure is reduced when the steam plant has been working for some while, and is thoroughly warmed through.

Coal *vs* gas

I had originally wanted to power the model by coal-firing, and to be able to stoke the boiler from both ends, which involved making a shared combustion chamber within the central section of the boiler. *Warrior*, and the later capital ships of the Channel Squadron which were to follow, were, in essence, all about coal, and I wanted to see and smell smoke coming out of the two funnels at once, and was prepared to pay the price of the filthy mess it would leave on the decks and the sails. A prototype boiler was contructed, but we became aware that with restricted access and only a very modest grate area, despite making the boiler as big as the hull would allow, this concept of coal-firing presented difficulties. The main ones would be how to stoke and trim a boiler efficiently in the middle of a voyage, as well as regulating the water feed and

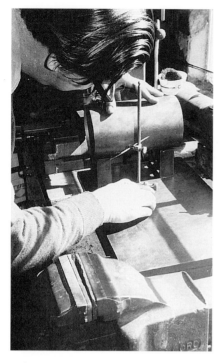

(Left)
Geoff Sheppard marking datum lines on the boiler shell for the model of SS *Great Britain*.

(Right)
lapping the endplate over the main firetube: note the spiral of crossflow tubes and the bronze stay rods (SS *Great Britain*).

steam pressure by remote control. These issues finally forced me to accept that bottled gas with a burner is the controllable answer, and this system has certainly served well over the years in my model of the *Great Britain*.

Boiler design

The design of boiler which has been found to work most efficiently in marine modelling terms is called a Scotch return flue boiler, with crossflow tubes fitted in the furnace tube. The appellation of return flue derives from the flow of heat which travels the length of the bottom furnace tube and returns in the form of hot gases from the front end of the boiler to the backhead plate *via* two smaller flues set above the main firepath. The importance of the crossflow tubes in the firehole is that they cause the water to bubble at the bottom of the boiler, and this has the effect of making the water circulate more efficiently with the hot water in the small tubes rising to the surface and drawing cold water in behind this disturbance, a

process known as ebullition.

Together, the tubing presents a good surface area of heated metal below the water level, and a practical amount of steam space at the top of the boiler, in which the steam is generated. A coal-fired boiler differs from this design in that a larger furnace tube is required to accommodate the grate and ashpan. Such boilers are heavier, and must allow access for stoking, as well as cleaning out accumulations of soot in the firetubes, and ashes beneath the firegrates. These considerations finally undid my initial ambitions. Nevertheless, a good compromise has been reached in that the newly-constructed boiler looks as though it is a coal-fired, multi-tubular boiler, complete with working furnace doors at either end and appropriate smokebox doors and uptakes but has, for the practical reasons mentioned above, been converted to gas.

Steam generation

To unaccustomed eyes, the boiler may look to be over-large for the task in hand, that is to say, the supply of steam to the Stuart Turner Score twin engine, which has a $3/4$in bore x $3/4$in stroke; however, these high revving engines are relatively greedy on steam, unless continuous fine adjustments are made to the reversing gear to obtain the ideal point of cut-off; the larger the model boiler fitted, the smoother the performance. It is also important to try to achieve a steady flow of steam for an engine which is running unattended, and because steam pressure rises as the water in the boiler diminishes, you are also involved in a balancing act of matching the demand for steam to the engine with pressure generated in the boiler and a rise and fall in water level. Steam pressure is very elastic, and a really big boiler that has a lot of middle ground for adjustment is therefore a desirable item. In practice what happens is this: when the operational heat has stabilised, the boiler safety valve can be set to approximately 25psi, after which, when the boiler pressure rises above this setting, the preset valve will automatically blow off, and delight onlookers with a column of steam, accompanied by suitable noises and smells.

Manufacture

No book of this sort can deal fully with a skill so scientific as boilermaking, but it is always interesting to know how things have been assembled, and what the necessary stages are to reach the production of a working steam pressure vessel.

The tooling represents some serious investment, namely, a metal turning lathe, a bandsaw, a pillar drill, taps, dies, measuring equipment, a forge, an industrial size propane heat gear, a bucket of acid pickle and a lot of courage and experience. To anyone who equates this sort of modelmaking as 'boys with toys' this will come as something of a shock. The reason for the seriousness with which boilermaking is regarded is quite simply that even a miniature boiler explosion differs very little from a full-sized blast bomb in its effect on bystanders. For this reason, every manufactured boiler must carry a certificate of inspection and safety, a requirement that has recently been reinforced by legislation from the European Community.

Having the machinery and other tackle in place, the next stage in boilermaking is to acquire the metals involved, not only the drawn copper tube for the boiler shell, but also the copper plate for the front and the two back ends of the boiler (wet and dry backs), and the tubing for the heating element. The copper vessel is also stayed with thin bronze rods in order to prevent the endplates blowing out as the pressure rises. Copper plate is surprisingly soft, so that the stays are necessary from a structural point of view. Before any work on the boiler takes place various formers must be made out of some sturdy pieces of aluminium plate, or plywood. The first of these comprises two discs which precisely fit the internal bore of the boiler shell, mounted at either end so that the shell ends can be accurately machined between centres on the lathe. A similar disc must be machined in order to act as a former around which the boiler endplates can be flanged, having been annealed (softened) several times at high temperature. The finished diameter of the former, on which the flanged endplate is to be made, will be equal to the internal diameter of the boiler shell minus twice the thickness of the material being used to make the endplate. Once the flange of the endplate has been carefully formed over this, the endplate should be a perfect push fit in the end of the boiler shell. There are three of these to be made, as well as a wet backhead, a wet front plate and a dry front cover, which is the cover plate at the front end of the boiler. This endplate reflects the heat generated in the firehole, allowing the hot gases to make the journey down the return flues to the backhead and heats the whole of the front end of the boiler by conduction.

Other preparations before the silver-soldering process can take place include drilling out the positions in the boiler shell and ends for the bronze bushes into

Fluxing up with Easy-Flo 2 paste (SS *Great Britain*).

Applying heat with industrial-sized nozzle on propane gas torch. Note the silver-solder stick and heat shield below the torch handle (SS *Great Britain*).

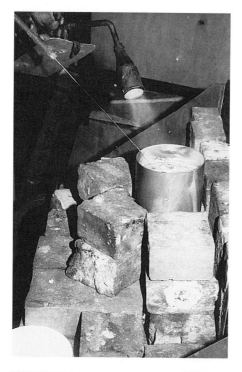

Placed back into the pickle bucket with tongs.

5. Johnson Matthey Silver-Flo 16, melting range 790-830ºC.

must have the matching furnace and fire-tube holes accurately cut out and reamed. Geoff Sheppard, who made both my boilers, has a device which raises a ring around the circumference of each of the smaller tubes, a short distance from its end, a process which gives them a slightly trumpeted lip at the point of contact with the endplate. This increases the surface area for the silver-solder to take hold, and provides a ring of strength at this critical annular point. The furnace tube has the crossflow tubes at its far end, silver-soldered with a higher temperature solder than the rest of the boiler.[5] This is because the boiler shell will have to be heated several times in the process of manufacture with the firetube *in situ*. This is called step-soldering, and more complicated boilers may have several such stages involved in their production. The cross tubes are also flared over where the ends protrude through the furnace tube, again increasing the strength of the joint.

The rest of the boiler will use either Silver-Flo 24 or Easy-Flo No 2 (melting range 608-617ºC) with matching flux. Each solder has a lower melting temperature than the other, but each requires the metal to reach red-heat, or close to it, before it disperses in the path of the flux. The flux is mixed into a white paste, which melts into a translucent state when sufficient heat has been applied.

When the flux appears as a clear liquid, that is the moment when the stick of silver-solder has to be applied, and the skill is judging just the right moment to do this. It is not long before it starts to burn out, and that is why one needs a burst of heat, taking the temperature up as quickly as possible, so that the flux is not spoiled by premature burnout. In contrast, the newly-soldered boiler shell must be allowed to cool down as slowly as possible, so that the contracting metal does not distort the structure. Differential contraction, caused by one piece of metal being thicker than the piece to which it is joined,

which the boiler fittings will be screwed later, and a thorough cleansing of all the component parts in acid pickle to make them all chemically clean. The endplates

(Above)
Broadside fire.

(Left)
First steaming of model
boiler.

boiler backhead is always crowded. The funnel uptakes have either to be cast, or fabricated as in the case of this model, and stay-bolts fitted to the boiler ends, to which smoke boxes can be attached. To make the casing of the smoke boxes gastight, packing material must be used as a gasket between the backhead plate and the uptake. Good boiler design must also include the fitting of a water gauge, with a blowdown cock, pressure gauge, water feed pipe, and steam take-off valve. On the top of the boiler, headroom must be allowed for the safety valves, the steam dome and manifold, and steam supplies to auxiliary equipment.

Both a mechanical water feed pump and a hand pump are fitted to the boiler. Logic dictates that the hand pump is used to prime the boiler until the boiler is in steam, whereupon the mechanical pump, which works off the crankshaft of the engine, can take over when the engine is in motion. The water for the feed supply is in a tank forward of the boiler room bulkhead, with a filler cap placed beneath the decking over the fo'c'sle hatch.

The displacement oiler which connects to the outflow of the steam line between the boiler and engine has been specially made in the old-fashioned style of a glass lantern. This ensures that the pistons are kept lubricated when the engine is in steam by saturating the steam with oil before it enters the steam chest and cylinder block. When the steam has performed its task, the exhaust line includes a separator (condenser) which removes the oil droplets into a sump before the purified steam is directed up to the adapted gun barrels, simulating gunfire.

can cause distortional havoc. At the end of the heating process a lid is put over the soldered boiler and the surrounding firebricks retain a good deal of heat, which means that the cooling process is lengthened.

When everything has cooled down an initial inspection can take place before putting the whole item back into the pickle bucket, which chemically removes the otherwise destructive flux. If all has gone well, the boiler is then pressure-tested hydraulically, normally to twice its working pressure, using a pump and with the boiler filled full of water. It must maintain this pressure for a twenty-four hour period before being certified as safe to use.

Boiler fittings

The surrounding pipework and fittings are added according to the needs of the vessel, although the available space on the

12
FLOATING OUT

In the great days of sail, when wooden walls reigned supreme in both grace and favour, the Admiralty were naturally sceptical about ship propulsion by propeller, and subsequently careful in its

Baseplate and plummer blocks supporting the ball bearing races to the mainshaft.

adoption. Given the problems of installing a propeller and lineshaft, approximately a quarter the length of the ship, one can well sympathise with their Lordships, as well as with the engineers who had to make such things work. Wherever one has revolving shafts and alignment with more than two bearings, the accuracy called for in both machining and fitting will be of a high order.

Water ingress

Where the bearing surfaces are sited below the waterline, there is likely to be trouble with water ingress. In full-sized ships, the stern bearing of the propeller shaft and the boss (set within the stern run of the hull) house a stuffing gland which is of constant concern to the Chief Engineer, being the most likely source of leakage into the hull. No stuffing gland can be perfectly watertight for long: neoprene O-seals are how the modern modeller gets over the issue. In theory they are an excellent solution: they will stand a great deal of punishment, and are easily fitted in a groove machined into the tailshaft. The groove must match the dimensions of the ring, which should be allowed to protrude approximately 0.004in more than the diameter of the shaft. With the squash factor, a difficult thing to calculate, the shaft should be a sliding fit and the ring(s) give a watertight seal without causing undue friction. If you feel a slight caution in the narrative at this point, it is because there is no guarantee that it will work as it should, and one is mindful of the troubles which the American Space Programme has had with these little marvels of technology.

Essentials of design

This lineshaft ought to be fitted and tested before putting the main and upper decks onto the model. Unfortunately, logic and life do not always hold hands and my own delay in doing this essential piece of work had to do with an apprehension about how it could best be designed. As you may deduce from the schematic sketch, under the floor of the model was to have been water ballast, so that the bedding plates which support the pedestals for the plummer blocks could not be bolted through the floor, and would therefore have to be set in epoxy resin.

Universal couplings

The other concern I had was that the lineshaft has to be horizontal at the head and tail, but sloping in the intermediate section in order to bring the tailshaft below the waterline. This means using universal couplings, being aware that extra energy is absorbed by these joints, which ideally run best in the straightest line possible. However, they would have been employed whatever the circumstances, because these couplings remove the problem of mis-alignment and vibration which any lineshaft of this length would bring about.

Ball-bearing races

The length of the shafting runs in ball-bearing races, which means constructing three bearing housings set on pedestals, fabricated from brass. This means that the whole lineshaft can be removed, complete with bearing housings if necessary. These plummer blocks, in line with common full-sized practice, should have oil cups fitted, particularly as the bearings being used are open on one side so that an external drip feed is appropriate.

Removability and access

A personal mantra is to insist that access to working parts is always possible: not necessarily easy, but possible. Apart from the base plates and bolts, all the couplings

Schematic sketch on four deck levels.
(Author)

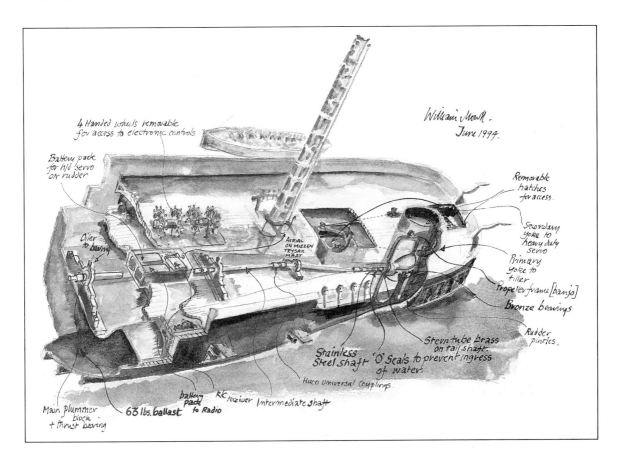

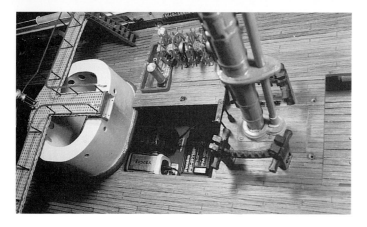

Radio control centre
sited beneath the helm.

can be reached either via the engine room, or through the hatches directly overhead. The most likely need to remove these in the future will be to renew the O-seals but, of course, the hope is that this will not be for a few years. (See the later description of the launch of the model for further discussion of this point.)

Electrochemistry

The baseplate bolts are of some concern, in that they are set in a block of aluminium and have therefore to be made of brass, rather than steel. Many modellers will be aware that steel and aluminium on the Galvanic Scale are electrochemically very active in the presence of sea water. Brass is a much better companion to aluminium and a quote from Ron Warring's book, *Radio-Controlled Model Boats*, is worth considering: 'When two dissimilar metals are in contact, and wetted with any solution which is an active electrolyte, (eg salt water) the more anodic metal will corrode'.[1] In the case of the *Warrior* model, this means that the aluminium would corrode long before the brass bolts were attacked. The hope is that sea water will not find its way into the hull at all, but I also know enough about the practicalities of boating to be cautious. Salt water is very bad news to everything except fish.

Fitting the radio control

Radio control is at once both completely magical and an utter mystery to the author. The transmitter uses the 40Mhz band, has seven channels, and it all functions according to the instructions. These do mention keeping the bits and pieces of radio-control well away from coal dust, oil, bilge water and even rain water. The R/C receiver centre, which includes two batteries and a junction box, is therefore sited pretty well directly under the armoured rifle tower, in a separately suspended metal box. In full scale, the rifle tower marked the first step in the Royal Navy's eventual concept of central control, a single point from whence all the orders for the ship could be issued. This ties in neatly with the general idea of its being the nerve centre of the model. It also means that the considerable amount of wiring associated with it can be hidden away under the main deck, and not spoil the look of the gun deck with festoons of anachronistic cabling.

Rudder control

The rudder has a heavy-duty servo attached to it, because a good deal of displaced weight has to be steered on the tiller arms. The original full-sized rudder had a complex pulley system using sheaved blocks to activate it. The model has a simplified version, using stainless steel wire with a breaking strain of approximately 30lb stretched between a primary and secondary yoke. It will be a matter of experiment to find out whether or not the rudder is efficient enough not to require attaching an extra surface area in the form of a false rudder; if this is required, then obviously the heavy-duty servo will have to work even harder. It has a separate battery pack to power it, housed in the control centre.

Floating out trials

Ideal conditions for floating out trials are difficult to come by, but 25 June 1994 was, in terms of the weather, a day of total

1. Warring, Ron, *Radio-Controlled Model Boats* (Watford: MAP/Argus, 1981), p119. Another useful publication is John Cundell's *Installing Radio Control in Boats* (Hemel Hempstead: Argus Books, 1990); his *Introducing Model Marine Steam* (also Argus, 1990) is a further source of general information.

calm. Certain vital things were of major concern once the launch had been executed, foremost of which were the internal water ballasting arrangements; secondly, would the complicated joint between the hull and the tailshaft tube be watertight? Thirdly, would the vessel float to the waterline in trim? Fourthly, would the stern tube and fitted O-rings be watertight?

At first, things went well; it took 63lb of water to bring the vessel into trim and there were no leaks in vital places. Household bricks were shifted about on the internal floor of the ship, substituting for the then absent machinery, and the propeller was brought into action by use of a temporarily fixed, battery-powered screwdriver. Household bricks weigh 6lb apiece; it took four of these to trim out to the load waterline so that the total displaced weight was three buckets of water at 21lb each, four household bricks and the weight of the model as well (58lb): a total of approximately 145lb. It was proved to be an incredibly heavy object, but it did float, and for over an hour the vessel tasted freedom and motion for the first time ever.

A qualified success

Exciting as this preliminary launch was, the shadow of a big issue emerged from the experiment. The original calculations required the wing tanks to be fitted above the floor of the vessel. Unless the wing tanks were full, the water could move about, thus destabilising the hull, and that was not good news. In short, it meant that the whole idea of water-ballasting would now be ruled out, reverting to ballasting the keel more traditionally, with 63lb of lead. (This is not to say that large model boats cannot be ballasted with water, but it is almost impossible to calculate at the outset where the greatest volume of water will be required in the hull, and how that water can be kept confined.)

The launching trials had shown that the ballasted weight for this model has to be placed directly under the mainmast, aft of the ship's central point of balance and astern beneath the propeller shaft, in order to counterbalance the weight of the boiler: a serious 23lb when filled with water. The boiler also represents top weight, that is to say it is sited above the metacentric level of the hull, and must be counterbalanced in order to avoid destabilisation, particularly under sailing conditions.

Up with the floor

The GRP floor of the model had to be cut in order to insert long strips of lead from midships to the stern quarters beneath the

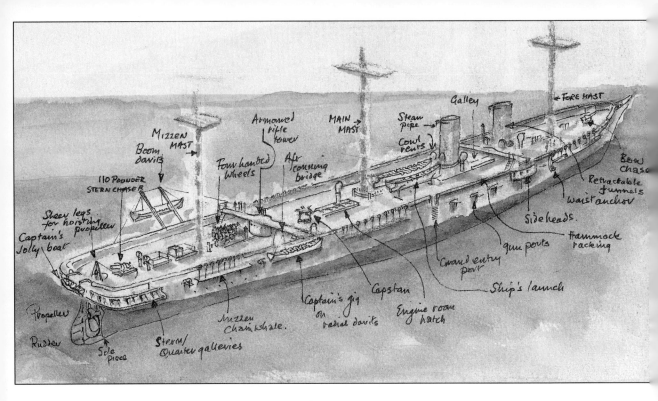

Labels on the sketch:

MIZZEN MAST
Boom davits
110 POUNDER STERN CHASER
Sheer legs for hoisting propeller
Captain's Jolly boat
Propeller
Rudder
Sole pieces
Stern/Quarter galleries
Mizzen Chain whale.
Captain's gig on radial davits
Capstan
Engine room hatch
Four handed wheels
Armoured rifle tower
Aft conning bridge
MAIN MAST
Steam pipe
Cowl vents
Galley
FORE MAST
Bow chase
Retractable funnels
waist anchor
Sideheads.
Hammock racking
gun ports
Grand entry port
Ship's launch

Sketch of general arrangements. (Author)

floor beams. Twenty-two of these long lengths, eleven strips either side of the keelson, added up to a total of 63lb, and under test conditions brought the model to the correct load waterline at the stern, balanced by an unfilled boiler forward of midships. The bow was at this point marginally light but that would be evened out with the feedwater tank supplying the boiler, placed in the forepeak of the boat. Any further forward ballast required could be provided with chain.

Some crumbs of comfort were derived from the knowledge that the original *Warrior* also had weight distribution problems, mainly arising from the heavy iron knee forming the clipper bow, which made her prone to snouting. This was somewhat cured during her second major refit, with the addition of a poop deck weighing 340 tons, trying to combat the trim of a hull whose forward draught was 7in lower than her stern. Her present problem at Portsmouth is in reverse order, in that she cannot be laden to the waterline due to the shallowness of the water alongside the quay and the lack of machin-

ery weight. Such ballast as she does carry is largely made up of cast iron railway track chairs.

The launching cradle

In order to move what has become a similar weight to a baby crocodile, it has been necessary to construct a launching cradle in which the model is now permanently placed, with particular regard to supporting the length of the ballasted keel. The cradle has a maximum of six carrying points, which are three chrome steel crossbars with lengths of hardwood timber inserted in them for extra strength. These cross poles can be removed when the vessel is in display mode, and means that she is at all times fully supported, and can be carried without having to handle the hull. It is at the point of launching and retrieving that the model is at its most vulnerable, and one is necessarily reliant on volunteers, often with no previous experience of lifting heavy but fragile objects. One is always working with a new team, because if they have ever been asked to participate in the past, they know never to volunteer again!

EPILOGUE
THE LAUNCH

The launch of the original *Warrior* on 29 December 1860 was a very protracted affair. In that very bleak midwinter the newly-constructed ship was frozen solid in the slipway and unsuccessful attempts were made to melt the frozen grease down the rails of the inclined plane, using any receptacle from the shipyard in which a fire could be lit. Extra tugs were sent for and hydraulic rams were also used in the attempt to free her, as well as hundreds of dockers, who ran from one side of the upper deck to the other to induce a rocking motion; finally all these efforts bore fruit and she moved slowly down the slipway into the solidly frozen and snow-covered London River.

There have been hints throughout the account of the building of my model of this vessel that my ultimate intention was for her to be launched into the sea, because I have always thought of her as a miniature replica down to the last detail, and a truly working model. Part of the realisation of my dream would be to see her riding through waves, justifying her full wardrobe of sails, and the 63lb of lead ballast carried along her keelson. I also had a deeply held desire to see how she would perform under the stressful conditions of a reasonable sea breeze, in a real tideway, straining every sinew.

Weather conditions on 28 August 1996, the date chosen for the launch, were such that, had I been on my own, I would have turned back, but it is surprising how brave one becomes with a television camera crew urging one on, reinforced by the consciousness that there is a hired lorry waiting in the yacht club car park as well as another group of well-wishers on the sea wall, some of whom had taken time off work just to see the ship finally take to the open sea. With all these onlookers waiting for action, there could be no question of turning back, despite a bracing 20knot onshore breeze.

A small group of young people arranged in a flank along the seashore were the official launching party for the replica vessel. Some suitably chosen words were spoken over the newly-commissioned ship as she lay in her launching cradle, and there was a fluttering of flags, the Union flag and the national one of St George, valiantly held in position by the colour party, as the tide raced across the foreshore. A miniature bottle of Navy rum was placed aboard for the crew, at the same time as the incoming tide began to lap determinedly against the offshore side of the ship. Operationally speaking, there

Down the slipway on the foreshore; note the essential launching cradle and carrying handles which keep the personnel away from the model.

was no question of being able to control her, conditions being far too rough for anything other than straight running with a fixed rudder.

With the wind coming off the sea, and the tide running up the shoreline, I wondered how we would ever get her off without either losing her to the open sea, or seeing her founder against the nearest breakwater; either way the vision of the sixteen years' work that she symbolised seemed to me in imminent danger of being lost forever! Despite the fact that it took four men to launch this vessel, once on the water her intentions were very obvious. She wished to join the Channel Squadron, and was tugging to be let off the lead like a greyhound pup.

Under sail alone

I have always found it very hard to believe in the efficiency of sail; one can hold a suit of model sails in the palm of one's hand, weighing next to nothing, yet they have the energy to move a displaced weight of over 100lb, powering a model ship across water in an apparently effortless manner, and the model *Warrior*'s sea outing proves to me that this ship was first and foremost a sailing ship. Her sea-keeping qualities were fascinating, in that she did not ride on top of the waves but cut through them

in an unyielding way, demonstrating the strength of the iron hull design, and its ability to cope with adverse and difficult conditions. Even at this reduced scale, one could also see clearly that the long low profile of the hull would act as a much more stable gun-platform than the three-decker wooden-walled ships of the line which immediately preceded her. Equally obvious was the inference that under these conditions at full scale, ships concerned with broadside fire would not have been capable of firing a single shot in anger. All the effort would have been put into sailing and controlling the ship. My guess is also that it would have been nearly impossible to stoke boilers and keep the furnace fires trimmed under such extremes of weather, and it makes one realise that an engined hybrid vessel must have been extremely difficult to manage in such a seaway.

Damage

On maiden voyages one expects both damage and loss. The surprise for me was how little injury there was to the structure of the ship, and the fine lines of rigging. The martingale chain is always vulnerable in small scale, but can be repaired quite easily. The spanker boom was broken, at the weak point where the cheek sheaves are fitted, and I lost the propeller well cover

Free at last in the English Channel with a 20knot onshore breeze, and a sixteen-year dream fulfilled.

when the following sea pooped the stern in the rescue operation to drag her clear of the waves breaking on the shore. Of much greater concern were the electrics, which had been awash with seawater, despite the fact that they were below decks and in separate housings.

On arrival back into the workshop, this issue needed to receive priority attention as electrolytic action starts immediately sea water becomes involved with electrical current. Realising this, John Cundell, Editor of *Model Boats*, removed the radio receiver before the homeward journey and doused it in a freshwater puddle behind the sea wall; this was of course not ideal, but was a great help in a crisis. Back in the workshop, the battery packs were removed and revealed electrolysis on the move; likewise the switches and leads. The plastic-moulded covers had to come off the rudder servo and the winch servo, although the latter had proved to be totally watertight, as promised in the Abel brochure. I was tempted to use WD40 moisture repellent to try and counteract the effects of the seawater on these items, but do not do this, as it could actually seal in the water. Instead, use a high pressure aerosol electronic switch/contact cleaner, available from radio component stores, as this blows out the moisture without leaving any residue. This ought to be part of the maintenance kit which is carried wherever this sort of problem is going to arise.

Stripped bare

I had not thought that I was going to have to strip this vessel down again quite so soon after assembling it all, but in order to rid the hull of fine sand, as well as salt water, the drive lineshaft had to come out, and this involved removing the boiler housing, the feedwater tank and the bearings, which were grinding with minute particles of sand and sea-shells. There was also a draping of seaweed, which had wrapped itself around the mizzen shrouds

in a very authentic manner. That trophy will stay put as proof of the conditions endured, and as silent witness that she has survived the ultimate test of sailing in the English Channel.

Anyone contemplating a similar launch needs to consider carefully the sanity of doing such a thing, and the considerable risks involved, but if you still feel determined on such a rash act, the following points should be borne in mind.

First, check the tide tables: an ebb tide is easier to deal with than an incoming tide. For transportation, you will need a lorry with a 12ft flatbed because of the height and width of the model - this is not the sort of item to be carried casually in the back of a van. You will also need a very strong launching cradle, with lifting crossbars fitted, and preferably with wheels or rollers on it. A useful tip is to use two full-sized inflatable rubber fenders (available from yacht chandlers) as rollers under the launching cradle.

The launching site must have a slipway or ramp nearby, to enable the vessel to get from lorry to beach without undue difficulties. To assist you, you will need four people who are prepared to get their feet (and more) wet; for lifting the ship out again at the end of the voyage, when the hull has shipped a considerable amount of water and become much heavier, strength and a good pair of waders, or wellington boots, are almost indispensable. Needless

An anxious moment for Joe Brewer guiding the model onto the cradle. An improvement would be to attach buoyancy to the carrying handles. Always something new to learn!

to say, these helpers should be free of cameras and other impedimenta which might hinder their ability to plunge enthusiastically into the sea.

Sea-cocks should be fitted to the hull bottom in order to drain off the water in the bilge (large brass nuts set into the hull with epoxy resin, and brass bolts with rubber washers work well), and if you can run to a rescue boat, that is an added luxury.

There are always over-excited beach dogs to contend with; no one knows where they come from, but they are a guaranteed audience, and they usually arrive in pairs without a collar between them.

Feelings

Overall, it was an exhilarating experience, too fraught for true enjoyment at the time, but wonderful to look back on. I do not in any way regret the necessary repairs involved or the considerable experience gained by having launched her into the same waters as her big sister sailed all those years ago, when the Channel Squadron was a familiar sight off the East Kent coastline. What a sight that must have been!

* * *

I wrote at the beginning of this book about the challenge to build a model of *Warrior* as a 'roaring lion': one which could neither be ignored, nor would it slink away of its own accord.

This challenge was also faced by the original builders. An often quoted exchange is one which took place between Sir John Pakington, First Lord of the Admiralty, and Mr Peter Rolt, Chairman of the

Thames Iron Works & Shipbuilding Company, when they were admiring the results of their labours. Packington said to Rolt, 'I often wonder how I mustered sufficient courage to order such a novel vessel.' Rolt's response was 'I often wonder how I mustered sufficient courage to undertake its construction.'

My roaring lion has temporarily left the scene of the kill, and slunk off back to the edge of the jungle, but I am also aware that the jungle has many more animals to its name, and that like creation, it never sleeps.

Craftsmanship

Some ever would be where they're not,
Would ever have that they've not got.
True happiness - contented mind
Sufficient near at hand will find.
Absorbing interests lie all round,
Will by observant mind be found,
Create something however small,
There lies the truest joy all,
When brain and hand together strive,
Real happiness becomes alive.
In the pursuit the pleasure lies,
The how and wherefore to devise.
Though vision dreamed will far excel
The work achieved, yet it is well,
To have attempted is not in vain.
Failure urges one on again.
Great craftsman, asked once to decide
Which was his greatest work, replied
Simply with these two words 'My next'.
For 'ever better' was his text.

CHARLES WADE[1]

1. I am grateful to the Curator of Snowshill Manor, Snowshill Village, Gloucester (a National Trust property) for permission to quote this poem.

Bibliography

Abell, Sir Westcott, *The Shipwright's Trade* (1948) (London, Conway Maritime Press edn, 1981)

Armstrong, Richard, *Powered Ships: The Beginnings* (London: Benn, 1974)

Aspin, B Terry, *The Backyard Foundry* (Watford: MAP/Argus, 1978)

Ballard, Admiral G A, *The Black Battlefleet* (London: Society for Nautical Research, 1980)

Bramwell, Martyn, *The International Book of Wood* (London: Mitchell Beazley, 1979)

Brinnin, John Malcolm, *The Sway of the Grand Saloon* (London: Macmillan, 1972)

Brown, D K, and John Wells, *'HMS Warrior'*, Paper No 2, Royal Institute of Naval Architects, Spring Meeting 1986

Brownlee, Walter, with drawings by John E Wigston, *Warrior: The First Modern Battleship* (Cambridge: Cambridge University Press, 1985)

Bullen, F L, *The Ventilation of Ships* (Liverpool: 3rd edn, 1950)

Cantwell, Anthony, and Peter Sprack, *The Needles Defences*, The Solent Papers No 2 (Ryde, IOW: Redoubt Consultancy, 1986)

Corlett, Ewan, *The Iron Ship* (Bradford-on-Avon: Moonraker Press, 1975)

Cossons, Neil, *Industrial Archaeology*.

Cundell, John, *Installing Radio Control in Boats* (Hemel Hempstead: Argus, 1990), and Jim King, *Introducing Model Marine Steam* (Hemel Hempstead: Argus, 1990)

Emmerson, George, S, *John Scott Russell: A Great Victorian Engineer and Naval Architect* (London, 1977)

Health and Safety Leaflet (Reading: Tiranti, 1991)

Kemp, Peter, (ed), *The Oxford Companion to Ships and the Sea* (Oxford: Oxford University Press, 1976)

Lavery, Brian, *The Arming and Fitting of English Ships of War 1600-1815* (London: Conway Maritime Press, 1987)

Lees, J, *The Masting and Rigging of English Ships of War 1625-1860* (London: Conway Maritime Press, 1984 edn)

Longridge, C Nepean, *The Anatomy of Nelson's Ships*, revised by E Bowness (Watford: MAP/Argus, 1977)

Macquorn Rankine, W J, (ed), *Shipbuilding Theoretical and Practical* (London: Wm Mackenzie, 1863)

Main, Thomas J, and Thomas Brown, *The Marine Steam Engine, Designed Chiefly for the Use of the Officers of Her Majesty's Navy* (Longman, 1865)

Mowll, William, *SS Great Britain: The Model Ship* (Watford: MAP/Argus, 1982)

Nares, Lieut George S, *Seamanship* (1862), first published in 1860 as *The Naval Cadet's Guide: or Seaman's Companion*), facsimile of second edition, introduced by David R Macgregor (Woking: Gresham Books, 1979)

Paasch, Capt H, *Illustrated Marine Encyclopedia* (1890), facsimile reprint edition with an introduction by David R Macgregor (Watford: MAP/Argus, 1977)

Perlmutter, Tom, (ed), *War Machines at Sea* (London: Octopus Books, 1975)

Ropp, Theodore, *The Development of a Modern Navy: French Naval Policy 1871-1904* (Annapolis, Maryland: Naval Institute Press, 1987)

Russell, John Scott, *Ships of War* (London: ?1866)

Spratt, H P, *Marine Engineering Descriptive Catalogue* (London: Science Museum, u/d)

Stammer, M K, *Ships' Figureheads* (Prince's Risborough, Bucks: Shire Publications, 1983)

Underhill, H, *Masting and Rigging the Clipper Ship and Ocean Carrier* (Glasgow: Brown Son & Ferguson, 1988)

Warring, Ron, *Radio-Controlled Model Boats* (Watford: MAP/Argus, 1981)

Warrior News, Issue No 5 (1983)

Wells, Capt John, *The Immortal Warrior* (Emsworth, Hants: Kenneth Mason, 1987)

Further Reading

Engineering History

Bourne, John, *A Catechism of the Steam Engine* (Longmans, Green & Co, 1885)

Sothern, J W M, *"Verbal" Notes and Sketches for Marine Engineers*, 12th edition (London: Technical Press, 1939)

Thearle, Samuel J P, *Naval Architecture: Laying Off and Building Wood Iron and Composite Ships* (London: William Collins, ?1900)

Engineering and Metal

Bradley, Ian, *The Amateur's Workshop* (Watford: MAP/Argus, 1976)

———————, *Myford Series 7 Manual* (Watford: MAP/Argus, 1982)

Britten, F J, *Britten's Watch and Clock Maker's Handbook, Dictionary and Guide*, 10th edn, revised by Richard Good (London: Methuen, 1987)

Calvert, N G, *Steam Engine Principles: Their Application on a Small Scale* (Southampton: Calvert Technical Press, 1991)

Dyer, Herbert J, *How to Work Sheet Metal* (Watford: MAP/Argus, 1948)

Horth, A C, *Repoussé Metalwork* (London: Methuen, 1905)

Kronquist, Emil F, *Metalcraft and Jewelry* (Peroia, Illinois: Manual Arts Press, 1926)

Rolt, L T C, *Victorian Engineering* (Harmondsworth: Penguin, 1970)

Sparey, Laurence, *The Amateur's Lathe* (Watford: MAP/Argus, 1948)

Throp, Arnold, *Vertical Milling in the Home Workshop* (Watford: MAP/Argus, 1977)

Vaughan, Adrian, *Isambard Kingdom Brunel: Engineering Knight Errant* (London: John Murray, 1991)

Ships and the Sea

Abramson, Erik, *Ships of the High Seas* (Eurobook, 1976)

Archibald, E H H, *The Fighting Ships of the Royal Navy 897-1984* (Dorset: Blandford, Press, 1984)

Barraclough, E M C, and W G Crampton,

Flags of the World (London: Frederick Warne, 1978)

Dixon, Conrad, *Ships of the Victorian Navy* (Shedfield, Hants: Ashford Press/Society for Nautical Research, 1987)

Emmerson, George S, *The Greatest Iron Ship: SS Great Eastern* (Newton Abbott: David & Charles, u/d)

Fabb, John, with an introduction by A C McGowan, *The Victorian and Edwardian Navy from Old Photographs* (London: Batsford, 1976)

Gardiner, Robert, *The Advent of Steam: The Merchant Steamship before 1900* (London: Conway Maritime Press, 1993)

Goodenough, Simon, *Sailing Ships* (London: Albany Books, 1981)

Goold-Adams, Richard, *The Return of the Great Britain* (London: Weidenfeld & Nicholson, 1976)

Greenhill, Basil, *The National Maritime Museum* (London: Philip Wilson, 1982)

Griffiths, Denis, *Brunel's Great Western* (Wellingborough, Northants: Thorsons, 1985)

Jane, Fred T, *The British Battle Fleet* (London: The Library Press, 1915)

Kemp, Peter, *The History of Ships* (London: Orbis, 1978)

———————, and Richard Ormond, *The Great Age of Sail: Treasures from the National Maritime Museum, Greenwich* (London: Phaidon, 1986)

Holdsworth, Richard, and Brian Lavery (Chatham Historic Dockyard Trust), *Wooden Walls: A Souvenir Guide* (Norwich: Jarrold Publishing, 1990)

———————, *The Ropery* (Norwich: Jarrold Publishing, 1990)

Marshall, Chris, (ed), *The Encyclopedia of Ships* (London: Orbis, 1995)

Mudie, Rosemary and Colin, *The Story of the Sailing Ship* (London: Marshall Cavendish, 1975)

Padfield, Peter, *Rule Britannia: The Victorian and Edwardian Navy* (London: Routledge & Kegan Paul, 1981)

Preston, Antony, and Louis S Casey, *Sea Power* (London: Phoebus Publishing, 1979)

Smith, Peter C, *Heritage of the Sea* (St Ives, Huntingdon: Balfour, 1974)

Smyth, Admiral W H, *The Sailor's Word Book of 1867: An Alphabetical Digest of Nautical Terms* (London: Conway Maritime Press, 1991)

Spectre, Peter, and David Larkin, *Wooden Ship: The Art, History and Revival of Wooden Boatbuilding* (Boston, Mass: Mifflin, 1991)

Visual Dictionary of Ships and Sailing (London: Dorling Kindersley, 1991)

Models

Darch, Malcolm, *Modelling Maritime History: A Guide to the Research and Construction of Authentic Historic Ship Models* (Newton Abbott: David & Charles, 1988)

Lavery, Brian, and Simon Stephens, *Ship Models: Their Purpose and Development from*

1650 to the Present (London: Zwemmer, 1995)

Macgregor, David R, *Square Rigged Sailing Ships* (Watford: MAP/Argus, 1977)

McNarry, Donald, *Ship Models in Miniature* (Newton Abbott: David & Charles, 1975)

Williams, Guy R, *The World of Model Ships and Boats* (London: André Deutsch, 1971)

Wingrove, Gerald A, *The Techniques of Ship Modelling* (Watford: MAP/Argus, 1974)

Other Materials

Budworthy, Geoffrey, *The Knot Book* (Kingswood, Surrey: Elliot Right Way Books, 1983)

Sanctuary, Anthony, *Rope, Twine and Netmaking* (Princes Risborough, Bucks: Shire Publications 1980)

Seymour, John, *The Forgotten Arts: A Practical Guide to Traditional Skills* (London: Dorling Kindersley, 1984)

Warring, R H, *The New Glassfibre Book* (Watford: MAP/Argus, 1978)

Suppliers

Engineers' Suppliers

Unless otherwise stated, the following companies all stock a wide range of model engineering supplies.

MJ Allen Founders, Hilton Road, Cobbs Wood Industrial Estate, Ashford, Kent TN12 6DW; tel 01233 622214 (foundry).

Blackgates Engineering, 209 Wakefield Road, Drighlinton, Bradford, West Yorkshire BD11 1EB; tel 01132 853652.

Bruce Engineering, Hollow Tree, Penny Lane, Walton Bridge Road, Shepperton, Middlesex TW17 8NF; tel 01932 245529.

Chronos Ltd, 95 Victoria Street, St Albans, Hertfordshire AL1 3TJ; tel 01727 832793 (small-scale engineering products).

Clerkenwell Screws, 109 Clerkenwell Road, London EC1R 5BY; tel 0171-405 6504 (screws in all sizes).

Diamond Machining Technology Inc, 85 Hayes Memorial Drive, Marlborough, MA 01752, USA; tel (508) 481-5944 (knife/tool sharpeners).

Fyne Fort Fittings, Clarence Boatyard, East Cowes, Isle of Wight PO32 6EZ; tel 01983 293633 (steam fittings).

Graham Engineering Ltd, Alpine House, Roebuck Lane, West Bromwich, Birmingham B70 6QP; tel 0121-525 3133 (machinery and tooling).

Maidstone Engineering Services, 50 Hedley Street, Maidstone, Kent ME14 5AD; tel 01622 691308 (stock ferrous and non-ferrous materials in small lengths).

Microflame Ltd, Vices Road, Diss, Norfolk IP22 2HQ; tel 01379 644813 (small drills/blowlamps/Dremel tools).

David Proops (Sales) Ltd, 21 Masons Avenue, Harrow, Middlesex HA3 5AH; tel 0181-861 5258 (tools; electrics; electronics; much ex-stock material).

Proops Bros, Technology House, 34 Saddington Road, Fleckney, Leicester LE8 0AW; tel 01533 403400.

Proops Educational Packages, Unit 24 Fiddlebridge Industrial Centre, Lemsford Road, Hatfield, Hertfordshire AL10 0DE; tel 01707 261276 (small gears, etc).

Reeves & Co, Holly Lane, Marston Green, Birmingham B37 7AW; tel 0121-779 6831/2/3 (castings; materials; established as one of the biggest stockists of all material for model engineering).

Rotagrip Ltd, 16-20 Lodge Road, Hockley, Birmingham B18 5PN; tel 0121-551 1566/554 5177 (chucks and lathes; accessories; measuring equipment).

Severn Lamb Ltd, Stratford on Avon; tel 01789 400140 (professional model engineers - bull-headed aluminium rail).

Shesto Ltd, Unit 2 Sapcote Trading Centre, 374 High Road, Willesden, London NW10 2DH; tel 0181-451 6188.

Simply Scissors, 48 Midholm, London NW11 6LN; tel 0181-458 4814 (scissors/tweezers).

Stuart Models, Braye Road Industrial Estate, Braye Road, Vale, Guernsey, Channel Islands GY3 5XA; tel 01481 49515 (Stuart Turner models).

Tracy Tools, 2 Mayors Avenue, Dartmouth, Devon TQ6 9NC; tel 01803 833134 (large stock of tooling for lathes, taps, dies, etc; good mail order service).

Specialist Tools

CeKa, Pwllheli, Gwynedd, N Wales LL53 5LH; 01758 701070 (excellent quality electronic tools).

Dockyard Model Company, PO Box 108, Florissant, CO80816, USA (micro carving tools).

Greenwood Electronics, Portman Road, Reading, Berkshire RG3 1NE; tel 01734 595843 (Portasol miniature gas soldering iron).

Record Tools Ltd, Parkway Works, Sheffield S9 3BL; tel 01742 449066 (full-size tools; vices; hammers; planes, etc).

Model Ship Supplies

Bassett Lowke, August Centre, 99 Sanders Road, Wellingborough, Northants NN8 4NL (model ship plans).

Cheddar Models, Sharpham Road, Cheddar, Somerset BS27 3DB; tel 01934 744634 (engines and boilers).

Euromodels, 35 Crown Road, St Margarets, Twickenham TW1 3EJ; tel 0181-891 0342 (model kits and tools; suppliers of ready-cut timber).

Maritime Models, 7 Nelson Road, Greenwich London SE10; tel 0181-858 5661 (model kits; books; ready-cut timber).

Nexus Special Interests, Nexus House, Boundary Way, Hemel Hempstead, Hertfordshire HP2 7ST; tel 01442 66551 (plans/books/magazines: specialists in hobby magazines and promotions; organise annual International Model Show - formerly the Model Engineer Exhibition).

Casting

Lego UK Ltd, Wrexham, Clwyd LL13 7TQ; tel 01978 290900.

Tiranti, 70 High Street, Reading, Berkshire RG7 5AR; tel 01734 302775 (casting, soldering, sculpture).

Woodworking Supplies

The Art Veneers Co Ltd, Industrial Estate, Mildenhall, Suffolk IP28 7AY; tel 01638 712550 (marquetry supplies).

Axminster Power Tool Centre, Chard Street, Axminster, Devon EX13 5DZ; tel 01297 33656 (large selection of power tools, etc).

Black & Decker, Westpoint, The Grove, Slough, Berkshire SL1 1QQ; tel 01753 511234.

John Boddy's Fine Wood and Tool Store Ltd, Riverside Sawmills, Boroughbridge, North Yorkshire YO5 9LJ; tel 01423 322370 (chisels, gouges, etc, for lathe turning).

Robert Bosch Ltd, PO Box 98, Broadwater Park, North Orbital Road, Denham, Uxbridge, Middlesex UB9 5HJ; tel 01895 838383 (power tools).

British Gates and Timbers Ltd, Biddenden, Ashford, Kent; tel 01580 291555 (wood and woodworking supplies; woodturning lathes).

Craft Supplies Ltd, The Mill, Millers Dale, Buxton, Derbyshire SK17 8SN; tel 01298 871636.

Elu Power Tools, Westpoint, The Grove, Slough, Berkshire SL1 1QQ; tel 01753 500805.

Hegner UK, Unit 8 North Crescent, Diplocks Way, Hailsham, East Sussex BN27 3JF; tel 01323 442440 (power fretsaw; circular saw; lathes).

Ashley Iles (Edge Tools) Ltd, East Kirkby, Spilsby, Lincolnshire; tel 01790 763372 (specialist chisels and gouges).

William Marples & Sons Ltd, Oscar Works, Meadow Street, Sheffield S3 7BQ; tel 01742 726662 (hand tools).

Myford Ltd, Chilwell Road, Beeston, Nottingham NG9 1ER; tel 0115-925 4222 (woodturning and metal screw-cutting lathes).

Skil UK, Unit 2 Beta Way, Thorpe Industrial Park, Egham, Surrey TW20 8RE; tel 01784 470784 (tools).

Robert Sorby Ltd, Athol Road, Sheffield S8 0PA; tel 01742 554231 (chisels/gouges).

Henry Taylor Tools, The Forge, Lowther Road, Sheffield S6 2DR.

Record Power Ltd, Parkway Works, Sheffield S9 3BL; tel 01742 449066 (lathes, etc).

Timberline, Unit 7 Munday Works, 58-66 Morley Road, Tonbridge, Kent TN9 1RP; tel 01732 355626 (hardwood, veneers, bobbins).

Art and Craft Supplies

Fred Aldous Ltd, 37 Lever Street, Manchester M60 1UX; tel 0161 236 2477 (craft supplies including sheet pewter and copper).

Balco Group, 49 Vyse Street, Hockley, Birmingham B18 6HJ; tel 0121-554 1026/523 2926 (pliers, tweezers: everything for jewellers).

Barbour Threads, Lisburn, N Ireland (mercerised thread for ropemaking).

Geliot Whitman Mail Order Warehouse, Herschell Road, London SE23 1EQ; tel

0181-699 9262 (fine art, craft and graphic supplies).
The Guild of Master Craftsman Publications Ltd, 166 High Street, Lewes, East Sussex BN7 1YE; tel 01273 478449 (publications; source of information for craftworkers/repairers).
Philip & Tacey Ltd, North Way, Andover, Hampshire SP10 5BA; tel 01264 332171 (Pebeo Setacolor fabric paints).
RM Trading Co (K&S Metals), 646 High Road, North Finchley, London N12 0NL; tel 0181-445 6531 (miniature sections of non-ferrous stock).
Slater's (Plastikard) Ltd, Royal Bank Buildings, Temple Road, Matlock Bath, Matlock, Derbyshire DE4 3PG.
The Wheatsheaf Art Shop, 56 Baker Street, London W1M 1DJ; tel 0171-935 5284.

Finishes

Picreator Enterprises Ltd, 44 Park View Gardens, Hendon, London NW4 2PN; tel 0181-202 8973 (micro-crystalline wax polish; restoration suppliers).
E Ploton, 273 Archway Road, London N6 5AA; 0171-348 0315/348 2838 (bronze, gold leaf, etc).

Soldering

Techno-Weld Ltd, Aston Works, Back Lane, Aston, Oxon OX18 2BX; tel 01993 851028

(low temperature aluminium welding).

Resins & Silicone

Fleming Services (Resins) Ltd, 10 Barrington Road, Shepreth, Royston, Hertfordshire SG8 6QB; tel 01763 60598 (silicone rubber).
Rota (Fibreglass) Developments, Hanover Street, Herne Bay, Kent; tel 01227 368 687.
Strand Retail, Scott Bader Company Ltd, Wollaston, Wellingborough, Northamptonshire NN9 7RL; tel 01933 663100 (resins and glassfibre).

Useful Addresses

HMS Warrior 1860, Victory Gate, HM Naval Base, Portsmouth PO1 3QX; tel 01705 291379, fax 01705 821283.

The American Museum in Britain, Claverton Manor, Bath BA2 7BD; tel 01225 460503.
Bournemouth and Poole College of Art and Design, Wallace Down, Poole, Dorset BH12 5HH; tel 01202 533011.
Chatham Historic Dockyard Trust, The Old Pay Office, Church Lane, Chatham Historic Dockyard, Chatham, Kent ME4 4TQ; tel 01634 812551.

The SS Great Britain Project, Great Western Dock, Gas Ferry Road, Bristol BS1 6TY; tel 01179 260680, fax 01179 255788.
Illustrated London News Picture Library, 20 Upper Ground, London SE1 9PS; tel 0171-928 6969.
Maritime Trust, 16 Ebury Street, London SW1W 7AW; tel 0171-730 0096.
Mary Evans Picture Library, 59 Tranquil Vale, Blackheath, London SE3 0BS; 0181-318 0034.
Museums Association, 34 Bloomsbury Way, London WC1A 2SF.
The National Maritime Museum, Greenwich, London SE10 9NF; tel 0181-312 6747. Also the home of the Historic Ships Committee, c/o C G Allen (formerly Captain of HMS *Warrior*).
The Science Museum Library, London SW7 5NH; tel 0171-589 3456.
The Smithsonian Institution, Washington DC20560, USA.
The Society for Nautical Research (South), c/o the Vice Chairman, P A Moore MA, 20 Stourvale Gardens, Chandlers Ford, Hampshire SO5 3NE, or contact the National Maritime Museum as above.
West Hartlepool - restoration of historic ships (now working on *Foudroyant*), The Custom House, Victoria Terrace, Hartlepool, Cleveland; tel 01429 33051.

INDEX